RENEWING DEMOCRACY
INTO THE MILLENNIUM

RENEWING DEMOCRACY INTO THE MILLENNIUM

The Jamaican Experience in Perspective

TREVOR MUNROE

THE PRESS UNIVERSITY OF THE WEST INDIES

Barbados • Jamaica • Trinidad and Tobago

The Press University of the West Indies
1A Aqueduct Flats Mona
Kingston 7 Jamaica

Printed in Canada

ISBN 976-640-078-4

03   02   01   00   99   5   4   3   2   1

CATALOGUING IN PUBLICATION DATA

Munroe, Trevor
Renewing democracy into the millennium: the Jamaican
experience in perspective / Trevor Munroe
p. cm.
Includes bibliographical references and index.

ISBN 976-640-078-4

1. Democracy – Jamaica. 2. Jamaica – Politics and government.
3. Elections – Jamaica. 4. Jamaica – Social conditions.
I. Title

F1887.M7665 1999   320.9'7292 – dc 20

Set in Adobe Garamond 11/14 x 24
Cover and book design by Robert Harris

Cover photos: Election 1997 activities, courtesy of
The Gleaner Company Limited; burning tyres used
to block Slipe Road, courtesy of Norman Grindley,
The Gleaner Company Limited

*Dedicated to the Jamaican people who continue
to inspire me by their determined struggle
for more meaningful democracy*

Contents

Tables and Figures

(Appendix, pages 115 to 139)

Preface
and
Acknowledgments

Renewing Democracy into the Millennium is about a race that is taking place in Jamaica and, in one form or another, in many other countries as well. It is a race between two competitors: deepening democracy and anarchic disorder. In Jamaica the race is advanced, and it is neck and neck. The race is linked to a similar contestation in the transnational sphere between uncountable sites of authority and a global citizenry demanding increased involvement and accountability.

The argument of the book is simple: democratic renewal can and must win, otherwise the man in the street is going to turn to his own devices. Furthermore, if democratic renewal is slow and is overtaken by anarchy, sooner or later there will be a backlash of authoritarianism. To complicate matters, the identities of the competitors, their performance and their ultimate fate in Jamaica is connected not only to local and national factors but as well to global considerations.

Moreover, the Jamaican experience is by no means unique. Amidst the admitted peculiarities of the Jamaican case are broad similarities with other states facing a central contradiction on the eve of the millennium. The more the citizenry have embraced democracy, the greater their dissatisfaction with existing democracies. This book both draws on the experience of other countries as well as sheds light on their dilemma in seeking to evaluate the quality of Jamaican democracy and to suggest the way forward.

Many people need to be thanked for their contribution, direct and indirect, to the conception and completion of this work over the last two years. First, my graduate students in the Democracy seminar in the Department of Government at the University of the West Indies (UWI), Mona. Coping with their questions, comments and insights helped considerably to form and develop my own ideas. So too did interaction with colleagues in the Department of Government, especially those who, like Brian Meeks, Louis Lindsay and Christine Cummings, share similar interests. This intellectual stimulation continued during my year on sabbatical as a visiting scholar (1997–98), at the Weatherhead Center for International Affairs at Harvard University. The comments of graduate students and academics at the seminars that I presented there were very useful. In this regard, I would wish to specially acknowledge the thoughtful and informed suggestions of Jorge Dominguez, the Clarence Dillon Professor of International Relations at Harvard.

Beyond the purely academic, the book has benefited from long practical engagement in Jamaican civic life. For the many ideas derived from this dimension, I wish to thank colleagues in the Citizens' Action for Free and Fair Elections (CAFFE), in the University and Allied Workers' Union, and on "The Breakfast Club". These and other interactions in the civic sphere always help to ground the ivory tower of concepts in the real world of everyday life.

A number of agencies of the Jamaican state and civil society were particularly helpful in providing data and making available information for the book. Amongst these, I wish to particularly acknowledge assistance from the Ministry of Foreign Affairs, the Electoral Office of Jamaica, the Jamaica Constabulary Force (the Commissioner's Office, the Narcotics Division, the Community Relations Division and the Police Information Centre in particular), the Supreme Court, the Social Development Commission, the 4H Clubs, the Seventh Day Adventist, Anglican, Baptist, Roman Catholic and United Churches and, of course, the People's National Party, the Jamaica Labour Party and the National Democratic Movement. As usual, the librarians at the Institute of Social and Economic Research, UWI, Mona were always willing to go the extra mile in providing help. Special thanks to my research assistants at different stages of the work – Garfield Ferguson, Diana Thorburn, Lisa Taylor – and to those who painstakingly typed the manuscript – Theresa Spinale at Harvard's Weatherhead Center for International Affairs, Denise Brown and Adlyn Smith at the Department of Government, UWI. Acknowledgments and appreciation as well to American Airlines and to Air Jamaica who facilitated frequent trips between the United States and Jamaica to collect data during my sabbatical year.

Thanks to Ivelaw Griffith at the Florida International University and to Doug Payne at the Center for Strategic and International Studies in Washington for serving as readers of the manuscript and for providing very perceptive and constructive criticisms.

To my wife and most constructive critic Ingrid, and son Tarik, I say special thanks for enduring my long absences on sabbatical and my speechless hours while working on the book.

Last but by no means least, I wish to express my deepest appreciation to The Press UWI, in particular to their indefatigable director Pansy Benn and to Shivaun Hearne who supervised the proofreading and without whose contribution this work would have taken much longer to come to fruition.

In one way or another all these institutions and personalities have left their imprint on this book though I have to claim overall responsibility for the final product.

Mona, Jamaica
December 1998

Introduction

This book arises out of an interest in identifying deficiencies in the treatment of democracy in the 1990s and in helping to make the democratic system more meaningful for the man in the street. It is an interest which started in my high school days and has continued, through many twists and turns, ever since. Most recently this general concern has been stimulated by one of the great and continuing puzzles of politics and of political science as the twentieth century draws to a close, namely, the unprecedented, near universal acceptance of the legitimacy of democracy and yet the unprecedented, near universal discontent with the performance of democracies. Among the more 'mature' democracies of Western Europe and North America, in the 'established' democracies of the Anglophone Caribbean, and in the Latin American, African and East European states that are in varying degrees of transition from different forms of authoritarianism, popular dissatisfactions with democratic government have been, in recent times, persistent and, in some cases, growing. Interestingly, these discontents do not seem so much to fuel a generalized desire for authoritarian rule as to drive a more or less conscious search for appropriate democratic reforms.

As such, in country after country, the main thrust of popular movements is to deepen rather than to weaken democracy; a central focus of scholars and policy makers to redesign rather than abandon democratic institutions so as to improve democracy's effectiveness. The critical challenge is how to renovate a system formed (and deformed) by industrial capitalism and the Cold War, how to transform it to better meet the realities and the needs of post-Cold War politics and post-industrial society.

Amongst the more important of these realities are some new elements. Not the least of these is a citizen who at the beginning of the millennium is in significant ways different even from his mid twentieth century parents and grandparents, a citizen more informed, more critical, more confident, less deferential, less governable in old traditional ways. There is a new quality state – more confined, less in control, less welfare, more subject to transnational and subnational forces. Then there is a more powerful market imparting new qualities to governmental institutions, civil society and economic relations – threatening to reduce all to the 'cash nexus' and to render porous as well as permeable territorial and other demarcations of all types. It is as if mankind is not so much at the 'end of history' as at the 'end of geography'. To the extent that this is even partially so, must not the end of geography carry with it fundamental renewal of a democracy concept and structure apparently prem-ised from day one on the primacy and obduracy of geographical boundaries?

At any rate, these are some of the underlying realities which condition a general feeling that while democracy is unquestionably legitimate, existing democracy is equally unquestionably inadequate. What appears to be needed is more democracy not less; transformation rather than abandonment of that which is viable in established forms, innovation with the new as much supplements as alternatives to the old.

In any event, these are some of the perceptions which helped motivate the writing of this book. Its more immediate intellectual genesis lay in two critical reviews which I did of two of the more important works on democracy produced in the early 1990s.[1] To differing degrees, these works reflected a short-sighted triumphalism at the time too evident in the Western scholarly community following the fall of the Berlin Wall and the collapse of commu-nism. They projected an undue complacency regarding the complexity of the issues which would face not only new democracies in transition from authori-tarian rule but also well-established systems coming to grips with the informa-tion age and knowledge driven society. My reviews were intended to caution against idealizing existing democracy, to call for more thought in identifying deficiencies and, most of all, to suggest the need for new institutional designs to overcome these weaknesses. This book, in a sense, continues the argument of those essays.

At the same time, this general concern of comparative politics was reinforced by the specifics of the Jamaican experience of the 1990s. Here was an 'established democracy', the first predominantly black state to win universal adult suffrage in the 1940s, widely regarded as a model for the Third World in the 1960s, a leader of the non-aligned movement in the 1970s with strong political institutions and a vibrant democratic culture. Yet by the 1990s, it was apparent that significant sections of Jamaican people had become increasingly alienated from the country's democratic institutions whilst retaining their loyalty to the democratic system. Intriguingly, disenchantment was leading not so much to all-pervasive apathy but to apathy primarily within established political channels. Outside these channels, much of the population demonstrated great energy and even aggressiveness in non-traditional, sometimes illegal, channels of interest articulation. How unique, the question naturally arose, was this contradiction between apathy and activism, often existing in the very same people?

This situation also posed other issues. To what extent was popular withdrawal from the established system providing that system with an increasing incentive to move towards reform and self-renewal? Could it provide that incentive at all? How far was the emerging agenda of democratic reform in Jamaica and the basis for it related to global experience and trends elsewhere? Were the causes of disquiet with democracy in Jamaica the same or different from those in other countries? Are the issues being addressed similar or divergent from experience in other democracies? Are the solutions and proposals being contemplated adequate or do they fall short? What about the very concept of democracy and measures of 'democraticness' as well as notions of democratic renewal – do the realities of the nineties expose gaps and require rethinking on any count? Does current rethinking and 'institutional-engineering' match up to the needs of the times? Most of all, what are the ways in which ordinary people can become less objects and more subjects of meaningful decision making?

These are but some of the questions arising from the Jamaican and the more general experience that this book seeks to address. In one sense they are not new. Jamaica and Jamaicans, particularly those of my generation who came to adolescence in the 1960s, have been wrestling with the issue of taking more effective control of their country and of their destiny for as long as one can remember. The end of chattel slavery, the working-class revolt of the 1930s, decolonization, the Black Power movement of the 1960s, socialism in its various tendencies during the 1970s, 'free enterprise' of the 1980s – each of these episodes reflected, to one degree or another, more or less political manifestations of that search for meaningful self-determination and self-direction. No less have been the twists and turns of different segments of mankind over the last two hundred years from mercantilism to *laissez faire* capitalism back to 'statism' of different Eastern as well as Western varieties and then again to neoliberalism; from colonialism to independence to dependence and inter-dependence. On reflection, each of these episodes had positive and negative content and consequences. Clearly the sum total of the achievement and the current moment in the journey represents a significant advance but is far from satisfactory for most of mankind in most countries in the modern world. The majority of Jamaicans are among the majority of the global dissatisfied. Helping to uncover some of the sources and manifestations of political dissatisfaction; suggesting some of the challenges and lines of democratic renewal are part of the purposes of this book.

Chapter 1 looks at some of the more general issues: questions relating to defining and measuring democracy. It examines some central challenges posed for democracy by growing 'globalization' and takes up a fundamental and often ignored concern: the quality of democracy. The chapter suggests dimensions in which democratic quality may be evaluated. Specifically in relation to Jamaica, chapter 1 proposes a number of accepted propositions on which this particular case appears to shed new light – not least of all the contention that democracy requires economic growth to be viable and sustainable.

Chapter 2 deals with the 1997 general elections in Jamaica. In that context, the chapter looks at the recent pervasiveness of electoral irregularities in Jamaica, analyses the growth of a citizen backlash against the deterioration in Jamaican democracy, the significance of the unprecedented presence of na-tional and international observers in the 1997 elections, the electoral reforms and the election results. The chapter identifies ways in which these elections reflected similarities and differences with other countries and also raises the issue of how far the elections could represent part of a 'new beginning' for Jamaica's democracy.

Chapter 3 takes up the origin, content and course of Jamaican debate on constitutional reform. It looks at the growth of popular discontent as one important basis of proposals for change, both radical as well as moderate. The chapter also examines the debate in Jamaica on whether to change the parliamentary Westminster model for a presidential system and places this discussion in a comparative perspective. Similarly, proposals for moving towards a more participatory democracy are reviewed within the context of a global trend towards more direct forms of democracy. Some deficiencies in the Jamaican debate on constitutional reform are also pointed out.

Chapter 4 explores a critical policy issue – the question of illicit drugs – and its implications for Jamaican democracy. The Jamaican experience is reviewed within a comparative perspective and the extent to which the country has coped or succumbed to the drug menace is probed. Without in any way detracting from and whilst spelling out different levels of the danger to democracy, the chapter argues for a more nuanced analysis of the factors which influence the extent to which democracies survive or succumb to the multidimensional threat posed by the global narcotics industry. The need for regional and transnational responses to the drug menace, particularly within the Caribbean context, is explored as are the ways in which such responses may either constrain or augment democracy on the national level. In terms of narcotics policy, the suggestion is made that more flexible approaches to decriminalization have the potential to enhance the quality of Jamaican democracy.

Chapter 5 takes up the issue of 'civil society', its meaning and significance to modern democracy. The current state of critical groups in Jamaican civil society is reviewed. In this context the trade unions, the churches and other voluntary associations are assessed and the direction of their development evaluated. The chapter suggests that tendencies to both decline and renewal are evident in Jamaican civil society, tendencies not dissimilar to experience elsewhere in other democracies. Important gaps in research and policy are also identified in this chapter.

Chapter 6, entitled "Global Reforms and the Jamaican Agenda", presents some conclusions and recommendations. Much of the discussion relates to the extent to which popular discontent with political corruption of one sort or another has driven much of the reform agenda across the democratic world. The main lines of Jamaica's reform process are reviewed; the importance of new approaches to foreign relations and to leadership qualities are stressed as highly significant to democratic renewal in Jamaica as elsewhere.

Note

1. Samuel P. Huntington, *The Third Wave: Democratization in the late Twentieth Century* (Norman and London: University of Oklahoma Press, 1991); and Francis Fukuyama, *The End of History and the Last Man* (New York: Fress Press, 1992). See also my reviews in *Social and Economic Studies*, Vols. 41 and 43.

Abbreviations

CAFFE	Citizens' Action for Free and Fair Elections
CARICOM	Caribbean Community
FPTP	First Past the Post
IGO	Intergovernmental Organization
IMF	International Monetary Fund
INGO	International Nongovernmental Organization
JCFTU	Jamaica Confederation of Trade Unions
JLP	Jamaica Labour Party
JTURDC	Jamaica Trade Union Research and Development Centre
MP	Member of Parliament
NDM	National Democratic Movement
OAS	Organization of American States
OCADA	Latin American Energy Organization
PNP	People's National Party
SDC	Social Development Commission
UAWU	University and Allied Workers' Union
UN	United Nations
WTO	World Trade Organization

1

Challenges of
Democratic
Renewal

Introduction: Moderating Mood Swings

Not unexpectedly, 1997 was typical of recent times in the continued profusion of writing on democracy.[1] Not so typical however was the mood evident in much of this work a mood of doubt, even of declining confidence in the future of democracy, certainly when compared to the euphoria of the early 1990s. A cursory glance at some of the more representative titles is indicative of the mood swing: "Was democracy just a moment?"[2] "Will volatility kill market democracy?"[3] "The rise of illiberal democracy."[4] "The crash of Western civilization: the limits of market democracy."[5] "Unequal participation: democracy's unresolved dilemma."[6] Interestingly these converging conclusions of doubt regarding democracy derive, in general, from two quite different anxieties. One is the apparent impotence of democracy in the face of economic oligarchies, transnational capital, international organizations, and the like; the other is the apparent omnipotence of illiberal democracy over individual rights, the rule of law and constitutional constraints.

Of course, pessimism has by no means been the only theme. Much of the writing in this vein has been hotly contested.[7] Robustly optimistic currents in respect of democracy's future are still very much evident in the literature. But no doubt influenced by the somewhat chastening experiences of "really existing democracy" in the second half of the 1990s, optimism has happily shed some

1

of its triumphalist character and contemplates a more sober, more complex path of democratic development.[8] Indeed there appears to be an emerging consensus that for democracy to remain worthwhile and valued, it cannot stand still; its institutions, processes and culture must undergo renewal in the context of changing circumstances and of new challenges.[9]

To my mind, reflection on the need for reform and on the possible lines of renewal is a more productive enterprise than succumbing to successive moods of optimism or pessimism. Not least of all because some of the issues involved are complex, difficult and global in scope. Indeed the imperative of renewal appears to apply as much, though in different ways and for different reasons, to the established 'first wave' liberal democracies as to the new 'third wave' democracies and to those 'in between'.[10]

In that last category belong countries like Jamaica and other states of the Anglophone Caribbean. Somewhat peculiar among the 'second wave', mainly ex-colonial, countries in its long, sustained practice of democracy, Jamaica has nevertheless experienced ups and downs in its democratic politics. Even more so, analysts of the Jamaican process have been as prone to the mood swings between optimism and pessimism typical of scholars of both established and new democracies elsewhere. Concern at imminent demise in the mid 1970s gave way by the mid 1980s to confidence that it was "most unlikely" that Jamaican democratic institutions "will collapse or crumble".[11] Then in the early 1990s anxiety reappeared that Jamaican democracy had become "fragile and vulnerable".[12] Now it appears the pendulum is once again swinging to the pole of optimism.

It seems to me of some importance to get a better understanding of these mood swings evident on the question of democracy. Doubtless each mood and each swing must have some basis in reality. But could it be that what Plattner calls "alternating cycles" of "euphoria and despair"[13] take up and exaggerate positive or negative aspects, respectively, of that reality? Could it be further that this feeds a tendency to absolutize each pole rather than to understand the dynamism inherent in the relationship between the positive and negative elements of any prevailing democratic reality? For example, absolutizing the positives in the fall of communist dictatorships, one-party states and military regimes obviously led to a triumphalism which ignored or underestimated the backlash for democracy of transition states with much freedom but declining order and rising inequality. Conversely, in the Jamaican case, absolutizing the negatives in the growth of violence in electoral contestation probably encouraged underestimation of the consequent potential for regeneration of civil society and the reform of political institutions arising from widespread political alienation. No doubt each mood, whatever the cause or combination of causes, produces, if at the same time exaggerates, valuable insights. Yet it is obviously necessary to reduce the zig-zags of analysis and of evaluation. One way to help in achieving this objective as well as in developing a more meaningful democracy is to reject determinism in any form and to reaffirm the open-endedness of the present. This would encourage a focus more on issues of renewal and reform in the rapidly changing circumstances prevailing at the end of the millennium. This chapter proposes to reflect on some of these questions and to pose some answers, drawing on material from the Jamaican case.

Defining and Measuring Democracy – How Far Does it Matter?

Obviously, as we all recall from Government 101, definitions do matter. Without defining a concept or a material phenomenon we would be unable to meaningfully discuss it, much less systematically relate to it. There would be no way of grouping and separating phenomena with similar and contrasting characteristics respectively. Less abstractly, to talk about the renewal of democracy one has to be clear on the systems to which one is referring and those to which one is not. Without clear definition of democracy a problem obviously arises; equally, if not more so, with too many definitions of democracy other problems arise.

To illustrate with perhaps an extreme, but not unpersuasive, example, Jeff Haynes, in an interesting, recently published work[14] distinguishes between what he calls "formal", "substantive" and "facade" democracy. Formal democracies and facade democracies, as the adjectives suggest, are identified respectively "by regular 'free and fair' competitive elections"[15] on the one hand and by "outward appearance", "fig-leaf elections"[16] on the other. Of both of these, there is a large number in the Third World. "Substantive democracy", on the other hand, is quite a different kettle of fish. Haynes takes this to exist where "all citizens have easy access to the governmental process and a say in collective decision-making [where] there are effective channels of accountability for public officials. Substantive democracy is concerned with the development of equity and justice, civil liberties and human rights."[17] Not surprisingly, with such a definition, as far as Haynes is concerned, there is now no "substantive democracy" in the Third World nor perhaps for that matter in any other part of the world. Certainly, such a democracy does not exist in Jamaica nor anywhere else in the Caribbean. Equally clearly, one could not discuss the renewal of democracy, substantively understood, since by definition such a system does not exist anywhere.

One may, of course, sidestep this issue by regarding Haynes' definition of substantive democracy as idealistic and therefore not very useful in application to the real world. But this would hardly solve the problem – there are many others where Haynes is coming from or going to. A recent study out of the Department of Political Science at the University of California, Berkeley, identified "more than 550 subtypes of democracy".[18] Forty years prior to this, another study had come up with a list of 311 definitions of democracy – found in surveying the literature from Plato's time to the 1950s.[19] More worryingly, the very originator of the Survey of Freedom, used most authoritatively to determine which countries are democratic and which are not, recently commented: "We are still in the midst of defining what democracy means, and we may always be."[20] Be this as it may, we do use the term *democracy* and its definition is obviously not a matter of indifference to framing the project of renewal.

To illustrate, let us take the 'electoralist', 'minimalist' or 'proceduralist' definition of democracy undoubtedly dominant in Western political science from Joseph Schumpeter in the early 1940s to Huntington in the early 1990s. In the words of the latter, a "twentieth-century political system is democratic to the extent that its most powerful collective decision-makers are selected through fair, honest and periodic elections in which candidates freely compete for votes and in which virtually all the adult population is eligible to vote."[21] In this definition, the "central procedure of democracy is the selection of leaders through competitive elections by the people they govern."[22] Clearly in this concept of democracy, civil liberties are less important than political rights; how and on whose behalf the politician governs is of little significance so long as the government is "democratically" elected, the power of "special interest" on the outputs from the political system is neither here nor there, and, most important, the extent of popular empowerment outside of periodic elections does not arise at all. From this perspective, the argument that democracy is "government of the people, by the people, and for the people" has useful rhetorical purposes but is analytically and empirically meaningless. Equally meaningless, therefore, within this definitional framework would be concern for either equity in outcomes or popular involvement in governance.

Programmes of democratic renewal in the minimalist perspective attempt nothing but to fulfil the important (but highly inadequate, from my point of view) task of ensuring free and fair elections. This electoral definition of democracy and, consequently, the electoral understanding of democratic renewal was not significantly nor successfully challenged during the Cold War. Democracy and non-democracy (or authoritarian rule) were, in the more authoritive works, regarded as dichotomous variables, as labels for two boxes into which all states could be put depending on their electoral credentials. With the end of the Cold War, in East and West, North and South, the passing of the common enemy disorganized and 'complexified' previously relatively ordered and simple global as well as national realities. Amongst the bewildering variety of changes in the East, people were now free to vote without fear of persecution from communists; in the West and South, on the contrary, people were now free to question the efficacy of the vote itself as a counter-balance to the market without fear of being regarded as communists. The warming of political landscapes, long frozen during the Cold War melted old realities and encouraged redesign of politics, ideologies, parties, leaders, social movements, civic associations as well as popular and other concerns.

In this context, the deficiencies of democracies hitherto defined as such in exclusively electoral terms became more fully exposed as did, consequently, the inadequacies of electoral conceptions of democratic renewal. The minimalist understanding of democracy was accused of the 'fallacy of electoralism', that is, of privileging the electoral dimension to the detriment of other domains, in particular of civil liberties. 'Electoral democracies' or 'formal democracies' were now explicitly distinguished from 'liberal democracies',[23] the latter, in addition to free and fair elections, being defined in terms of elected governments upholding the rule of law, observing and protecting the human rights of the citizenry (including minorities), promoting free and independent media, public discussion. More importantly, on this definition, "during the 1990s the gap between electoral and liberal democracy has steadily grown".[24] This latter understanding of democracy clearly requires an agenda for renewal which goes beyond preserving free and fair elections. It extends to strengthening both the vertical and horizontal accountability of the executive,[25] deepening the recognition of human rights and enhancing the quality of civil society.

In a sense, however, despite their differences both the electoral and liberal definitions (and their corresponding renewal agendas) share at least one feature in common – they both ignore two dimensions of more substantive understandings of democracy: the quality of economic outcomes from state action and the degree of popular participation in governance. These dimensions are of particular relevance to Latin America and the Caribbean where enormous socioeconomic inequity and popular disempowerment *vis-à-vis* powerful oligarchies undermine public satisfaction with a democracy confined to electoral and liberal terms. Hence "one of the paramount imperatives of democratic consolidation in Latin America . . . is reducing the levels of poverty and inequality".[26] This, I would suggest, has to be more than an 'imperative'; it has to be a defining feature in the prevailing circumstances of the region.

This raises the question of whether definitions of democracy and therefore agendas for democratic renewal are appropriately influenced by popular perceptions. I believe this influence to be unavoidable and desirable. Public attitudes and understanding of the meaning of democracy set the context and criteria for evaluation of the political system. The fact is that in Latin American and the Caribbean popular conceptions of democracy are at least as much social as liberal and electoral. A substantial majority regard it as a responsibility of the state "to reduce the differences between the rich and the poor".[27] In Jamaica, popular attachment to equality and justice has been traditionally not far behind attachment to freedom and liberty. Amongst the lower classes, better living conditions rank ahead of free speech as a value preference.[28] Any agenda for democratic renewal needs to give due weight, without uncritical subordination, to such value preferences if democratic legitimacy is to be strengthened.

In sum, how one defines democracy is not only, nor even primarily, an academic question. It does matter immensely in determining the assessment of the state of democracy and, therefore, the necessity for reform. Moreover, the notion that democracy and non-democracy are dichotomous is increasingly being left behind.[29] In its place, there is now greater recognition that in between extreme poles there are degrees of electoral democracy, of liberal democracy, and of substantive democracy. This undoubtedly complicates the picture but does allow more nuanced approaches to analysis, evaluation and policy reform. The global map of democracy is now more than ever varying shades of grey in between a few, if relatively large, patches of black and white.

This raises the question of the adequacy of existing measures of degrees of 'democraticness'. By and large these measures rate and rank countries by assigning numerical values to the more important indicators of democracy: "political rights and civil liberties";[30] "political rights and political freedoms";[31] "fair elections, freedom of expression, media pluralism, freedom of organization";[32] "degree of competition, degree of participation, index of democratization";[33] "competitiveness of political participation, regulation of political participation, competitiveness of executive recruitment and constraints on the chief executive".[34] As is apparent from even the most cursory review of these indicators, the measures of democracy are almost exclusively derived from liberal and electoral concepts of democracy. By and large, indicators (however imperfectly developed) quantifying democratic outcomes or levels of socioeconomic inequality are not among the bases for scoring and ranking democratic states.

Nevertheless these measures are useful as far as they go. Generally, they accord with qualitative judgements and common sense perceptions. They each concur, for example, in rating Jamaica as a democracy throughout the post-independence period while scoring both absolute and relative decline in the level of the country's 'democraticness'. Using Diamond's eight-category classification of Latin American and Caribbean countries (based on Freedom House scores) Jamaica slipped from the second highest category of democracy in 1987 to category three "partially illiberal democracy"[35] by 1994 (and continuing into 1997). Interestingly, this fall off in formal rating coincided with a marked growth during the decade in popular political alienation amongst the Jamaican people and a corresponding acceleration of the political reform process.

Despite their utility, however, there is a highly significant and huge deficiency in these existing measures of democracy. *None includes any adequate indicator nor measure of the "democratic deficit"* [36] *the extent to which modern democracy is subject to unaccountable "spheres of authority"*[37] *particularly, but not exclusively, of a transnational character* [authors emphasis]. Some authors do recognize that external power resources "may improve or decrease the chances of democracy . . ."[38] Gastil in discussing the authoritative "Comparative Survey of Freedom" does recognize that "leaders in many Central American and Caribbean countries have reason to fear the North American pressure",[39] and by implication this impacts on democratic decision-making. Moreover one of the questions scored in constructing the Comparative Survey of Freedom asks "are the people free from domination by . . . foreign powers . . . economic oligarchies or any other powerful group?"[40] But this is one of 21 equally weighted questions. Pointedly David Beetham's democratic audit proposes to check "how far does any supranational level of government meet the criteria of popular control and political equality, whether through national parliaments or through representative institutions of its own?"[41] Here again this is but one of 30 questions. The point is that the measures of democracy have neither realistically "attempted to . . . estimate the significance of external power resources used in domestic politics"[42] nor have they accorded such factors significant weight in determining degrees of democraticness. In contemporary circumstances of globalization, this is a near fatal flaw not only conceptually but also operationally. Existing measures of democracy, therefore, simply fail to indicate what must be a main line of reform in raising levels of democracy and any meaningful democratic renewal into the millennium: the necessity to tackle the 'democratic deficit'.

Globalization and the 'Democratic Deficit'

Put squarely, modern democracy, however defined, whether established, consolidated or transitional, faces a fundamental mismatch. The geography of major problems is transnational; yet the geography (and philosophy) of democratic problem-solving remains national. James Rosenau makes the point graphically: "Goods, services, money, ideas, polluted air and water, drugs, AIDS, terrorists, immigrants, crime . . . move too quickly across established political boundaries for governments to control sufficiently to satisfy their constituents."[43] Hence with varying degrees of reluctance, governments, are yielding to other authorities unavoidably and inexorably, the challenges of 'control' or of 'liberalization', of regulation or of standard-setting. The problem is that none of these authorities – intergovernmental or nongovernmental, transnational corporations or capital – are accountable in any meaningfully democratic sense.

The problem would be small or at least more confined if two things were not happening – one, if national publics were not becoming more democratic and, two, if national democracies were not experiencing daily contracting space for purely national decision making. In respect of the first point, a hundred years ago the growth of supranational authority would be primarily, if not exclusively, a concern of international lawyers or government officials debating appropriate redefinitions of sovereignty. Then, the man-in-the-street had by and large neither internalized the social values nor achieved political systems whose legitimacy rested on decision-making and decision-makers having at least to enjoy majority endorsement in regular, periodic 'free and fair' elections. Now that democratic values and democracies are increasingly universal, publics are not easily accepting that kings, queens and emperors, presidents, prime ministers and parliamentarians previously responsive to minority elites, having become after decades of struggle at least partially accountable to the people, should now themselves become subject to unaccountable authorities and unelected bureaucracies.

Which leads to the second point. Were these bodies as few or their spheres of authority as limited as a hundred years ago, then perhaps the 'democratic deficit' would be relatively small, manageable and probably acceptable. But the development of non-state authorities in what has been properly called a "multi-centric world"[44] has grown exponentially in the last hundred years. On one count "in 1909 there were 37 international governmental organizations (IGOs) and 176 international nongovernmental organizations (INGOs), while in 1989 there were nearly 300 IGOs and 4,624 INGOs. In the middle of the century there were two or three conferences or congresses per annum sponsored by IGOs; today the number totals close to 4,000 annually."[45] On another count, "1,700 INGOs were active in the mid 1980s and in excess of 35,000, transnational corporations with some 150,000 foreign subsidiaries were operating in 1990".[46] There are now clear disjunctures between decision-making at the national level which is at least democratic in the minimal, electoral sense on the one hand, and rule-making in no sense democratic at the international level in the most varied spheres of law, politics, economy, security, communications and the environment.[47]

The issue here is not whether this rule-making is necessary or beneficial. There can be no doubt that much of it is. Rather the question is whether it is legitimate in terms of democratic norms. In much the same way, the recognition of any beneficial decision-making under authoritarian regimes does not make such regimes any more acceptable nor compatible with democratic values. The question then becomes not how or whether to reverse such beneficial rules but how to make their sources more legitimate and accountable. Equally, the issue is not how to dismantle but to democratize transnational rule-making structures.

This question is easier posed than answered. By definition, answers require some reconceptualization of democracy away from foundations on which is has rested whatever the differences of theory and definition for over two thousand years: the foundation of territorially bounded space. But if this question is not more persistently posed and more effectively answered, the democratic deficit is bound to widen with the most negative consequences. Put crudely, to the extent that critical areas of traditional nation-state responsibility such as security, economy, environment can no longer be conceptualized much less dealt with in national terms, why should any democrat bother to vote for increasingly powerless national ministers of security, economy, or environment? In the same vein, to the extent that transnational spheres of authority and rule-making are unaccountable, is it not more likely that national legislatures and citizenries will reject or resist cooperation even with beneficial agreements and acceptable compromises because they were arrived at through undemocratic processes? Clearly what is at stake in the short run is the delegitimization of transnational structures (particularly when they embody asymmetries of power) and, in the medium or longer term, the delegitimization of democracy itself at the national level. Hence it is a matter of some urgency that not only theorists of international relations but also of comparative politics give more thought and come up with better, more realistic answers to the democratization of global governance. Democracies cannot long endure in an external environment "wherein democratic principles are systematically ignored, grossly violated or paid only superficial lip service".[48]

Whilst the deficit affects all states, it is obviously greatest in relation to those states at the bottom of the global hierarchy. In this context the Jamaican case is instructive. Here is an example of a smaller consolidated democracy with membership in approximately 50 IGOs and a signatory to over 100 multi-lateral treaties.[49] These figures exclude the large number of INGOs to which Jamaica belongs and the many bilateral treaties to which Jamaica is also a signatory. The point is readily conceded that the IGOs of which the country is a member vary considerably in authority from the relatively powerless group of 77 at one pole to the International Monetary Fund (IMF) and the World Trade Organization (WTO) at the other. Similarly, the domestic implications of the multilateral treaties also differ immensely in their significance from the relatively innocuous agreement establishing the Latin American Energy Organization (OLADE) to the United Nations Vienna Convention against illicit traffic in narcotics drugs and psychotropic substances (1988). In each case, albeit with varying degrees of autonomy, the democratically elected Jamaican government acceded to the various treaties and to membership in the IGOs.

But, in democratic terms, this is as far as the legitimacy goes, of the organizational memberships, the international instruments and their attendant obligations. Legislative oversight is weak and executive attention for the most part is inadequate. Partly because of this, media attention and public discussion of related issues is low. In the normal course of affairs, neither the elite nor the mass public is aware or involved in determining the extent of the country's incorporation within unaccountable transnational "sites of authority". The objective democratic deficit, unavoidable in such international relations, therefore takes on added dimension in a sense, a subjective deficit as well. When such relations do not involve controversial issues, there is hardly a problem.

When, however, complex or disagreeable items are placed on the national agenda, because of membership in IGOs or accession to treaties of one sort or another, both the legitimacy and the effectiveness of the country's democracy often come into question. Such was the case in respect of Jamaica's implementing conditionalities arising out of successive multiple agreements with the IMF and other multi-lateral agencies.[50] Again the matter arose in relation to Jamaica enacting domestic legislation to give effect to its ratification of the 1988 UN Vienna Convention.[51] In each instance the lack of democracy in the IMF and, to a lesser extent, the UN Organization became matters of great public concern. More so, the question was hotly disputed as to whether Jamaican democracy had any meaning if "foreigners" with no accountability to the Jamaican people could dictate to the country's elected government. Why vote if whichever government results from elections is either unable or unwilling to practice greater transparency in relation to international obligations or to more adequately secure the national interest in the course of making such arrangements? There can be no doubt that questions such as this contribute to public dissatisfaction with democracy in countries such as Jamaica, if not to actual erosion of the legitimacy of democracy itself.

The case in turn confirms that sustaining and renewing democracy not only amongst smaller states is going to require continued attention to making transnational 'sites of authority' more accountable and national executives more amenable to legislative oversight and responsive to public opinion on international affairs. This is not to suggest that smaller democracies, even in current arrangements, are mere ciphers on the international scene and, as some dependency and world systems theories suggest, have no room for manoeuvre in relations with more powerful entities. There is some Jamaican and Caribbean experience to suggest that tough negotiation, skilful diplomacy, professional lobbying and astute coalition-building, backed by a strong national consensus, can make a difference in both bilateral and multilateral contexts.[52] This however does not weaken the point that the drive to make such contexts more responsive in a democratic sense remains fundamental to democratic renewal.

So far, regrettably, the thinking on the democratic deficit has failed to produce convincing and effective proposals on closing the gap. Much less has there been practical movement in this direction. This is not to say that some ideas are not useful and do not hold some promise of reducing the deficit. Amongst the more interesting of these are the many recommendations within the framework of what has been called "cosmopolitan democracy"[53] as well as the reform of global governance. But many even relatively modest measures appear 'pipe dreams' in the prevailing international environment and, in particular, in the context of fairly deep and broad resistance amongst American elites even to meeting existing financial obligations to organizations over which the United States currently exercises inordinate power. Thus reform of the IMF to make it more democratic, of the UN Security Council to give developing countries a significant voice, or creation of a more directly representative UN second chamber, inevitably meet strong opposition.[54] Less so perhaps proposals to create or to strengthen regional parliaments and to use referenda, national and transnational, to validate recommendations which impact the legitimacy or effectiveness of democracy at the national level.

Other, perhaps less utopian, thinkers take a different tack in addressing the democratic deficit. They place hope not so much in what could be regarded as step by step empowerment of a global citizenry but in the very proliferation of groups in the multi-centric world. Their very numbers, the argument goes, particularly of the transnational corporations and the INGOs in a sense reduces excessive concentration of power. Moreover, the transnational movements supporting NGOs such as Amnesty International or Friends of the Earth might well develop into a system of checks and balances, admittedly little more than "a ramshackle assembly of conflicting sources of authority."[55] Rosenau looks in the same direction for less autocracy over the widening frontier between the national and the transnational "in the degree to which ad hoc control mechanisms evolve to steer . . . in the direction of more checks on the excesses of power, more opportunities for interests to be heard and heeded, and more balanced constraints among the multiplicity of actors that seek to extend their command of issue areas."[56] The attractiveness of these notions is their apparent realism – their extrapolation from ongoing processes of a growing multiplicity of groups and centres which one day may have some veto capability. But need we remind ourselves that neither at the national nor the transnational level are checks and balances, necessary though they be, equivalent to democracy?

This leads us back to the unavoidable necessity to give more thought to making the transnational corporations, the IGOs and the INGOs (and, in a different sense, the transnational criminal networks) more accountable to democratic power and authority. If it is a pipe dream to expect acceptance or implementation of some of the more coherent proposals already on the table, it is even more of a pipe dream to expect that national democracy can long endure in the context of what amounts to transnational autocracy. In this context, it is hardly inappropriate to recall that the WTO rules require that "each member [be it the United States or Jamaica] shall ensure the conformity of its laws, regulations and administrative procedures with its obligations as provided in the annexed agreement . . ."[57] How many international economists, much less legislators, much less citizens, have even read much less digested the "annexed agreement"? If the governments we elect are subject to forces which are not democratized, then in most countries "the casting of a vote from time to time becomes merely a symbolic act. Democracy is as apt to decline as a result of boredom and frustration as the violent overthrow of constitutional government".[58] This would undoubtedly precipitate a "legitimacy crisis" to the extent that "citzens [in democratic societies] perceive effective governing authority to have dissipated into a supranational ether".[59]

From Consolidating Democracy to the 'Quality of Democracy'

Coming more effectively to grips with the challenge of democratic renewal obviously requires careful attention to those factors that remain primarily national. But this attention needs to shift focus somewhat from preoccupation with the question of consolidation to more complex issues associated with the quality of democracy. It is important to understand both the distinction and the relationship between consolidation and quality.

The former is primarily a quantitative concept, referring to the length of time freely elected governments have lasted; the number of times opposition parties have formed the government and ruling parties been removed from office by elections. More generally the term *consolidated democracy* is taken to mean "a political regime in which democracy as a complex system of institutions, rules and patterned incentives and disincentives has become . . . 'the only game in town' ".[60] It would follow that consolidation implies that "even in the face of severe political and economic crisis, the overwhelming majority of the people believe that any further political change must emerge from within the parameters of democratic procedures".[61] Obviously this condition would not rule out the existence of fringe groups with non-democratic agendas but these would, for all intents and purposes, be isolated from the mainstream.

It follows that the prelude to consolidation is emergence and the obverse is collapse or breakdown. Understandably, in the first half of the 1990s, a major, if not *the* major, preoccupation of the literature has been issues related to the transition of "third wave democracies", to the conditions and prospects for consolidation or breakdown. In that context, a lively debate has resurfaced around the relative importance of economic, cultural and institutional factors in the sustainability or otherwise of new democracies. Economic growth, rising per capita income and decreasing economic inequalities; the rootedness of democratic values, attachment to freedom and equality as well as rejection of authoritarianism; the appropriate design of executives, legislatures, political parties, and electoral systems – each of these three clusters of variables has been put forward by one or another school of thought as critical to democratic sustainability.[62]

Somewhat surprisingly, despite numerous studies, particularly on the relationship between economic factors and democracy, evidence remains ambiguous on the main economic issue. "Researchers have yet to reach a consensus on the precise relationship between growth and democracy: about one-fifth of the studies find a positive relationship, one-fifth a negative relationship, and the rest are inconclusive."[63] Moreover, the 1997 World Development Report continued, "economic performance among developing countries classified as sustained democracies has varied considerably".[64] Without denying this observation, the most consistent investigators of this relationship have nevertheless concluded that "democracy is more likely to survive when the economy grows"[65] and is therefore "vulnerable to bad economic performance".[66]

Interestingly, the Jamaican case tends to question this conclusion. There has been little or no net economic growth in 25 years; on most indicators, including inflation and income inequality, the economy has performed badly. Yet on any measure Jamaican democracy remains among the most consolidated in the world. Parties have alternated in office by way of relatively free and fair elections; constitutional rule has been unbroken, the rule of law upheld and human rights largely observed for over half a century spanning a period from decolonization to the post-colonial state. This certainly suggests a clear case where popular faith in democracy, the character of political organization and the nature of political leadership have achieved democratic consolidation and prevented breakdown despite severe strains, not least of all arising out of poor economic performance.[67]

This then leads us to the issue of quality. In everyday affairs most of us recognize a clear distinction between a long life and a satisfactory life, between longevity and contentment. So too in political science we need to more clearly differentiate democratic consolidation from the quality of democracy.[68] The differentiation becomes ever more important as fewer democracies break down, and more endure but with obviously high levels of popular dissatisfaction. It is far from clear whether these two conditions – consolidation and dissatisfaction – can permanently coexist, particularly in the context of sharp crisis. What is obvious however is that "within the category of consolidated democracies there is a continuum from low-quality to high-quality democracies".[69]

The project of democratic renewal requires us to confront what Linz correctly calls the "gigantic" [70] task of identifying the elements which go into the make-up of quality, develop comparative indicators and delineate at least general lines of reform. This is clearly a complex problem. For one, it will not be easy to get agreement on the elements of quality, particularly across political traditions, which while clearly democratic, may differ significantly in positioning on a liberal (in a European sense) social/democratic continuum. Having managed to achieve some consensus on indicators, there is then the hurdle of assigning weights to the different dimensions, assuming that each is not to have the same value. Within each dimension and across indicators there will be clearly higher or lower levels of quality. Is it necessary to develop a threshold or 'quality line' (analogous to a 'poverty line') below which the quality of democracy, however 'consolidated', is regarded as unacceptably poor? Or is it acceptable simply to develop country ratings and rankings (as with the Human Development Index) and leave it at that? Finally, in my opinion, the elements indicating quality ought to include subjective factors, such as the degree and dimensions of citizens' satisfaction with democracy, alongside more objective elements. To revert to our earlier metaphor as one grows older the doctor may pronounce vital organs in great shape but surely how one feels, one's mood, must also enter into any meaningful assessment of quality of life.

Taking these considerations into account and while recognizing the complexity of the issue, I would nevertheless suggest that the following be included in any measure of the quality of democracy:

The quality of political participation: This indicator proposes to look primarily not so much at the level but at how far political participation takes place through conventional or unconventional channels; what is the balance between voting in elections, writing petitions, representations to or lobbying of legislators and other government authorities, on the one hand, and, on the other, protests, demonstrations, boycotts, roadblocks and other more unconventional (elite-challenging as distinct from elite-sanctioned/directed)[71] forms of political participation on the other. Clearly a healthy combination of both probably points to high quality whereas an imbalance in either direction may suggest high or low, depending on the context.

The quality of political contestation or competition: At the level of political discourse, what is the balance between partisanship and adversarialism weighed against accommodation and cooperation? Are the language and rhetoric more aggressive and belligerent, the metaphors and images those of war in which the opposition is the enemy to be 'vanquished' at the polls or is the discourse one of strong, vigorous, but nevertheless 'friendly' competition in a non-zero sum game in which the players contemplate at least some levels of collaboration? Relatedly, at the level of political behaviour, how far do leaders and followers engage in, collaborate with or turn a blind eye to acts of intimidation and even politically related violence?

The level of development and quality of civil society:[72] Is the number of civic groups high and the degree of associational life considerable or is it relatively low and insignificant? How uniform is the pattern across social, economic, ethnic, age, gender, geographical divides? How far are the groups themselves exclusivistic or inclusive, divisive or bridge-building? What is the extent of their formal structure? To what degree are the groups local or national, democratic or undemocratic? How far do the social groups allow not only for checks on the state but also for popular participation in governance? What is the extent of balance or imbalance amongst various groups in influence on the process of governance and on political outcomes?

The degree of corruption in the public and private sectors: How far is there abuse of public power for private gain as well as private power for private gain? To what extent are procurement and allocation systems influenced by cronyism, partisanship, and clientelism? How far do formal checks from the justice system (rules of transparency, effectiveness of prosecution and so on) and informal checks from the mass public work in exposing and reducing corruption?

The quality of socioeconomic outcomes from state policy: How far does state policy contribute to the widening or reduction of socioeconomic gaps? Is there economic growth with equity or otherwise? Are disadvantaged sectors, for example, women or the poor, facilitated in self-empowerment?

The attitude to government: To what extent do people trust or distrust government, hold offices and officials in high or low esteem? How far is the public satisfied with the performance of government and of politicians? How willing are the people to participate in reforming the system and in the very process of democratic governance itself?

Some comments on these indicators are in order. In the first place, they are obviously rough and in need of much refinement. For example, there is some overlap not only among the various elements but also between some of the questions and indicators taken up in existing measures of democracy. More significantly, there is a very strong case (with which I am very sympathetic) for including the character of political leadership as a separate indicator. On reflection, however, it seems to me that leadership is an indispensable aspect of each of the indicators and should therefore probably better be evaluated in the context of each rather than be singled out as an independent element. Finally, much valuable work is under way on each of the elements I have proposed. What appears to be missing is some bridging of this work and bringing it together. The ultimate aim would be the development of some broadly acceptable check-list and composite index of the quality of democracy. This index would be distinct from but obviously related to measures of consolidation or of degree of democracy and allowing for clearer specification of lines of renewal.

In applying this approach to the Jamaican case, it is pretty clear that here we find a classic case of a highly consolidated democracy – democracy is very definitely the 'only game in town' – but of low and (until recently, at least) declining quality. Hence, in recent times, while the country has maintained relatively high scores in relation to political rights and civil liberties, levels of public confidence and satisfaction are low, corruption is high, the quality of political participation and contestation has been, on balance, negative and the character of civil society at best mixed. This is certainly not a general phenomenon of the Anglophone Caribbean where countries such as Barbados have held the top rung in the Comparative Survey of Freedom and would undoubtedly also score highly on any Quality of Democracy Index.

It appears to me, however, that in global terms Barbados may be more the exception and Jamaica the rule. Certainly there is justifiably growing concern about the quality of political life in the established liberal democracies despite the highest levels of 'freedom' and of democratic consolidation. In this regard, Larry Diamond has pointed to "the social decay, economic stagnation, political corruption and general sclerosis of the most powerful practitioners and promoters of democracy in Europe and North America".[73] Schmitter has spoken of "new strains"[74] in these states and Putnam of "democratic disarray"[75] in the United States itself. The 1996 Survey of American Political Culture provides much data which corroborates these judgements. Whilst there remains general agreement on the core "ideals of public life", the survey found high levels of "pessimism about America . . . disaffection toward the government [and] . . . cynicism toward political leadership".[76]

This situation quite rightly calls for "a research agenda that reduces the unknowns"[77] regarding the causes of growing public distrust and the extent of actual deterioration in the quality of democracy. It also suggests that "the established democracies – and not least – the United States – must 'heal themselves' ".[78] Regrettably there are few signs that this healing is under way. To the extent that this process is slowed by the absence of research and appropriate policy recommendations, then obviously action on that front needs to be speeded up. Or, perhaps, things have to get worse before they get better, before strategic elites and critical segments of the mass public are moved to more effective action on the front of political reform and renewal.

Certainly, this latter appears to be what is happening in Jamaica. As the quality of democracy deteriorated, political alienation grew exponentially, spontaneous protests and public demonstrations on the widest range of issues multiplied, mass criticism of the performance of politicians and the political system reached a crescendo, 'normlessness' and disorder increasingly threatened to displace civility and order in everyday relations. Paradoxically, it is at least in part this obvious process of decay which has fuelled elements of renewal and is broadening consensus around the need for a new democratic order.

In this context, national dialogue and reform programmes, with varying degrees of public involvement, are emerging and being developed along a number of dimensions.

The redesign of critical public institutions: Democratizing the constitution, reform of the electoral system and electoral administration, police and prison reform, strengthened anti-corruption legislation, restructuring of local government, rethinking party organization and party finance.

The revival of civil society: Mainly around churches connected to fundamentalist religious tendencies, sporting associations, neighbourhood groups and action networks supportive of electoral and political reform.

The renovation of democratic political culture: Mainly campaigns and greater law enforcement against intimidation, aggressiveness and violence in elections and political contestation as well as less partisan and more inclusive attitudes to political life.

Reform of the labour market: Mainly to preserve traditional rights of freedom of association and some degree of job security in the context of economic liberalization while at the same time encouraging foreign investment, and ensuring a broader base of participation in ownership and significantly greater employee involvement in corporate structures.

Deepening and broadening of regional and hemispheric relations: Mainly in the form of extending ties beyond the Anglophone Caribbean to Haiti, the Dominican Republic and Cuba, the development of the Caribbean community in terms of the establishment of a regional parliament, closer collaboration in bilateral and multilateral relations with non-Caribbean states, IGOs and NGOs.

Finally, it is worth mentioning that these impulses to renewal, as yet unconsolidated, are developing within an economy that is still stagnating, though now showing some signs of partial stabilization.

Conclusion

What might we conclude from these observations? First, the continuing swings between euphoria and depression regarding the present performance and future prospects of democracy are not very helpful. One approach to better regulating disconcerting highs and lows is to assume that there will be thorns in every rosy picture, and, conversely, positive possibilities in the most negative of situations. This mindset better allows us to more easily escape being bogged down in either over-optimism or excessive pessimism and focus research as well as policy more single-mindedly on what is evidently a truly universal imperative – better understanding and more fully applying the specifics of democratic renewal in 'first', 'second' and 'third wave' states. Secondly, how we define democracy – whether in primarily 'electoral', 'liberal' or substantive terms – does matter in terms of influencing the focus and dimensions of the renewal project. Thirdly, existing measures of democracy are helpful in evaluating the varying degrees of democraticness, but primarily in internal, national terms. In a rapidly globalizing world in which the borders between the local, national and international are everyday becoming more porous, the flow of authority in smaller democracies is increasingly from the transnational downwards and inwards. (In 1995, 87 of the 192 countries of the world had a population of less than 5 million.) At each national level, a democratic deficit develops which existing indices of democracy are not designed to measure and are therefore in urgent need of fundamental reconstruction. Fourthly, the growth of the democratic deficit ultimately threatens democratic legitimacy, to one degree or another, everywhere. This threat presents both a necessity and an opportunity for carrying forward existing, thoughtful but inadequate analysis into more realistic prescriptions for democratizing the transnational sphere (or what is called in somewhat utopian terms "global governance"). To put it starkly, either democracy beyond the national is extended or democracy within the national is diminished. The conclusion follows that at the same time, within the primarily national frontier, greater attention needs to be paid to the issue of raising the quality of democracy. This requires going beyond the preoccupations with consolidation, primarily a quantitative concept, to developing research on indicators, indices, ratings, and recommendations to do with the quality of democratic life. In this regard, I suggest a composite of the following six elements: the character (not primarily the level) of *political participation; political contestation; civil society; corruption; state outcomes*, and *public attitude to government*. (Perhaps a seventh as well: the *quality of leadership*.)

Finally, the Jamaican case appears to raise a number of questions for further investigation: Cannot consolidated democracy coexist for a long time with poor economic performance, and even with high levels of economic inequality? Do not economic variables impact more directly on the quality of democracy rather than on the degree of democratic consolidation? Are not factors of political culture and institutions more critical for democratic consolidation than economic considerations in conditions of poor economic performance? Less tentatively, Jamaica confirms that the democratic deficit is particularly harmful for democratic legitimacy in smaller and weaker states, but that this need not mean paralysis nor loss of autonomy. To sum up, declining quality of democracy need not be a 'free fall' but can provide the impetus and incentive for stimulating wide-ranging projects for renewal. In this last point, perhaps, lies much encouragement for further research, policy-relevant scholarship and even civic re-engagement.

2

The 1997
Elections:
A New Beginning?

In terms of measures of the quality of democracy suggested in chapter 1, the falling level of participation, violent contestation and the ineffectualness of civil society as a force for upholding democracy in elections from the late 1970s to the early 1990s indicated a decline in Jamaican democracy. Hence the 1997 general elections in Jamaica were a relatively rare occurrence as far as established democracies are concerned. The elections, contrary to the norm in such states, were anything but routine. Rather, these elections had a watershed character and a contradictory potential: either to bring new elements to the renewal of Jamaican democracy or to leave the status quo untouched and contribute to further serious erosion of the system. To this extent, the 1997 Jamaica elections prefigured a choice which mature democracies shall increasingly, in one form or another, have to recognize: to leave things as they are and face decay as well as further growth of popular dissatisfaction with the 'existing democracy' or to reform the system and renew public confidence in the performance of democracy.

As it turned out, the elections combined elements of the old and the new, of decay as well as of renewal. At the end of the day, the result of the elections, which gave Prime Minister P. J. Patterson's People's National Party (PNP) an unprecedented third term in office and, conversely, Opposition Leader Edward Seaga's Jamaican Labour Party (JLP) an unprecedented third consecutive defeat, were accepted as reflecting the collective will of the Jamaica people.[1] Moreover there were signs of "major improvements in both freeness and fairness of the election process". At the same time alongside "the most sophisticated democratic politics" were juxtaposed elements of "the most primitive form of coercive and violent politics".[2] While, on balance, it was the former which predominated as "far less violence occurred than in previous elections" and "the elections were certainly the most peaceful in recent times", the fact is that irregularities of one kind or another provide some basis for the judgement that "the elections met only a minimum of democratic standards".[3]

Electoral Irregularities, Reforms and Observers

The defects in the Jamaica system were apparent in the 1980s and became acute in the 1990s. Electoral irregularities and malpractice took multiple forms: flawed voters' lists, impersonation, multiple voting, but, most of all, intimidation and violence on Nomination Day, during election campaigns and on Election Day itself. In 1980, at the height of the global Cold War and ideological polarization in Jamaica, there were over 500 political killings in election-related violence. In 1986, during the local government elections, massive intimidation reflected the continued erosion of Jamaica's democracy. A Commission of Enquiry into that election found "the evidence . . . abundantly clear that the electoral process . . . was neither fair nor free from fear in may polling divisions particularly in the parish of Kingston and St Andrew . . ."[4] The Report went on to speak of:

Evidence of considerable violence and intimidation of election officers and of electors . . . the most serious aspect . . . was the presence of roving bands of hooligans purporting to be supporters or activists of the two major parties . . . Members of these gangs were armed with guns, knives, sticks and other weapons. The police were heavily outnumbered and unable to prevent them entering the polling stations where they terrified the election officers and in some cases assaulted them and inflicted injuries. They forcibly seized ballots and marked them for their chosen candidate, forcing the presiding officers to sign the counter foils . . .[5]

This Commission went on to identify the existence of "certain urban areas . . . known to be either pro-JLP or pro-PNP and woe betide any person entering these areas unless he is a known supporter of the party holding supremacy in the area".

These last areas had developed into "garrison communities" which, in the perception of the Carter Center, became "a socioeconomic and political phenomenon unique to Jamaica".[6] By the 1990s sufficient numbers of these had been built by the political parties to make 12 of the 60 constituencies electing members of parliament into garrison constituencies. These were defined as constituencies dominated by communities:

in which anyone who seeks to oppose, raise opposition to or organize against the dominant party would definitely be in danger of suffering serious damage to their possessions or person thus making continued residence in the area extremely difficult if not impossible. A garrison, as the name suggests, is a political stronghold, a veritable fortress completely controlled by a party. Any significant social, political, economic or cultural development within the garrison can only take place with the tacit approval of the leadership (whether local or national) of the dominant party.[7]

In effect, in these constituencies, created primarily on the basis of partisan distribution of scarce benefits, housing in particular, one-party rule and homogeneous voting were institutionalized; democracy, in large measure, non-existent.

Garrison politics and generalized electoral malpractice continued into the 1993 general election and stained the legitimacy of the election results. While violence was considerably reduced compared to the 1980 election, approximately 12 people died in election-related incidents. Independent members of the Electoral Advisory commission "were shocked . . . [by] . . . the intensity of violence and thuggery . . . in some of the areas mentioned, no election really took place".[8] Leaders of the church for their part "noted that incidents of fraud and thuggery took place in both PNP and JLP strongholds".[9] Not surprisingly, but very dangerously, following the 1993 elections 44 percent of all voters, including approximately 25 percent of all those who voted for the victorious PNP, felt that the election was not free and fair.[10] On top of this, the system's failure to successfully prosecute and punish electoral malpractice as well as the degree of perceived fraud and force in those elections led to the dire predictions that followed and, paradoxically, strengthened the base to ultimately galvanize civil society into action. In the words of Jamaica's political Ombudsman, "we are heading for a time when violence will be the determinant factor and the electoral process so undermined as to render the results no longer reflective of the popular will".[11] This element of pervasive electoral violence and intimidatory politics was both a major source of alienation from the established parties as well as of consolidation of the growing 'uncommitted' tendency in the electorate. As such, electoral reform leading to the reduction or elimination of violence became a main condition for re-engagement by significant sections of Jamaican society in conventional politics. It also became a principal demand of the opposition JLP and a condition for ending a parliamentary boycott it initiated following its defeat in 1993.

In these circumstances, it was hardly surprising that the agenda of electoral reforms was substantial and that the process produced significant reforms leading up to the 1997 general elections. Amongst the more important of these were provisions which for the first time allowed electoral authorities to abort as well as void elections in the face of significant malpractice in the specific constituencies.[12] In addition, the law governing the enumeration process was amended to allow for parties other than the PNP and the JLP, having met certain criteria, to have the right to nominate persons to be appointed as scrutineers.[13] In effect, provision was being made for the first time in the country's modern politics to grant some legal status to parties other than the PNP and the JLP. Moreover, to facilitate a continuous rather than periodic process of voter registration, fixed enumeration centres were to be established, a system of finger printing of electors was to be introduced and identification cards, with encrypted personal data, were to be produced and distributed to each elector. Not least of all, the reforms substantially increased the penal sanctions for offences against the Election Law. Arguably, however, the most significant change was the amendent of the law to permit election observers to enter polling stations.

The observer issue and its resolution represented perhaps one of the most positive aspects of the 1997 elections, reflected a citizen backlash against the erosion of the country's democracy and brought Jamaica into the forefront of one of the more significant trends in late twentieth century democratic governance. As Elklit has observed in relation to international observers: "Over the past decade, countless election observers have been dispatched to every region of the globe."[14] This practice, begun by the United Nations in the mid 1950s in relation to referendums on independence in a number of decolonizing states, was developed during the third wave of democratization under the aegis of a variety of international as well as regional governmental and non-governmental organizations. Subsequently, monitoring of elections by domestic observer groups also developed, so much so that during recent years there has been a "growing prominence of domestic observation groups alongside international observers in a numbers of countries".[15] These domestic groups have invariably not only performed the function of watchdogs of the electoral process, often pronouncing on their freedom and fairness, but they have also, more generally, been an important channel through which often critical segments of civil society, unwilling for one or another reason to be party political activists, become involved in the system of governance.

Not suprisingly, both international and domestic observers groups have tended, in the main, to operate in contexts where 'free and fair elections' are in doubt. Hence, election monitoring has developed primarily in relation to transitional or 'first time' democracies and in countries where democracy is being resumed following periods of authoritarian rule. Traditionally, observers were neither proposed nor accepted in established democracies, though in the 1990s a secondary tendency begun to develop which regarded election observation as a norm of an increasingly interdependent global democratic community rather than a symptom of democracy's insecurity in a particular state.[16] Nevertheless, for the Carter Center and the Council of Freely Elected Heads of Government, "Aside from the Council's 1992 US election observation, Jamaica's were the first elections we observed in a country with an established democracy".[17]

These considerations concerning the modern election observer phenomenon all entered, for the first time, into Jamaican politics prior to and during the 1997 elections. Initially, the matter arose out of widespread concern primarily outside but also inside the political parties that the extent of electoral irregularity and malpractice associated with the 1993 election seriously questioned how far that election was indeed free and fair. Indeed, the political ombudsman reported that in 1993 "interference with the electoral process reached an unprecended extent and brazenry".[18] This concern and the failure to effectively monitor the 1993 election motivated the leadership of the Roman Catholic Church to bring together a group of non-partisan citizens to perform a watchdog role in relation to the 1997 general elections. This initiative coincided with significant and growing voter de-alignment[19] and a developing inclination in the citizenry to speak out against negative features of Jamaican democracy. Within a relatively short time, the Church's invitation galvanized a substantial response, ultimately among all social classes, and led to the establishment three months before the election of the first Jamaican domestic election observer group, Citizens' Action for Free and Fair Elections (CAFFE). The development of this group attracted sympathy from broad sections of the people and support from the international donor community. Drawing largely on the uncommitted, independent tendency in the electorate, CAFFE was in a relatively short time able to attract over 2,000 volunteers and play a significant role in deterring election-related intimidation and violence.[20] The Jamaican experience was once again confirming that detachment from party activism in modern democracy often does not indicate political apathy. On the contrary, in many countries such detachment signals greater readiness for unconventional political participation. "Evidence . . . indicates that, although they may vote less regularly, most publics are not becoming apathetic . . . They are becoming increasingly interested in politics."[21]

The issue of domestic observers became connected, somewhat controversially in the Jamaican context, with the question of international observers. The latter very soon became a subject of partisan division as the opposition JLP and the National Democratic Movement (NDM) made the case for and the governing PNP against inviting international observers to Jamaica for the upcoming elections. The opposition argued that the extent and character of electoral irregularities in Jamaica required the kind of experienced, influential, neutral and credible deterrent that could only come from established international organizations independently observing the Jamaican elections. The government countered by arguing that Jamaica had been and remained one of the longest established democracies in the Third World, and that the electoral reform process under way could successfully achieve its objectives assisted by monitoring from Jamaicans themselves in domestic observer groups. Not suprisingly each side, consistent with its perceived interest, tended to absolutize the advantages and disadvantages of domestic and international observer groups, counterpoising one against the other and thereby threatening to undermine any broad non-partisan acceptance of each by associating the call for international observers with opposition parties and that for domestic observers with the government position. The Carter Center and CAFFE each had occasion to be critical of opposition and government party positions respectively, thereby undermining any images of one-sided partisan associations. Ultimately, with some tact and flexibility on all sides, the initial divide was bridged, the opposition parties acknowledged the utility of a domestic observer group and the government modified its position and facilitated an official invitation to the Carter Center to send an observer team to monitor the elections.[22]

On Election Day itself, the coverage provided by CAFFE and the Carter Center was extensive and significant. CAFFE had a volunteer presence in all 60 of the island's constituencies "albeit in widely ranging numbers . . . from just one observer in five constituencies . . . to full coverage of all polling divisions in St Andrew, North Eastern".[23] The coverage was particularly intense in the urban Kingston and St Andrew constituences. Indeed, "Observers did not shy away from 'garrison' constituencies and served in sections of Western Kingston, South St Andrew, South West St Andrew, Central Kingston and in areas of pre-election violence such as August Town in East St Andrew and Grants Pen in North East St Andrew."[24] Whereas the CAFFE volunteers were, in the main, stationed at polling sites, the Carter Center, for its part, deployed its 58 international observers in mobile teams of two persons each throughout the country. In all, these teams "observed the vote in 52 of 60 constituencies . . . covered rural areas and all important cities, concentrating on constituencies deemed closely contested". They too did not shy away from the garrisons and "were deployed to the most dangerous neighbourhoods in the corporate area".[25]

It is clear however that while the CAFFE and Carter Center deployments were broad, extensive and relatively effective each lacked depth and intensity. In the case of CAFFE its volunteer numbers allowed it to station observers in some 965 polling stations, 15 percent of the total. The Carter Center mobile teams visited 1,098 polling stations constituting 17 percent of the number. "In almost half of the sixty constituencies in which CAFFE observers served, volunteers were present in under 10 percent of the constituencies polling divisions."[26] Nevertheless, the coverage was acknowledged as more than adequate to be effective and to allow meaningful evaluation of the elections. In this regard, both the international and domestic observers came independently to essentially the same assessment – despite significant administrative breakdown and evidence of continuing political irregularities, the Jamaican election was the most peaceful in recent times and the results reflected the will of the people.

Overall, the presence and role of international and domestic observers in the elections contributed significantly to their relative success, in particular to its comparatively non-violent character. In fact, this feature was signalled early in the campaign when on Nomination Day (when candidates hand in their election documents) there was a significant reduction in tension and acts of violence. Instead there was widespread peace and calm, as well as, on occasion, manifestations of goodwill and friendship between competing groups of party supporters. Carter Center staff who attended Nomination Day ceremonies in two urban constituencies "reported seeing supporters from all parties ringing bells and dancing in the streets. Jamaicans commented they had not seen such camaraderie in decades."[27]

This relative peace continued on Election Day. The Police High Command indicated that there was one death only that could be linked to the elections. Both domestic and international groups of observers reported low levels of violence compared to past Jamaican elections . . ." Carter Center delegates reported intimidation and harassment in only 24 stations (2 percent of their sample) . . . "all . . . in urban zones".[28] CAFFE noted "nineteen instances . . . in nine of the constituencies . . ."[29] The relatively low violence level was the more significant as this had become a major threat to Jamaica's democracy; indeed, anticipation of electoral violence had been high and some predictions of bloodshed even dire.[30] No doubt this outcome was also connected to a less inflammatory and confrontational campaign than in previous years by the political parties and, in particular, by the party leaders. Moreover, the professionalism and election preparedness of the security forces had been significantly upgraded. There can hardly be any question that these positive developments, at least in part, emanated from the breadth and depth of public revulsion at the erosion of Jamaica's democracy, reflected not least of all in alienation from traditional politics. To the extent that this withdrawal has begun to convert itself into a positive tendency for democratic renewal, reflected in the establishment of CAFFE and the formation of NDM, the 1997 elections could well mark a 'new beginning' in Jamaica's politics. In other respects, the election in large measure continued traditions of Jamaican democracy.

The Campaign

The campaign leading up to the elections was, overall, consistent with Jamaican tradition while revealing both similarities and differences with campaigns in other established democracies. In the first place, candidate selection reflected a combination of local and national party influences, with the latter exercising the decisive say, especially in contexts where there was division in the party's constituency organization. A secondary tendency was for the party constituency membership and supporters to choose the candidates with little or no subordination to the national leadership. This was manifested primarily in the NDM, formed two years before the election. Whatever the selection process, however, the candidates who faced the electorate and, even more so, those who were elected to the House of Representatives, reflected what Pippa Norris has appropriately called the "iron law of social bias".[31] They were, as Table 2.1 shows, in the main, male, over 40 and from the professional middle class.

This 'iron law' predominated despite some deviation in the past Jamaican elections and definite effort within recent years to break with tradition. For example, it was not always the case that the "over 40s" represented the majority of candidates, MPs and even cabinet members. In an earlier period, younger age cohorts were less alienated from politics and this reflected itself in more significant participation of the "under 40s" in the political system. Not so, however, with women, who in Jamaica, as elsewhere, despite dominance of lower levels of party organizational structure,[32] have never been meaningfully represented in party candidacy, much less in legislative and executive positions. (See Table 2.1.) Some effort to break with this pattern took organizational form in the years up to the 1997 general elections. A Women's Political Caucus was established which cut across parties and which provided moral and material support for increased female candidacy in the electoral process. Whilst this work marked an encouraging start, it did not produce any immediate positive result for the 1997 elections in terms of raising the proportion of the female candidates or of female members of parliament. The Jamaican experience appears to bear out the general conclusion that more than rhetorical or token support is required to significantly increase women's legislative and executive presence. One form or another of affirmative action at the level of the party leadership and party organization would seem to be required to help to rectify female under-representation.[33]

Similarly reflective, at least in part of past Jamaican experience and current global trends, was the nature of the election campaign. A marked feature was its significantly increased cost compared to the 1993 general elections. The combined spending in 1997 of the two major political parties was estimated at over J$100 million during the six weeks leading up to the 18 December poll.[34] Each depended heavily on big business and on the Jamaican economic elite, though the PNP appeared to raise significantly more support from the overseas Jamaican community. Very often major corporate donors gave to both the PNP and the JLP. The political importance of financial support from this source was confirmed in the credible allegation by the newly formed NDM that one decisive reason for its low campaign profile was the result of elements in the business community reneging on financial pledges to the party.

The 1997 election, therefore, reflected the tendency for Jamaican campaigns to become more expensive and for much the same reason as in other states – the growing role of the media, the escalating costs of media advertisement, and the increasing professionalization (indeed Americanization) of election campaigns.[35] To this extent, the global trend towards more 'capital intensive' electioneering was apparent in the Jamaican experience. This was, however, not at the expense of the traditional 'labour intensity' of the Jamaican election.[36] Door to door canvassing during the registration-enumeration exercise, face to face meetings in local districts and communities, preparation and mobilization for mass meetings, manning of polling stations on election day – each of these and other elements of the 1997 campaign required significant 'grass-roots' involvement. The PNP, in particular, placed considerable emphasis on "extensive and intensive training of party workers to win the enumeration as well as the election". This required major expenditures on training and on sustaining a field force which at its peak numbered 12,000 party workers. The JLP, in contrast, placed much greater emphasis on what Mr Seaga later called "street activity to whip up enthusiasm",[37] on mass rallies, for example, the biggest and the most important of which in major urban centres cost up to J$1 million each, not least of all in expenses for transport of supporters, refeshments for activities, and motorcades. To this extent, the 1997 Jamaican elections could be regarded as both capital and labour intensive.

For this reason, the election and the election process raised the issue of campaign finance reform, a subject justifiably at the centre of debates on the future of democracy in many countries of the world. Concern to reduce, if not eliminate, undue influence by special interests, particularly big business, on the political directorate has led most democracies to introduce regulatory frameworks which include elements of public funding of political parties and of election campaigns.[38] These range, as Figure 2.1 indicates, from government support of parties by way of provision of free broadcast time to transparency in reporting requirements relating to party finance, maximum caps on party income and expenditure, direct state funding for bona fide political parties and election campaigns. By and large, existing mechanisms remain under review in many countries; in a number of cases, they are regarded as inadequate guarantors of both political transparency and protection of the public interest against excessive influence by big money.

Jamaica remains an exception to the rule in so far as there is no public funding of political parties. At the same time, the level of dependence by Jamaican political parties and election campaigns on private sector interests is as great as in any other established democracy. This contradiction has from time to time posed the question of public funding of parties.[39] Favourable public consideration of this issue has, however, been seriously affected by generalized negative perceptions of politicians as corrupt, self-seeking and unconcerned with the natonal interest. Hence, the argument goes, neither the politician nor the political party should receive tax payers' money. Needless to say, this argument ignores the reality that for the foreseeable future the political party and the politicians are an integral part of Jamaica's democratic system. The victor in any election inevitably exercises significant control over billions of dollars of public funds and of public assets. Hence the necessity for the public to assure itself through an appropriate regulatory framework that no party is either unduly benefited nor excessively disadvantaged in seeking electoral support by access or lack of access to private sector financial support. The electorate has a clear and obvious interest in ensuring that all political parties are transparent and that no party is either a captive of special interests or handicapped by rejection of subordination to such interests.

Nevertheless, the Jamaican electorate remained at best divided and a majority more than likely opposed to public funding of political parties. Despite this, prior to the 1997 elections, the leadership of each of the two major political parties, whilst sensitive to prevailing public opinion, was giving consideration to how "the state might strengthen the electoral and representational process".[40] Obviously such consideration had to involve strengthening the quality of party involvement in the process. This concern has led in turn to increases in the payments to party scrutineers who play an important role in voter registration and, for the first time, payment of party indoor agents by the state. It also led to duty concessions by government on motor vehicles, designated by the parties as required for the 1997 election campaign, up to a maximum of 60 for each one. Further consideration is also being given to public provision of or a subsidy for constituency offices for members of parliament, separate and distinct from constituency party offices. Favourable examination of ways in which the state might facilitate and assist the political parties in getting their messages to the people is also taking place. In that regard, one recommendation is to provide support for the publication of party manifestos. In these, albeit somewhat oblique ways, the 1997 elections provided the occasion for the Jamaican party leadership to edge closer toward some public funding, thereby beginning to meet a need of the Jamaican process and, at the same, catch up with one positive element of most modern democracies.

In terms of the campaign itself, the many issues raised in the final analysis essentially boiled down to two questions.: Who would be the best leader for Jamaica going into the twenty-first century? Which party would perform better in running the government? The PNP and its supporters projected the party president, Prime Minister Patterson as a 'born ya' Jamaican from humble origins, belonging to the black majority, reflecting a caring, consensual approach to leadership. The JLP, in contrast, presented its leader, former Prime Minister Edward Seaga, as a sound manager, technically competent, with the experience and know-how to stabilize and ultimately guide to a path of growth a Jamaican economy in continuing crisis. Consistent with this focus, "the issues which dominated the campaign advertising in both print and the electronic media were predominantly criticism and promotion of the party leaders and candidates".[41] In terms of performance records, the PNP cast its case for re-election to a "third term as government in terms of the need to complete the work it had begun", which was to consolidate the economic stabilization and to sustain social programmes, for example low-income housing, designed to benefit the disadvantaged majority. The JLP, on the other hand, drew comparisons predictably unfavourable to the government, between the JLP and PNP terms of office in relation to levels of inflation, employment creation, crime, rates of growth, and the transfer of wealth from the poor to the rich. Another campaign issue reflecting the connection between national and the transnational related to the IMF. The PNP promoted the government's ending of its borrowing relationship with the IMF as a premier achievement, in effect, thereby reducing the country's democratic deficit and enhancing its sovereignty. Seaga and the JLP, on the other hand, argued that this termination was unsustainable and that the PNP was secretly returning to the IMF. Behind the scenes, of course, each party and its supporters ran 'unofficial' campaigns of a somewhat more scurrilous nature. PNP supporters depicted Seaga as alien to Jamaica both literally (with reference to his place of birth in the United States and Middle Eastern ethnic character) and metaphorically in terms of leadership style which was confrontational, divisive as well as associated with violence. The JLP for their part depicted Patterson as racist, prone to corrupt use of public assets for partisan gain and inclined to homosexual tendencies.

Opinion polls revealed an interesting response on the part of the Jamaica electorate. On the one hand, a majority regarded its economic conditions as worse off under the governing PNP than under previous JLP administrations. A majority also considered the leader of the JLP as a better economic manager than the leader of the PNP. At the same time, however, the opinion polls revealed deep distrust of Seaga, rejection of his leadership style and concern that the internal state of the JLP (disunity, distrust, low levels of teamwork) did not make them ready to lead the country. This perception was reinforced by the resignation from the JLP of its chairman (and Seaga's heir apparent) Bruce Golding in October 1995 together with a section of party leaders and activists, mainly on grounds of Seaga's dictatorial character. Conversely, Patterson was seen as a better team leader, a crusader against violence and confrontation, an advocate of national unity and reconciliation. The PNP Patterson election victory proved consistent with the poll results and predictions.[42] They were as much, if not more, a rejection of Seaga as an embrace of Patterson. In this regard, the Jamaican elections confirmed two tendencies of note in modern democracies. One relates to the issue of the economy. "In studies of individuals' 'choices'," Helmut Norpoth observed, "the economic issue often drowns in a sea of voter responses to other topics and concerns."[43] In Jamaica it is clear that such "other topics" included approach to leadership and the perception of leadership character. One insightful scholar of the Jamaican process had noted this clear tendency in relation to the results in 1989 general elections. At that time,

Seaga's politics were weak but his economics were strong. Manleys's politics were strong but his economics were weak. On 9 February 1989, Jamaican voters voted heavily for politics over economics much to the surprise of the international press. Seaga's backers in the world's financial centres, and the Jamaican middle class and business community.[44]

This raises a second general tendency, historically evident in Jamaica and carrying over into the 1997 election: ". . . because most voters will find it easier to evaluate personalities than policies, appraising leaders is arguably the central component of democratic selection within liberal democracies."[45] This is a finding which the Jamaican experience would certainly appear to bear out.

Voter De-alignment and Political Participation

So, too, were the Jamaican elections consistent, but only in part, with global patterns relating to political participation. Of one aspect of these, Arend Lijphart has commented, "voter turnout is not only low but also declining in the most countries."[46] As Table 2.2(a) indicates, 1997 voter turnout at 67 percent was undoubtedly low in the Jamaican elections, relative to both Jamaican averages of the 1980s and 1970s as well as to global patterns. In that latter regard, up until the mid 1990s Jamaica ranked in the lowest quartile of democracies in relation to electoral participation. (See Table 2.2[b].) The country's ranking fell significantly because of the dramatic decline in both voter registration and electoral participation levels in the 1993 elections. By this time, significant sections of the Jamaican people "perceived [a] lack of connection . . . between election outcomes and public policy"[47] and regarded public policy as failing to come to grips with important national issues such as crime and unemployment. In earlier years, particularly in the 1970s and 1980s, the major parties appeared clearly differentiated on programme, performance, ideology and leadership. To the vast majority of the electorate, it appeared to matter which party won and therefore there was a point in voting.

The 1997 election, whilst confirming the decline of this perception reflected in the low turnout, nevertheless revealed a secondary element. This was a slight upturn in voter registration. This had to do with a number of factors. One was the voter registration campaign by the Electoral Office of Jamaica. Another was more focused efforts by the political parties, in particular the ruling PNP, to contend with citizen electoral apathy and to motivate higher levels of enumeration and voting. Finally, as the party campaigning gained momentum, the perception undoubtedly began to grow on all sides that it did matter who won the elections.

Despite this element, there can be no doubt that the main factor affecting the 1997 Jamaican elections and the politics of the 1990s has been the phenomenon of voter "de-alignment".[48] In Jamaica, as elsewhere, this has taken the form of a sharp decline in traditional party attachment and loyalist voting behaviour. Concomitantly there has been an increase and consolidation in the proportion of the electorate regarding itself as uncommitted to either of the two established political parties and as independent of conventional politics. Of those who vote, there has been a growth in issue-oriented behaviour rather than voter choices determined primarily by socioeconomic standing or traditional party ties. This voter de-alignment has been most evident among the younger age cohorts and has driven many of the changes in Jamaican democracy in the 1990s. These changes have given rise to 'unconventional politics' at a number of different levels, some in accordance with global tendencies, others more or less specific to Jamaican experience. Among the latter has been the dramatic growth in popular protest, road blocks and demonstrations. These have taken place in the main around 'parish pump' issues related to the deteriorated economic and social infrastructure of the country, such as poor water supplies, bad roads, and inadequate transportation services. However protests have also occurred relatively frequently on human rights issues related primarily to excessive use of force and extra-judicial killings by the police. The demonstrations have not been confined to urban areas but affect rural areas as well and have been islandwide in scope. In the decade of 1986–96 these popular outbursts grew eight-fold, not least of all because the demonstrations have been relatively effective in attracting public attention and in producing some remedial response from the authorities. (See Table 2.3.)

A number of observations appear relevant on this definite change in the Jamaican political environment. In the first place, the sustained, largely spontaneous, extensive and intensive nature of unconventional forms of political participation paralleled the decade of diminishing electoral turnout. This would seem to question the idea that the Jamaican electorate was apathetic and suggests in its stead a certain quality of rationality. That is to say, significant segments of the electorate tend to withdraw from forms of political action which prove ineffective and gravitate to those, however unconventional or aggressive, which appear to produce some beneficial result. In this context, Franklin's comment in relation to global experience applies as forcibly to Jamaica: "Voters are not fools and an unresponsive system will motivate many fewer of them to vote."[49] At the same time, I will add: as it, in certain conditions, motivates many more of them to demonstrate to the extent that demonstrations produce positive results.

Secondly, however, the Jamaican phenomenon appears to depart from the pattern elsewhere in at least one important respect. Lijphart it is who observed that, generally speaking, levels of participation have been "unequal".[50] In most countries, "it is especially the more advantaged citizens who engage in . . . both conventional activities such as working in election campaigns . . . and unconventional activities like participation in demonstrations . . . blocking traffic".[51] In Jamaica, there can be no question that it has been the less "advantaged citizens" (to use Lijphart's phrase) who have dominated both conventional and, even more so in recent years, unconventional forms of political participation. This further suggests a peculiarity of a Jamaican political culture which is clearly in need of deeper and more profound analysis.

The extent of voter de-alignment in Jamaica and the nature of the uncommitted, independent trend amongst the Jamaican electorate also provided the basis for other important changes in Jamaica's politics. One of these has been the emergence of a relatively viable, partially anti-system party reflecting one dimension of the growth of an "anti-politics politics"[52] typical of many modern democracies. A major reason for this phenomenon in Jamaica and elsewhere has been an over-institutionalization of the traditional parties and a lack of openness to newly emerging social interests. In addition, particularly in the post-Cold War period, a convergence among the established parties developed, which, in many respects, limits both party representativeness and electoral choice. As a consequence, interests and positions from both the right and the left critical of middle and upper class male political hegemony, neoliberal economics and politics as well as existing forms of representative democracy, are in effect marginalized from the political mainstream. This lays the basis, under appropriate combinations of local circumstances, for the emergence and viability of anti-politics parties and personalities (from business, the media, the military, the Church).[53]

In Jamaica, these circumstances centred around long-standing disaffection within the JLP elite with Seaga's authoritarian leadership of the party. This discontent came to a head with the resignation of his heir apparent, Bruce Golding, and the latter's decision to form a new party, launched in October 1995, under the name, National Democratic Movement. The party's main slogan "Change the System"[54] reflected its central concern to change Jamaica's parliamentary system to a presidential order with separation of powers and effective checks and balances on what the NDM regarded as an almost omnipotent executive. In its economic programme, the new party was less clearly radical; even further were its anti-system credentials brought into doubt by the predominantly JLP background of many of its co-founders and the upper middle class character of much of its leadership. Nevertheless, the party signed up 10,000 members, gathered over 50,000 signatures necessary to win the right to appoint scrutineers and, three months after its formation, was able to attract a more than respectable 17 percent electoral support in national opinion polls. These were achievements no previous third party had been able to attain and, at base, reflected the strength and resilience of voter de-alignment as it had developed in Jamaica of the 1990s.

The fact that in the December 1997 elections the NDM was able to get only 5 percent of the national vote and did not win a single parliamentary seat does not substantially detract from the significance of the party's emergence nor of the importance of the tendency for democractic renewal amongst the people, which the party's emergence in part reflected. Rather, the NDM's relatively poor performance reflected deficiencies in the party itself as well as in the Jamaican political system. The party's middle class social character and predominantly JLP political origins separated it from the disadvantaged classes and sections of the uncommitted while the track record of service by its main candidates did not allow these gaps to be bridged. Added to this, Jamaica's first-past-the-post electoral system and total absence of public funding for political parties militated against the party's greater electoral success. Nevertheless, the NDM's formation and activity re-established some connection with the Jamaican political process among important sections of the younger professional and business elites and also strengthened the debate on important issues of constitutional and political reform in the 1997 elections.

The Result

One such issue was the nature of the electoral system and its influence on election results in Jamaica. In the first place, the decisiveness of the seat and, to a lesser extent, the vote majority of the PNP in 1997, maintained one of the most consistent traditions of Jamaican elections. In the eight previous general elections since Independence in 1962, the winning party had received not only a majority of the seats but also a majority of the votes cast. (See Table 2.4.) In terms of seat majorities, the Jamaican experience was very much in accord with other first-past-the-post (FPTP) electoral systems. This system unlike the various forms of proportional representation has a strong, though not universal, tendency to produce single party majorities in the legislature.[55] Much less evident elsewhere is the tendency of FPTP in Jamaica to produce, in addition, a popular vote majority and not just a plurality for the winning party. To that extent, Jamaica could hardly present a more stark contrast to the British FPTP prototype (from which the Jamaican system was copied) which has, over the past six decades, never produced a vote of 50 percent or over for the winning party in British elections.[56]

One reason for this peculiarity lies in the tendency of the Jamaican electorate, in particular the 'swing' voters whose voting tendency, in effect, determines electoral outcomes, to behave in a uniform manner across geographical constituencies and to vote on perceptions of issues rather than of party loyalties. Swings in voting behaviour are therefore neither minimal nor uneven. The development across the island of a relatively dense transportation, communication and information network contributed to an erosion, if not the disappearance, of significant regional differences or of constituency-specific voting. As Carl Stone put it, "the electorate has come to behave as if the whole country were one constituency with no significant regional variations".[57] This fact, combined with the failure of new parties to attract a significant percentage of votes, has meant a majority and not just plurality electoral support for Jamaican's winning parties in successive elections.

This leads to two other continuities of the Jamaican situation, one consistent with the operation of the FPTP system elsewhere, the other more specific to Jamaican experience. The first is reflected in the considerable disparity in the 1997 election results between the proportion of votes received by the parties and the percentage of legislative seats allocated. (See Table 2.4.) Because of the uniformity of the vote swings, whoever wins and whoever loses, wins and loses across the board. In this sense, the parliamentary representation of the winning PNP and losing JLP was inflated and deflated respectively by this significant disproportionateness.[58] It also reflected another strong tradition of Jamaican election results and confirmed one of the more universal outcomes of the FPTP electoral system. This exaggeration of legislative majorities and the under-representation of the opposition minority in the Jamaican context facilitates serious deficiencies in the functioning of goverment. It has contributed to the reduction in effectiveness of legislative oversight, to the disregard of opposition views (whether from outside or within the government's parliamentary ranks) and hence to any meaningful independence of the legislature. The large parliamentary majorities to which the electoral system contributes, therefore, help to make the Jamaican legislature little more than a 'rubber stamp' for the executive and are one source of the legitimacy of the call for political and constitutional reform in Jamaica.

In a second way, the 1997 general election results were consistent with Jamaica's past but somewhat out of step with emerging global experience. This was in the near absolute two-party dominance of both the electoral vote and of legislative representation. In all contested elections since independence in 1962 and for all save one of the 13 general elections since universal adult suffrage was achieved in Jamaica over 50 years ago, the PNP and the JLP have won over 85 percent of the popular vote. Since 1995, they have together won all the parliamentary seats in each election. Amongst democracies, perhaps only the United States has a comparable record of two-party dominance. So much so that a recent study of 53 democracies worldwide found two countries only, Zambia and the United States, in which the most recent elections gave all legislative seats exclusively to two parties.[59] Even in states with FPTP electoral systems, multi-party legislative representation has been displacing one and two party monopolies (for example, Bangladesh, Malawi, the Philippines and Thailand).

In this context, not only legislatures but also executives have become more open to multi-party participation. Of the 53 democracies to which earlier reference was made, a majority of 29 had coalition governments in the first half of the 1990s. As one study revealed, "the past two decades have seen the opening up of the government to an increasingly wide range of political parties . . ."[60] This in turn has reflected a broadening of party competition and legislative representation. "Should these trends continue," Leiden surmised, "we might yet witness the progressive destruction of traditional patterns of party competition with formerly closed patterns increasingly giving way to a style that is at once more open and less predictable."[61] In contrast, the 1997 elections produced entirely predictable (though not uniformly predicted) results in a two-party parliament and a single-party government.

The results of the elections also reflected the continuation of one of the more unambiguous flaws in Jamaican democracy – the phenomenon of over-voting, in which more votes are being cast than there are electors on the list in a particular area. This occured traditionally in polling stations in garrison communities where ballot books were simply written up or ballot boxes stuffed by party activists with ballots fraudulently marked for their party. Intimidation or collusion brought connivance from local electoral officials. The persistence of overvoting is, therefore, invariably one clear sign of a garrison, of the geographical spread of this practice and an indication of the location of political garrisons. The 1997 election results revealed overvoting in 214 or 3.4 percent of the 6,294 polling divisions. Significantly, 161, or 75 percent of these divisions were in 10 percent of the 60 constituencies, all in the urban area of Kingston and St Andrew.[62]

New provisions of the electoral law, arising from the reform process, allows for the election to be promptly rerun in any constituency where the number of electors in polling divisions affected by overvoting was greater than the margin of the victory of the winning candidate. In one constituency, the new provision in the law was applied, the election rerun twice, and as a result the constituency changed hands.[63] Clearly, firm and decisive implementation of the law, prosecution and punishment of the law-breakers is one way of signalling that this form of electoral corruption will no longer be tolerated. But overvoting is simply one of the symptoms of the persistence of the garrison constituency, the main corrosive undermining Jamaican democracy. Overall, it is undoubtedly true that "the 1997 election offered an opportunity for a positive turning point for Jamaica democracy".[64] But for that opportunity to be seized and the promise of a new beginning fulfilled, Jamaicans shall have to more purposively implement measures to dismantle garrison communities.

Notwithstanding this major outstanding item on the national agenda, did the 1997 general elections indicate a further decline, stabilization or improvement in the quality of Jamaican democracy? Voter turnout remained stable while, at the same time, unconventional participation reflected in public protests also increased. In terms of contestation, violence in word and deed fell off significantly. Moreover, civil society, national and transnational, played a new and positive role. On balance, these elections could be regarded as marking a bottoming out of the decline of Jamaica's democracy, while helping to strengthen the basis for renewal.

3

Deciding
Constitutional
Reform

As was indicated in chapter 2, the 1997 elections offered some opportunity to stabilize and to renew Jamaica's democracy. How far this opportunity might be realized will depend in no small measure on the restructuring of the institutional framework of Jamaican politics. Of importance in this regard are issues relating to constitutional and political reform which appeared and remained on Jamaica's national agenda throughout the 1990s. These concerns have paralleled similar developments in established democracies of the Anglophone Caribbean such as Barbados and Trinidad and Tobago.[1] In relation to the Caribbean Community as a whole, the authoritative West Indian Commission concluded that reform of institutions of governance experiencing significant decay was an urgent priority.[2] Elsewhere in the hemisphere, political elites in Latin American states undergoing transitions from varying degrees of authoritarian rule also demonstrated preoccupation with constitutional reform. Beginning in the second half of the 1980s, commissions, legislatures, executives and the 'interested public' debated then accepted and rejected, to differing extents, proposals for changing governmental structures in Mexico, Argentina, Colombia, Chile, Brazil, Bolivia, the Dominican Republic, Ecuador, Guatemala and Nicaragua, to mention but a few of the more prominent examples.[3]

In the mature liberal democracies of North America, issues of constitutional and political reform took on a new salience. Canada saw two referendums on the boundaries and character of its federal system. In the United States, 'gridlock' between the executive and legislative branches leading to a temporary shutdown of the federal government in 1995 renewed debate concerning the working of the 'separation of powers' in the American system. At the same time, intense media, legislative and executive attention renewed focus on issues of campaign finance reform following the 1996 presidential elections.[4] Across the Atlantic, in perhaps the most venerable of Parliamentary democracies, the question of constitutional reform became an important issue in the 1996 British elections and, subsequently, a programmatic commitment of the new Tony Blair Labour Party government.[5] More expectedly, in countries undergoing transition from communist regimes in Europe and one-party systems in Africa, the need to transform previously authoritarian rule led to widespread constitution-making and 'institutional engineering'. Underlying these new processes everywhere, to one degree or another, was public dissatisfaction with existing politics.[6] Whether through protests in town squares or denunciations on talk shows, voter abstention in elections or public opinion surveys, the people signalled the need for change.

There is also another basis for this relatively intense focus on constitutions, constitution-making and constitutional reform towards the end of the 1980s and into the 1990s. This was a renewed recognition that, whilst social and economic factors were important, the particular design of a country's political institutions did, in fact, have significant impact on its government and politics.[7] This recognition had declined somewhat with the rise of behaviouralism in the 1960s and 1970s and the legitimate emphasis on the influence of social factors on politics: hence the preoccupation with the political impact of levels and patterns of class development, urbanization, education, ethnic and racial identity, communication and other changing areas. Similarly, concern focused on the political causes and consequences of economic growth, income inequality, industrialization and unemployment. Cultural attitudes and values were also assumed to be important elements in the politics of any country. The strength of this work was its emphasis on the social economy of politics, its avoidance of the formal-legal approach to political institutions; its weakness, however, was a disregard of the importance of the structure of political institutions as a relatively independent factor in the political process.

By the late 1980s, a 'new institutionalism' developed in response to this weakness.[8] Social and economic factors were recognized as important. But, to one degree or another, the politics of a country varied depending on the design of its political institutions. Social, economic or political cleavages, for example, could be widened or reduced in their significance depending on whether an electoral system was proportional or majoritarian. The potential for instability could be increased or moderated depending on whether legislatures or executives were structured to facilitate single-party dominance or power sharing. How far decision-making and decision-implementation were effective and legitimate might depend on whether legislative-executive relations were structured along parliamentary or presidential lines, and on whether there were effective mechanisms against 'special interest' dominance, corruption and the like. The design of new organs of governance and the reform of existing ones was therefore not a matter of insignificance. Such institutional engineering was important and took place, most meaningfully, not oblivious to but with full acknowledgement of the social, economic, and cultural specifics of particular countries.

Popular Discontent and Proposals for Radical Change

Jamaica was no exception to this rule. In June 1995, a landmark study of the country's political culture found, remarkably for a "consolidated democracy", less than 2 percent of Jamaicans indicating their constitution and government as that aspect of Jamaica of which they were most proud.[9] In the same vein, almost two-thirds of the people felt that Jamaican's democracy did not work well and was in need of a lot of fundamental changes.[10] Given the strong value preferences for free speech and the historical attachment to the right to vote, the changes desired pointed in the direction of more democracy, not less. Moreover, a major concern, reflecting locally a central preoccupation of scholars, statesman and the public globally, was the perception of excessive "special interest" influence on government by "the IMF/foreign banks, the private sector, and the upper class".[11] Consistent with this feeling, almost three-quarters of the Jamaican public rejected the view that "everyone in Jamaica has an equal say in government".[12]

Despite the fact that in recent times popular dissatisfaction with democracy is common to both transitional as well as established or consolidated democracies, the Jamaican level is undoubtedly toward the high end of the discontent continuum. (See Table 3.6.) In 1996, 35 percent of the population were very or fairly satisfied with the system. The available data suggests that no other consolidated democracy had as low a "satisfaction" score.[13] Among those 16 states with lower levels of satisfaction with democracy, all except Italy, could be regarded as "transitional" and part of the "third wave of democratization".

None were in the second wave as Jamaica had been nor had any sustained democracy for as long as Jamaica had done. Five of these (Spain, Chile, Greece, Brazil, Paraguay) were in varying degrees of progress to democracy from military rule dismantled within the last 25 years. One (Mexico) was moving from one-party authoritarianism and nine (Latvia, Slovak Republic, Lithuania, Hungary, Armenia, Ukraine, Belarus, Bulgaria and Russia) were in the process of establishing democracy out of previously communist regimes. Italy alone amongst democracies appears to harbour as much dissatisfaction with the inadequacies of the system as Jamaica.

Doubtless, this exception and sense of inadequacy with the Jamaican system amongst Jamaicans has to do with a number of special factors. One is the range of negative features – political violence, party patronage and clientelism, elite-dominated party organizations, to name a few – which matured in the competition structures and participation processes of Jamaican democracy by the 1980s.[14] Another is the relative non-performance of the governmental systems, reflected in economic indicators and in the quality of life of the majority of the population. Stagnant or declining per capita income, a significant proportion of citizens living below the poverty line, widening income inequality, rising levels of violent crime, high unemployment and low wage employment, deteriorating roads, inadequate water supply and sewerage systems,[15] these are among some of the features in the 1990s which would have heightened dissatisfaction with the political system amongst disadvantaged sectors. The fact that Jamaica ranked amongst states with the sharpest decline globally in rating on the UNDP's Human Development Index and has entered into the most agreements with the IMF[16] between the 1970s and the 1990s are but two reflections of the comparative severity, in global terms, of the non-performance of the political and economic system.

Objective non-performance and subjective discontent both fuelled and sustained the tendency toward constitutional and political reform in the 1990s. Among the earliest and most significant outgrowths as well as stimulants of the reform tendency was an official Committee appointed by Prime Minister Michael Manley in June 1990 "to examine ways of strengthening the role and performance of parliamentarians".[17] Manley, in fact, set up this body under the chairmanship of Carl Stone, Professor of Political Sociology at the University of the West Indies and the country's most prominent pollster, in response to widespread public opposition, reflected in national opinion polls, to significant increases in parliamentary salaries announced by the government despite the existence of an IMF wage restraint regime. The

Stone Committee, which was composed of parliamentarians as well as prominent public personalities from the church, the professions and the media, therefore, carried out its mandate in a context of explicit public disquiet with politics and politicians. The Committee itself commissioned national opinion surveys, received submissions from the public and submitted its report in April 1991.

The report acknowledged a basic choice facing Jamaican governance: "between gradual and incrementalist changes that preserve intact constitutional stability and continuity" on the one hand and, on the other, "more radical approaches that seek fundamentally to alter our political system".[18] The Committee, while recognizing the risk inherent in the latter, nevertheless opted for radical change in the Jamaican political system. It justified this on the grounds that only far-reaching and fundamental change had the possibility of arresting the sharp decline of public confidence in the system and restoring some credibility to government and politician alike. The extent of this decline was reflected in the public perception that the majority of MPs were self-seeking, corrupt, and made poor representatives.[19] Moreover, and no doubt partly as a consequence, there was a dramatic decline in interest in parliamentary affairs. "Only about 20 percent of voters", the Stone Report noted "now follow important parliamentary events such as the televised annual budget speeches featuring the country's top political leadership. This compares to a much higher 40 percent level in the early 1980s and an even higher 55 percent level in the 1970s."[20]

Against this background, the Stone Committee argued that radical institutional change was needed so as to provide a new framework for breaking with old habits and to lay out clear incentives for the development of new, more positive attitudes and behaviour at all levels in the political system. One fundamental negative with which the reform would need to come to grips was the overwhelming power of the prime minister in the Jamaican system and the consequent fact that the legislature was little more than a 'rubber stamp' for the executive.[21] Features which operated in some degree in the original British parliamentary prototype, such as the tabling of parliamentary questions and the operation of parliamentary select committees to check the executive had little significance in the Jamaican legislature.[22] This lack of independence together with the absence of any means whereby the electorate could hold their representatives to account in between elections was therefore a major problem with which the Stone Committee attempted to grapple.

In the final analysis, the Committee recommended two radical changes and a number of attendant proposals to cope with the central deficiency of

Jamaican governance. It proposed that Jamaica adopt a presidential system, with a clear separation of powers in place of the parliamentary system. Secondly, the Stone Committee proposed a duty to report to their constituents by elected representatives and a right to recall by the electorate of their representatives prior to the expiry of their term of office.[23] In relation to presidentialism, Stone argued that the separation of powers would induce much-needed checks and balances on the executive. On the other hand, the danger of gridlock under presidential government would be less real in a Jamaican system in which ideological and policy differences between the parties had become negligible and in which the executive would be likely to enjoy support from a relatively disciplined party within a two-party legislature. Moreover, a separation of legislative from executive responsibilities would free the members of each branch to attend to their respective primary responsibilities of constituency representation and executive oversight on the one hand and policy development and implementation on the other. As regards the right to recall, the Stone Committee was divided between a supportive majority and a minority which dissented from the proposal. The majority argued that, with appropriate safeguards against abuse, such a mechanism would both help to keep representatives 'on their toes' as well as encourage greater citizen interest in monitoring members of parliament.

The argument of the Stone Committee majority does find some substantiation in the American experience of the right to recall. Among the 26 states which have constitutional or statutory provision for this right, the use of recall petitions has been relatively infrequent. " . . . the fear of the opponents of the recall that it would be used often and disrupt representative government has proved to be unfounded . . . "[24] The reasons for this relative infrequency include (as Stone suggested for Jamaica) the requirement of voter signature thresholds which are relatively high and presuppose significant organization capability thereby discouraging frivolous applications. On the positive side there have been instances where the recall pattern has been used by citizens against representatives who have voted against their explicit wishes or who have in some way violated public trust.

In this latter regard, the Stone Committee recommendations included a pronounced participatory democratic dimension, alongside the controversial right of recall. It proposed the establishment of new institutions called "Constituency Consultative Committees". Each of these would be composed of representatives of civic bodies (such as churches, citizens' associations and youth organizations) within the constituency and would include the elected member of parliament for that area. Each such body would have the responsibility of assisting the MP in identifying worthwhile constituency projects, drawing up constituency budgets and monitoring implementation, all, hopefully, on a non-partisan basis. These committees, as well, would play an important role in managing the recall process, thereby helping to insulate it against abuse.

Initial response to what was properly considered a radical reform agenda was mixed. In regard to the change to a presidential form of government with separation of powers, public response was more or less evenly divided in early 1991 between 44 percent in favour, 46 percent against and 10 percent undecided. Interestingly, but perhaps unsurprisingly, the overwhelming majority of parliamentarians were against such a change. Similar, but much more decisive, was the conflict between the opinions of the political elite and that of the mass public on the issue of the right of recall. Over 70 percent of the public were supportive whilst an even greater proportion of past and present parliamentarians were against.[25] This divide certainly suggested a degree of dissatisfaction with Jamaican democracy and an openness to radical change significantly greater at the base and in the middle than at the apex of the political system. This perception was confirmed as the process of reform and, concomitantly, resistance to radical change unfolded in the aftermath of the Stone Report.

Moderate Reform of the Westminster Model

In the first place, whilst displaying a marked reluctance to discuss and conclude on the recommendation of the Stone Committee, the government and parliament set up, in effect, parallel structures to deal with constitutional reform. This began in 1991 with the formation of a Joint Select Committee of the Houses of Parliament on Constitutional and Electoral Reform "to recommend the precise form and content of Constitutional Amendments both with respect to an Electoral Commission and other aspects of Constitutional Reform" (p. 1). Subsequently, in February 1992, Parliament suspended the work of the Joint Select Committee and, on the recommendation of the leader of the opposition, established a Constitutional Commission. Unlike the Joint Select Committee on which membership was confined to parliamentary members of two major parties, the members of the Commission were drawn from representatives of educational institutions, trade unions, the legal fraternity, churches, the press and groups representing women, farmers, youth, and private sector organizations (p. 2). These representatives sat alongside substantial delegations from the parliamentary parties, whose views, as it turned out, nevertheless dominated the Commission's final recommendations.

The main body of these recommendations was finalized in August 1993 and, in regard to the question of Fundamental Rights and Freedoms, in February 1994. The Commission's Report and its recommendations were examined in detail by the reconvened Joint Select Committee of Houses of Parliament during 1994 and early 1995. The Committee's final recommendations and the contents of its report were agreed to at the end of May 1995. In contrast to the Stone Committee, the Constitutional Commission and the Joint Select Committee rejected radical change and opted for "incremental" reforms in the system of governance.

As such, the Joint Select Committee proposed to retain the parliamentary system and not accept the right to recall. In respect of the former, the Committee recorded that it "gave considerable attention to examining the public's views" such as that parliament was "merely a 'rubber stamp' for the cabinet's proposals, providing inadequate representation of the people [and was] more concerned about . . . the executive . . . at the expense of fulfilling their primary responsibility as representatives of the people" (p. 25). It also considered the criticism that Parliament "was perceived as . . . failing to provide an opportunity for representation of any groupings other than the two major political parties." In relation to the right of recall, the Committee noted that many members opposed the idea and "those members sympathetic to the idea could not devise a mechanism that would secure the benefits to be obtained without opening up the system of recall to abuse" (p. 27).

Nevertheless, in the light of criticisms and shortcomings of the existing system, the Committee did propose a number of reforms whilst recommending "the retention of the Westminster model"(p. 6). Amongst the more important of these was a limit or cap of 40 percent on the proportion of members of the legislature who could hold executive office. This proposal, it argued, was "designed to restrict the ability of the parliamentarians holding executive positions to dominate and control their parliamentary colleagues" (p. 27). In the same vein, the prime minister's unfettered discretion to dissolve the legislature should have some limit. He "should have no power to call a general election unless there is in existence a list of registered voters which has been completed for not more than six (6) months prior to the calling of the general elections" (p. 27). Moreover, the Committee recommended strengthening the

Fundamental Rights and Freedoms provisions so as to make them less amenable to incursions from the executive and so as to provide the citizen with more effective means of redress. Finally, provisions for impeachment of public officials, including members of the government and the executive, were recommended though the impeachment process proposed would itself be significantly subject to executive veto (p. 22).

Because of the centrality to the issue, it is worth summarizing the Joint Committee's argument for retaining the parliamentary form and rejecting the presidential system and the separation of powers. These were, in brief, the compatibility of "Jamaica's political culture" with the former and, given the country's "long working experience with it [the parliamentary system] our people are accustomed to it and our institutions have been fashioned under its influence" (p. 6). Secondly, "the Westminster model enables prompt implementation of programmes and policies with no likelihood of paralysis of the Executive and the Legislature" (p. 6). Conversely, the Committee argued that its recommendations would have some significant impact in circumscribing the admittedly overwhelming power of the prime minister vis-à-vis the legislature within the modified system.

Despite its own preference, the Committee recognized that the choice between retention of the parliamentary system and shifting to a presidential one was fundamental. Moreover, amongst the Jamaican people, "differing viewpoints [were] so strongly held that the question is not likely to be set at rest without some clear-cut expression by the Jamaican people as to which of the two systems commands greater support" (p. 37). Accordingly the Committee, recommended to parliament that "it should put in place" after "a full and effective public education programme", and before initiating the formal constitution amendment process, "an appropriate mechanism for determining the will of the Jamaican people in this regard". In this context, both the government and opposition parties committed themselves "in advance to abide by the result" (pp. 7, 37) of what would be an indicative referendum as to whether Jamaica should remain a parliamentary democracy or change to a presidential system. In effect, the people themselves would decide in general terms whether the reform path should follow the more radical direction of the Stone Committee or the more conservative course of the Joint Parliamentary Select Committee.

Participatory Democracy

The referral of this fundamental issue to a plebiscite was in itself an outgrowth of a more active public and reflected, in Jamaican circumstances, a wider global tendency on matters of constitutional and political reform. In fact, in the four years between the tabling and the Stone Committee (April 1991) and the Joint Select Committee Reports in Parliament (May 1995), with the latter's recommendation of a national poll to determine the structure of government, close to 70 referendums were held in a score of states around the world many on issues related to constitutional reform.[26] This represented an average of over 17 referendums per year in the 1990s, reflecting the highest ever global usage of this mechanism of direct democracy.[27] Moreover, this growing use of the referendum was not region specific; it was common to both North and South as well as to the First and the Third Worlds. It is interesting to note that at the subnational level in the United States, this method of decision-making also increased significantly in popularity during the 1990s.[28]

Of course, within the general pattern there were wide variations. At one end of the continuum, Switzerland as "the only nation in the world where political life truly revolves around the referendum"[29] had as many as all other states combined. In addition, the average annual number of referendums in Switzerland actually tripled in the decade after 1985, compared to the average for the previous 110 years. At the other end of the spectrum, over 60 countries (almost one-third of the membership of the UN) had not, up until 1995, held a national referendum since achieving independence though Bogdanor has observed that "there are only six democracies – the German Federal Republic, India, Israel, Japan, the Netherlands and the United States – which have never employed them at national level".[30] With the exception of Guyana in 1978, the Anglophone Caribbean democracies, including Jamaica, have not used this mechamism. Despite this unevenness, there can be no question that around the world there is a "growing use of direct democracy" in decision-making at the national and subnational levels.

The reasons for this trend are not hard to find. In a global context where distrust of politicians and government has grown, decisions by popular vote, especially on controversial issues, has obviously greater legitimacy. This consideration becomes all the more compelling given many of the circumstances of modern politics.[31] The historic gap in education levels between electorates and their representatives has narrowed considerably. The access of the 'man-in-the-street' to information has grown immensely contributing to what has been called a "skill revolution" and leisure time has increased as work hours per week have declined universally in the second half of the twentieth century. Moreover as evidence has accumulated of the subjection of legislatures and executives to the power of "special interests", more especially to the overwhelming influence of increasingly concentrated income and wealth, so too has grown the strength of the argument that the people should themselves decide critical issues. In any event, given that on any definition democracy does connote ultimate authority in the hands of the people, the position that this authority ought to be brought to bear directly on fundamental questions and exercised more frequently than at periodic elections for representatives carries much persuasiveness.

Experience does suggest however some caution against romanticizing the referendum. By and large, most are called by governments to suit their own "political convenience"[32] even though the outcome of the vote often goes against the wishes of the party or leader in office. Where the referendum proposal arises directly from popular initiative, sometimes the proposal lapses for want of the requisite level and timing of endorsement signatures (for example, New Zealand),[33] and at other times, particularly at the state level in the United States, the referendum result sometimes favours the side with the biggest financial backing and the highest campaign spending.[34] In terms of voter participation, the global tendency is for referendums to elicit lower turnout levels than elections to representative bodies.[35] Despite these factors arguing against idealization of direct democracy, there can be little doubt that at bottom a major consideration underlying the growing use of the referendum is the increased need to lend greater popular legitimacy to decisions of state on important matters.

High amongst these are constitutional issues and, especially in the context of disagreement on basic models, the desirability of ensuring at least majority endorsement of the option to be taken. In the Jamaican case, between the appointment of the Stone Committee in 1990 and the 1997 general election, a consensus emerged that the 1962 Independence Constitution had to be reformed. At the symbolic level this had to do with the need to abolish the monarchy inherited from the colonial period and move to a republican status. More substantively, there was agreement on the need to effectively protect and extend political rights and civil liberties. Most of all, there developed a consensus within and outside the political elite that there was an overwhelming dominance of the executive within the political system and any reform had to deal with this imbalance as a vital element. The fundamental disagreement centred on the issue of not whether but how this objective should be achieved. By the middle of the decade, the critical question had become: should Jamaica retain the Westminster parliamentary system or should Jamaica adopt a presidential system with the separation of powers?

Parliamentarianism versus Presidentialism

Within the political system, the alignment was as follows: for retention of the Westminster model, albeit with reforms, the leader of the opposition as well as the opposition JLP; opposed to the Westminster parliamentary system and for a presidential model, the newly formed NDM and its leader, Bruce Golding, formerly Seaga's heir apparent in the JLP; finally, supportive of a 'hybrid' system in which the head of government would be directly elected but the executive remain responsible to the legislature, the governing PNP. Outside the political parties, the picture was somewhat mixed. The major special interest groups (the private sector, the trade unions, churches) did not take organizational positions on this issue and opinion polls revealed, at best, secondary concern in the public at large in constitutional reform, posed in those terms. However, the majority of submissions to both the Stone Committee and the Joint Select Committee of Parliament which dealt with the structure of government favoured a change from the parliamentary model.[36] Moreover, by the mid 1990s, a majority of the electorate also favoured a separation of the election of the head of government from the election of the constituency representative.[37]

The argument in Jamaica about the system of government pretty much replicated, with local specifics, the global debate concerning the relative merits of parliamentarianism versus presidentialism.[38] The "perils of presidentialism" were consistently articulated by Seaga and the JLP. Such a system risked deadlock or gridlock when the executive and the legislature could not agree. Conversely, when the prime minister (or elected president) was at the same time leader of the majority party in the legislature, not only would the legislature fail to provide any check on executive power but it would also inordinately reinforce that power. Moreover, should the directly elected executive lose favour, either with the electorate or with the legislative majority during the executive's term of office, there would be no constitutional way to remove the executive from power. In addition, Seaga argued, under the presidential system, the members of the president's cabinet would suffer from two disadvantages: they would not enjoy the legitimacy of being elected legislators; not being members of Parliament, they would lack the legislative presence to pilot bills through debates in the House through the stage of law.

On the other side of the coin, the JLP argued that the parliamentary system was familiar to and an integral part of Jamaica's political culture. Admittedly the working of the system had led to an overconcentration of power in the hands of the prime minister. This however was not an inherent property and would be corrected by reforming the operations rather than changing the character of the parliamentary system. Such reforms, Seaga proposed and the Joint Select Committee and the parliament approved, should include: strengthening the Committee system in Parliament; making the standing orders regarding 'question time' and private members' motions more effective; introducing an impeachment process to deal with abuse of power by officials of state, a process to which the prime minister and other ministers would themselves be subject; dilution of the prime minister's power of appointment to sensitive state positions; and, most of all, placing a cap on the percentage of members of parliament who might be appointed to the executive, thereby automatically constraining their independence in exercising oversight functions in relation to the executive.

Within the political system, these arguments were most effectively critiqued by the NDM. The concentration of power in the hands of the prime minister was, the NDM argued, the single most important source of a number of evils plaguing the Jamaican political system and undermining the quality of Jamaican democracy. Amongst these were three particular negatives: the acute, often violent, nature of Jamaica's election campaigns as victory meant 'winner take all' for the triumphant prime minister and, conversely, 'loser lose all' for the defeated party leader (with attendant gains and losses for party supporters); the lack of independence of members of Parliament, and hence the ineffectiveness of checks on the executive, arising from the dependence of both their electoral candidacy and election prospects on endorsement by either the existing or alternative prime minister (that is, the leader of the parliamentary opposition); the poor quality of constituency representation arising in large measure from the difficulty of elected members successfully performing legislative representational and executive functions simultaneously. The NDM argued that these deficiencies had become inherent in Jamaica's parliamentary system as it had evolved by the third decade of national independence. The system had to be changed and not simply reformed in order to overcome the drawbacks which were disfiguring the country's politics.

Such a change to a presidential system with a more complete separation of powers than the parliamentary system allowed would go a long way to providing an institutional framework which would help modify some of the more negative behaviour of Jamaican politics. In the first place, separating the election of the constituency representative from the election of the prime minister would help to reduce the dependence of the former on the latter. The local candidate would no longer rise or fall depending exclusively on the elector's attitude to his party leader. The candidate's independent performance, inside or outside the legislature, could then count to an extent that it could not once there was no possibility of the elector 'splitting' his vote and once the candidate was, in effect, a proxy for the party leader. Moreover, once the life of the executive was no longer dependent on majority parliamentary support, legislative voting on issues 'on merit' rather than according to 'party line' would be facilitated in so far as voting for or against a measure could neither shorten the life of the government nor bring the opposition prematurely to power. No doubt the tradition of party-based voting would continue but could not be institutionally compelled by party whips preoccupied with the survival of the government or the accession of the opposition. These factors, the NDM argued, would not destroy 'party discipline'. Rather, together they would help move Jamaican parties from leader-dependent, highly centralized organizations to moderately disciplined bodies in which the members would have greater influence.

In this proposal, the dynamics of greater legislative independence within the framework of relatively disciplined parties would be reinforced and made meaningful by legislative prerogatives vis-à-vis the executive. These would include confirmation duties by way of a two-thirds majority for nominees of the prime minister to the Cabinet, to sensitive Commissions and to independent authorities (relating to the judiciary, public service, electoral administration and similar bodies), ambassadorships as well as other public offices.[30] parliamentary committees would exercise oversight in relation to executive proposals, including budget proposals. More effective constituency representation would be facilitated, first by the member of parliament having no executive responsibility. In addition, "a Constituency Development Fund to be financed by 5 percent of the annual budget" would be established and each member of parliament would be required to submit a five-year development plan, which, once approved by parliament, would guide the expenditure under the Constituency Development Fund. Moreover, a Constituency Consultative Committee would be established in each constituency, composed of members of civic organizations as well as members of other parties to oversee constituency projects and to report annually to parliament.

In regard to the issue of gridlock, the NDM argued that, in Jamaican circumstances, the absence of an automatic legislative majority, which would be encouraged by the separation of powers, would check the winner-take-all elective dictatorship which had developed under Jamaica's parliamentary system. This would, among other things, allow more careful examination and thoughtful scrutiny of controversial measures both by parliament and by the public. In order, however, to guard against governmental paralysis in the event of legislative-executive disagreement, there would be provision for executive proposals to become law unless, after resubmission, they were overridden by a two-thirds majority of the Parliament. Similarly, parliamentary positions would prevail against executive opposition if, after rejection by the executive, such positions won approval from a two-thirds majority of the legislature.

In the years preceding the 1997 general elections, intense debate developed inside and outside the Jamaican Parliament on the parliamentary and presidential systems as well as on possible variants of the main models. The mass media formed a particularly important forum for discussion. On talk shows, in letters to editors, in newspaper columns and series,[40] on television panels and radio forums, the issues were extensively debated. Outside the media, community groups and citizens' organizations of one sort or another took part in the debate. There can be no question that in the public discussion the issue of constitutional reform, so conceptualized, remained primarily a preoccupation of the middle and upper classes though the disadvantaged also took an interest in the debate. Equally clearly, however, the more practical matters to which the "structure of government debate" was related, such as more effective political representation or less violent party competition, were of considerable concern to the lower classes.

This contradiction between high levels of popular concern with social and economic issues such as crime and unemployment but relatively low interest in constitutional reform suggested one weakness in the national debate. An insufficiently clear connection was being made between the citizenry's everyday preoccupations and the constitutional reform issue. In part, this had to do with the indirectness and the real indeterminacy, in general terms, of the connection between types of democracy and, for example, levels of growth. Clearly a presidential system is not, in general terms, a concomitant of either economic growth or stagnation, employment creation or continued unemployment. Neither is a parliamentary system. Either has been accompanied by growth or stagnation and high or low levels of crime. Simplified, the argument ran as follows: the United States is a presidential system and crime is going down but crime is also going down in Barbados which has a parliamentary system. Conversely, Brazil is presidential and crime is rising; India is parliamentary and crime is also rising. Hence rates of crime, a major preoccupation, are unaffected by forms of government. A major challenge facing the reform process in Jamaica is therefore to uncover and explain the particular linkages in the specifics of Jamaican conditions between one or another position on constitutional change and the everyday concerns of the people.

A second shortcoming of the debate has been the counterpoising of the parliamentary and the presidential systems with insufficient recognition that variants within each type are often as important as the basic distinction between them.[41] For example, the European continental subtype of the parliamentary system has features very different from the British Westminster model and, in some ways, similar to the presidential system. In particular, the parliamentary executives in Europe are anything but "prime ministerial dictatorships" in the British mould. They are invariably composed of coalitions of different parties; decision-making by compromise within executives and between executives and multi-party legislatures is more the order of the day than rule by prime ministerial edict. This give and take places European parliamentarianism, at least in this respect, closer to American presidentialism than to the British Westminster model. The formal nature of executive-legislature relations (similar between British and European systems) is less important in influencing the less dictatorial nature of European parliamentarianism than are other factors, in particular, the proportional representation electoral systems and the multi-party cabinets. The parliamentary system need not, therefore, amount to executive dictatorship. To this extent, the relative absence of discussion of European parliamentary models from the Jamaican debate is undoubtedly a deficiency.

Conversely, presidential systems need not suffer from the extremes of presidents who are either impotent in the face of gridlock or omnipotent in the context of highly disciplined legislative majorities. Modification in the timing of executive-legislative elections and in the structure of parties, more particularly candidate selection, can influence the emergence of presidencies with enough power to govern but not too much to escape legislative "checks and balances".[42] The key is to facilitate the emergence of legislative parties that are disciplined enough to provide the presidential executive with a base to rule but, at the same time, one sufficiently independent not to be a pliant tool of presidential power. Moreover, much recent review of the available evidence is suggesting that even in the prototype presidential system, the United States, "divided government" has not, on the whole, meant governmental stalemate.[43]

One other deficiency in the Jamaican debate is worth mentioning – its relative unconcern with the basic issue of majoritarian versus consensual democracy.[44] In a sense, the Jamaican experience may be regarded as an extreme example of majoritarian democracy and the deformities to which it can contribute. Single-party cabinets, substantial single-party legislative majorities, single-party electoral majorities have in Jamaica characterized 50 years of universal adult suffrage through successive stages of decolonization and post-independence statehood. In a narrow sense, this has meant relatively stable government. But at an increasingly huge price. It has demanded the exclusion of the minority party from policy-making; the under-representation and relative ineffectiveness of the minority party in the legislature; policy discontinuities accompanying changes of government; most of all, victimization of the defeated minority by a winner-take-all majority. These negative features have grown over the years and have, in no small measure, eroded the quality of Jamaican democracy.

The question of a more consensual approach needs, therefore, to be put on the table as an alternative to this extreme majoritarianism. In this concept, the building of bridges between the major parties, at all levels, and between the parties and new formations, civic and political, would become an end in itself within the reform process. On this basis, the redesigning of government and the reform of the constitution would have as one aim the dilution of monopoly of power and the encouragement of power-sharing at all levels. Such a goal would have significant implications for modification in Jamaica's FPTP electoral system, for the composition of the legislature and the executive, for norms governing consultation between majority and minority parties, for appointments to state and parastate bodies, and for rules relating to the awarding of contracts and the disposal of public assets. Particularly in respect of the electoral system and the disproportionate legislative majorities, the system has invariably accorded single-party governments. The case is overwhelming for constitutional reform to propose some version of a mixed system (such as those that exist in Germany, New Zealand and the proposals being made in the UK). Such reform would preserve the value of constituency based on representation while ensuring proportionality in party legislative representation. Without a turn to more consensual forms and methods of governance, constitutional reform will insufficiently confront a major deficiency in Jamaican democracy.

In any event, by the middle of the decade, opinion polls showed that a majority of the people had moved away from support of the parliamentary system and were by then in favour of, at least, direct election of the executive and the separation of executive and legislative elections. Less clear is the depth of the popular understanding of the subsidiary issues and the state of public opinion on matters such as how to cope with gridlock. The fact is that opinion surveys have paid inadequate attention to stimulating and promoting the views of the mass public. To this extent, the Jamaican experience conforms to a global pattern whereby despite "constitutional and institutional reform on an unprecedented scale", insufficient effort has been made to tap the views of the people whose "opinions [are] generally absent from the research literature".[45] It is the strength of these opinions, however, in one direction or another, which have underlain the decision of the Jamaican government to take the unprecedented step of calling an indicative referendum on constitutional reform. Hopefully, the public education relating to the issues in the upcoming referendum will correct this weakness.

In this last regard, it is worthwhile noting that the Jamaican decision was not only in line with the growing use of referendums. It was directly influenced by such an experience in that the initial suggestion to hold a plebiscite was explicitly based on the 1992 New Zealand precedent. In that year, the decision to change New Zealand's long-established FPTP electoral system resulted from an indicative referendum following prolonged public debate, as well as considerable disagreement, within that country's political elite. On another level, it is interesting to note that the debate on constitutional reform in Jamaica represented, so to speak, the flip side of the coin to the parallel debate taking place in Latin America. In the latter case, the weight of scholarly and some public opinion was in the direction of highlighting the perils of presidentialism[46] and the virtues of the parliamentary system. In contrast, the Jamaican discussion trended in the converse direction. Perhaps it is that, especially in a period of discredited government, "the grass always seems greener on the other side" or, more prosaically, each system has both perils and attractions, vices and virtues.

The referendum process and outcome is, nevertheless, of great significance. To the extent that public education is significant and public participation meaningful, with or without the systemic institutional change, concentrations of power in winner-take-all structures are likely to be reduced, with positive consequences for the quality of Jamaican democracy.

4

Coping with the Drug Menace

Threats to Democracy

In assessing and enhancing the prospects of democratic renewal, a major concern must be the multidimensional threat posed by the 'drug menace' to democratic institutions. In Jamaica, the first serious public acknowledgement of the danger came from Prime Minister Michael Manley in April 1990 when he warned that Jamaica was "threatened" by an international criminal network in drug trafficking "that has no precedent in history".[1] Subsequent to this, at the regional level, the report of the important West Indian Commission set up by the governments of the Anglophone Caribbean Community (CARICOM) concluded that:

Nothing poses greater threats to civil society in CARICOM countries than the drug problem(s). The damage . . . to democratic society itself from the drug problem(s) is as great a menace as any dictator's repression . . . CARICOM countries are threatened today by an onslaught from illegal drugs as crushing as any military repression.[2]

At the global level, the international community had recognized, in the words of the 1998 Vienna Convention, that the "large financial profits and wealth" generated by the illicit drug industry were "enabling transnational criminal organizations to penetrate, contaminate, and corrupt the structures of government".[3] The size of the industry's total turnover "lies somewhere around the US $400 billion level . . . larger than the international trade in iron and steel, and motor vehicles, and about the same size as the total international trade in textiles".[4] The dimensions of this were, in the words of the 1988 UN Convention, such as to "undermine . . . legitimate economies and threaten . . . the sovereignty of state".

The dangers to democracy, however defined, are clear. To the extent that influence is bought so that illegal drug money and functionaries in the illicit narcotics industry can and do corrupt political parties and party representatives or elected legislators and executives, to that extent the will of the people is subverted. Moreover, the rule of law, a fundamental underpinning of democracy, is undermined when law enforcement agencies and officials in the justice system (customs officials, policemen, prosecutors, witnesses, jurors, judges) are successfully bribed, intimidated or otherwise corrupted by narco-criminals. Conversely, the rule of law is also undermined when, in the interest of dealing more effectively with the drug related crime and criminals, basic human rights are violated by the state and its law enforcement agencies. On a broader, macro-level, the authority of the elected government, and therefore the degree of democracy, is often reduced by subordination of state as well as non-state actors related to the narcotics industry. At the state level, to the extent that pressures from countries such as the United States coerce the international community or compel individual governments to conform to American demands against their better judgement, to that extent democratic sovereignty is compromised.[5] On the other hand, democratic sovereignty is also undermined to the degree that illegal transnational narcotics networks and organizations have and utilize the capability of violating the territorial integrity of a state with relative impunity.

It is, therefore, hardly an exaggeration to conclude that, in general, "powerful narcotics constituencies increasingly threaten electoral processes, the exercise of sovereignty and the rule of law (especially) in a number of Latin American and Asian States . . ."[6] In the Caribbean specifically, illicit drug "structures and networks", as one scholar observed, "could not exist without the collusion of people in government and private agencies in various positions and at all hierarchical levels; people in shipping companies, customs and immigration agencies, warehouses, police forces, the military, airlines, export and import companies, stores, cruise ships, trucking companies, farms, factories, bus and taxi operations and so on".[7] Moreover, in a number of territories, including St Kitts-Nevis, Antigua, Guyana, Jamaica, the Bahamas, the Cayman Islands, Turks and Caicos Islands, elements within political and economic elites have been convicted or credibly implicated in the drug trade. Not surprisingly, therefore, the Bridgetown Declaration, adopted in May 1997 by the Summit of Caribbean Heads of Government of the CARICOM and the United States, expressed deep concern at "the growing strength and capabilities of transnational criminal organizations and drug cartels, their attempts to distort and weaken our free economies and democratic systems and the effects which their activities and presence have on levels of violence and basic public order".[8] At the subnational levels, the danger has been acknowledged as going beyond threatening the state to supplanting its basic organs and functions in specific localities and communities. In some cases, narcotics organizations have taken over functions normally reserved to the state, especially in such areas as social welfare and (ironically) maintenance of law and order. In Mexico, Colombia, Bolivia and Peru, traffickers have devoted large sums to community development projects (such as roads, schools, and housing). Such activities have expanded drug capos' bases of political support among poor communities that governments were unable to reach.[9]

The implications for national economies are no less significant. Drug related activity in the informal, often illegal, economy, sometimes helps to inflate export earnings, increases the capacity to import, sustains artificial exchange rates and overvalued currencies and provides income and employment for significant segments of society. In fact, one United Nations study suggests that "the impact of the illicit drug industry on a producer country's trade balance tends to be positive for the simple reason that exports of illegal drugs generate inflows of foreign exchange".[10] In this vein, the World Drug Report cites the case of Bolivia where coca-cocaine exports are believed to have represented between 28 and 53 percent of the value of total exports that include the value of coca-cocaine exports or between 39 and 112 percent of those that exclude them.[11] Another study points out that in "the Andean countries . . . cocaine is the region's largest export (in fact, it is Latin America's second largest export after petroleum) . . . 3 to 4 percent of the gross domestic product of Peru and Bolivia and 8 percent of Colombia's".[12] Moreover, in terms of jobs, the illegal industry "employs 450,000 to 500,000 Andeans directly in farming, processing, transport, security, and money-laundering operations. Legions of others," the assessment concludes, "earn a living by providing goods and services essential to the industry."[13] In 1980, the incoming Jamaican prime minister, Edward Seaga, is quoted as having said that "the only healthy segment of the Jamaican economy" was marijuana production. "The US $1 billion business (had) been the economic lifeline of Jamaica for years, especially after traditional segments of the economy failed."[14]

These analyses concerning the multidimensional nature of the threat to democracy posed by the drug trade are persuasive and convincing as far as they go. Moreover, it is self-evident that "no nation . . . however robust its democracy, is immune to the adverse consequences of drug abuse and trafficking".[15] But important questions remain unanswered – sometimes not even posed – about the relationship between drugs and democracy. For example, to the extent that the impact of drugs is so corrosive, then there needs to be some explanation of the fact that half of the major drug-producing states and more than half of the major money-laundering centres in the Western hemisphere remain in the first rank of 'free' democracies. (See Table 4.1.) And if the answer is that the corrosive effect is just a matter of time, then the further question would arise as to how the majority of the remaining states have actually improved their rating on the Comparative Survey of Freedom at the very same time that the narcotics situation has deteriorated? Logically, this must mean that either the Survey is deficient as a measure of democracy or that the relationship between drugs and democracy is somewhat more complex than many analysts imply.

I believe the latter to be the case. The growth of the illicit narcotics industry does not appear to translate automatically on a one-to-one basis, either immediately or in the medium term, into a decline in democracy. Put more cautiously, the circumstances impacting on how far that relationship is apparent or not, in what forms and on what levels, needs to be more carefully examined and explained. Mediating structures, values and conditions which either impede or facilitate democratic erosion require probing. For example, the United States has for some been acknowledged as one of the major global money-laundering centres but remains a leading 'mature' democracy. What are the factors which blunt or neutralize the impact of money laundering on this particular democracy? Do these have to do primarily with the size or scale of the American political system vis-à-vis the money-laundering phenomenon? Or with the relative strength and immunity to corruption of state institutions and political elites? Or is it that the corrupting influence on democracy is apparent at the local and even state levels but not at the level of federal government? Similar questions may and need to be posed of countries such as Costa Rica (a major money-laundering centre) and of the Bahamas and Belize (major drug-producing/transit countries) which remain, for all intents and purposes, first rank democracies despite their 'high' status in the world of narcotics.

The Jamaican Experience

In relation to the Jamaican case, while there is room for debate, it appears that here again the country presents an example more of the resistance than the surrender of democracy to the illegal drugs industry. In the first place, Jamaica is not only a major drug producing territory but has for at least 20 years ranked in the top three (with Mexico and Colombia) marijuana-producing countries globally. Between 1991 and 1995, it was the third largest in terms of seizures of marijuana in the Caribbean (see also Table). The 1997 United Nations World Drug Report listed Jamaica as one of "the countries (20 in all) with the largest cultivation areas [of illicit drugs] relative to arable land . . ."[16] The Jamaican-based drug-related gangs or posses are regarded by some authorities as among the most significant, in global terms.[17] At the very minimum, they are ranked among "criminal organizations based on Korean, Filipino, Thai . . . Burmese, Pakistani, Israeli, Albanian, Nigerian . . . national bases (which) . . . have begun to cause serious worry to law enforcement officials"[18] on an international scale. The dimensions of the difficulty may be gathered from the fact that "by 1990 Jamaican criminals had garnered some 8 percent of the US $8.8 billion American cannabis (retail) market and were a significant player in the ($18 billion) cocaine and cocaine derivatives market".[19] Prior to this, estimates of local earnings from cannabis exports were in the region of "US $1 to 2 billion in the 1980s . . . with a high of some US $3.5 billion in the early 1980s".[20]

Equally important were the international linkages of the main gangs. In an examination of the "structural features" of 6 of the 41 identified gangs in the Kingston metropolitan area, Harriott found that all had "transnational structures".[21] There can be no question that "Jamaican criminal groups and organizations have moved since the late 1970s from being spatially limited to their immediate communities located in the urban slums to being truly international". In this context, while the US was and remains "the main foreign province of Jamaican gangs . . . they now operate in and have formed criminal networks in Europe . . . Latin and Central America, and other Caribbean states".[22] One ethnographic study accurately depicts the nature of linkages. "Cocaine deals generally are made in Panama and Colombia and shipments are dropped offshore either by ship or by small plane . . . picked up by boats and re-routed to Florida to trusted friends or family members. These offshore transactions apparently account for the majority of cocaine entering Jamaica."[23] In this way, the main Jamaican gangs manifest what has been appropriately described as one of the "key characteristics" of modern "transnational criminal enterprises". It is "the establishment of affiliates or cells abroad".[24] In fact, the organizational structure of these bodies very much approximates that of transnational corporations.[25] These drug-related phenomena have obviously placed multiple strains on the Jamaican democratic system. In the first place, the presence and operation of the Jamaican-based transnational criminal organizations contributes to the country's democratic deficit which is the extent to which decisions, decision-makers and activities of various types (in this case illegal) which affect Jamaica are beyond the authority of its democratically elected government and have no meaningful accountability to the Jamaican people. To the extent that the considerable resources and extra-territorial linkages of these gangs allow them to operate with impunity, to that extent they undermine the substance of Jamaican democracy and, further, suggest the corresponding need for matching or superior global linkages of an appropriate sort on the part of the Jamaican state.

Internally, the drug gangs are strongest in inner-city areas. However, in the Jamaican situation, unlike much experience elsewhere, the community influence and organizational outreach of the gangs interlink with the local economy and the base of the major political parties in a number of important constituencies. Recent police reports on three gangs reflect the overall situation:

1. Eastern Kingston Gang: A very sophisticated group seemingly with political connections. Its aim is to acquire most if not all the business community in Eastern Kingston. Whenever its offer of purchase for any business is refused, the business is systematically plagued with robberies . . . *betrays an interest in political office* [emphasis mine].

2. Cassie or Aallo gang: '*a politically affiliated group*, financed mainly from the proceeds of its robberies, drug distribution, and trafficking'

3. Marverly Crew or Patrick Mouth gang: '. . . highly political in nature . . . financed mainly by robberies and political handouts . . . their threat level was high, bordering on national security . . ."[26]

In his study, Harriott concludes that in "the garrison communities of the Kingston metropolitan area" there is a "tight integration between local party structures and criminal gang organizations".[27]

This tight integration allows for influence horizontally in the community concerned, but also vertically into the upper reaches of the party structure, depending on the significance of the gang and the nature of its linkages. In fact, beyond influence, these political drug connections "exercise a highly centralized control over social and political activity in these communities".

One basis of this control lies in the fact that "many of these criminal organizations perform both protective and allocative functions . . . not only armed defence against encroachment by political opponents and ordinary criminals, but also the function of control agents within these communities, often providing effective guarantees against predatory criminality in the context of ineffective policing".[28]

When this 'law and order' function is combined with community distribution of largesse from illicit narcotics activity and of contracts from political connections, it is easy to understand why "Drug 'dons', therefore, enjoy high status"[29] and great power.

This great power has at least two political consequences of some importance. Firstly, on the rare occasion (perhaps giving a glimpse of one possible future), the tail can end up wagging the dog. The local gangs and the drug dons can become so embedded that the party leadership concerned no longer exercises control and may even be compelled by circumstances to become deferential. In this regard, a recent admission by the former Prime Minister and leader of Jamaica's major opposition party, in relation to drug-related criminal elements in his Western Kingston constituency, is revealing:

I have no control over these persons, no control whatsoever . . . I have no intention of presiding over any area in which people can tell me that they are not listening to what I have to say . . . I have no reason to stay in a constituency in which people are being brutalized by men who are totally out of control . . . [30]

To the extent that the drug dons get 'out of control' of both the political party directorate – however undesirable that nexus is – and the criminal justice system, to that extent, Jamaica's democracy is seriously endangered by what could be termed a new "power elite".

The second level on which this threat exists is in the role played by the drug don – political leadership at the community level in maintaining the so-called garrison constituencies. These are areas in which one-party dominance is so complete that political rights and civil liberties do not exist for opposition parties or independent elements. The garrison is originated and sustained not only by one-sided partisan reward of party clients and punishment of party opponents through elaborate systems of patronage. What amounts to one-party dictatorship at the constituency level also depends on back-up support from gang members who function as armed enforcers on behalf of one or another political party. To the extent that the garrison constituency is acknowledged as the most serious blight on Jamaica's electoral democracy, to that extent the drug gangs, as major underpinnings of the phenomenon, constitute a basic threat to the system. Conversely, to the extent that inflows of drug money allow the dons to be more independent and to delink from the parties, the nature of the threat changes. From being a source of political violence, the gangs become combatants in drug-related turf wars. Political violence becomes displaced and mutates into drug violence. This has the potential of both making electoral competition less violent and of allowing focus on drug-related violence unencumbered by political connections.

One other dimension of potential threat, if not as yet actually documented, is the area of party finance. There is no system of public funding of political parties in Jamaica. Therefore, the parties have to depend exclusively on donations from private sources. As campaign costs have escalated and economic conditions have made contributions from the corporate sector both more difficult and less adequate, the parties have, from time to time, experienced severe financial straits. One 1994 report indicated that, "The People's National Party (PNP) is deep in debt, owing about J$33 million to various creditors . . . There are also rumours that the JLP (Jamaica Labour Party) was flat broke."[31] As the 1997 general elections drew closer, this situation did change significantly particularly for the PNP which raised substantial sums from corporate Jamaica. Nevertheless, given the general shortage of resources, there can be little doubt that, despite formal denials and even opposition by party officials at the national level, drug money does get into party coffers. Alongside this, drug dons and narcotics-related businessmen can obviously develop undue influence on individual MPs and, conceivably, on elements in party leadership.

Another major link between drugs and democracy in Jamaica relates to the justice system. This relationship manifests itself at different levels. In the first place, and most obviously, it is found in corrupt relations between elements in the police force and drug dons. The police high command itself has spoken of these linkages and of the need to eradicate drug-related corruption from the force. Internal oversight mechanisms within the police have also detected and attempted to deal with this connection.[32] The majority of the more well-established drug gangs have "linkages to the police".[33] The findings of an official inquiry into the police-drug connection in another CARICOM state may perhaps be indicative of the Jamaican situation:

Corruption can be described as endemic. It permeates all ranks . . . Corruption . . . also includes the protection of drug dealers, their supplies and their supply routes. This is where the corrupt core of the police service get its money. At the top is direct participation in crime or, more specifically, drug racketeering... police officers have been involved in the importation of cocaine, in growing marijuana, in transporting drugs, and selling them . . .[34]

Whether or not the Jamaican police are as corrupted by drugs as this report depicts the Trinidadian to have been is a matter of debate. What is not is the reality of the police-drug connection and its deleterious impact on the rule of law in Jamaica.

A second pressure on the criminal justice system is perhaps the converse of the first. Instead of the police being protective of drug dons and narcotics criminals, they go after suspects with excessive, sometimes lethal, use of force. This charge and the basis for it in the annual number of killings and shootings by the police has been and remains one of the most enduring blemishes on Jamaica's human rights record. The annual reports of Jamaican and foreign human rights organizations are replete with "allegations of police murder".[35] In the four years between 1994 and 1997, police killing of civilians averaged 132 per annum or well over 2 per week. Many of these incidents are related to alleged shootouts with members of drug gangs. On occasion, these incidents result in charges being laid against the police and "the number of police actually charged with murder rose from single digits in 1993 to 35 in both 1994 and 1995".[36]

At the same time, there can be no question that this is not a one-sided affair. The growth of the illicit drug industry has brought with it an intensification of violent crime in Jamaica. The number of murders committed annually has grown significantly and in 1990, "Jamaica's homicide rate . . . was four times above the global average"[37] and twice that of the United States.[38] In recent years, over one-third of all murders in Jamaica have been drug-related.[39] Kingston ranks among the most violent cities in the hemisphere. The use of guns in the commission of violent crimes has increased as has their availability, primarily through the narcotics networks, and use in the increased incidence of gang-related killings. The significance of this phenomenon for eroding the quality of Jamaican democracy can hardly be overestimated. To the ordinary citizen, crime and violence are often the greatest problem. What is regarded as government's failure to adequately cope with this issue in turn shakes confidence in the system and encourages ordinary citizens to take things into their own hands through various forms of "vigilantism".[40]

In one other way, drugs put pressure on Jamaica's democracy – it is a major source of 'overload' on the criminal justice system, and hence a major cause of 'justice delayed' for the ordinary citizen. The increase in drug-related offences has put new strains on already inadequate police lock-ups, overpopulated prisons, undermanned correctional services and overworked judiciary. The 1996 State Department Human Rights Report and the 1997 Economic and Social Survey of Jamaica correctly identified "overcrowding" as a main cause of poor prison and jail conditions and the overburdened judicial system as a major reason for the prevalence of "lengthy delays in trial".[41] The dimensions of this difficulty can be better appreciated from the fact that while between 1989 and 1996 the number of cases before the Resident Magistrate courts almost doubled, the number of judges remained almost static. This in turn meant a double case load, a massive increase in the number of cases pending each year and hence, in part, the inordinate delays in matters being finally brought to trial. (See Table 4.2; Figure 4.1.) Narcotics-related cases are a major source of this burden on the police, the prisons, and the judges, a burden which is undoubtedly weakening the justice system, a main pillar of Jamaica's democracy.

Coping or Crumbling?

How has the system coped with these burdens? In the first place, given the weight of illicit narcotics in the Jamaican economic and sociopolitical order, it is not easy to explain the country's survival as a relatively healthy democracy. Why, after 20-odd years, has not any substantial element of the legislature or the executive been bought off or come under the influence of drug money? Why has not any significant element of the directorate of the criminal justice system been corrupted by the funds and functionaries of the illicit narcotics industry? Why has not the legislative process or law enforcement been significantly subordinated to the dictates of narco-dollars? In one or another of the Caribbean and Latin American states such deleterious effects on the democratic process have been apparent. In Colombia, for example, "President Ernesto Samper's 1994 election campaign was awash in millions of dollars in drug money and all branches of government have been so compromised by traffickers that Colombia warrants definition as a narco-state."[42] Within the English-speaking Caribbean, prime ministers and ministers have been credibly implicated in narcotics corruption in Antigua-Barbuda, St Kitts-Nevis, the Bahamas and the Turks and Caicos Islands. Commissioners of Police have been fired or have had to resign for connections with the illicit drugs industry in Trinidad and Tobago as well as St Lucia; in Antigua, the Commander of the Antigua-

Barbuda Defence Force was implicated in the 1989/90 arms trafficking affair. Finally, drug Mafias "are reported to have bought and corrupted everything of value in Aruba: casino, hotels, real estate, banks . . . the prime minister, the justice minister and the ruling and opposition parties".[43]

Against this background and given Jamaica's centrality in the global narcotics system, there can be little doubt concerning the corrosive effect of drugs on the sociopolitical order. On the contrary, the question must be posed as to why drug-related institutionalized corruption has not been worse, has not, for example, bought wholesale state and economic elites. It seems to me that this question cannot be convincingly answered without reference to what are undoubtedly some peculiarities of the Jamaican system. One is the "rule of law" tradition. Contemporary judges and prosecutors, court and public service elites inherit a colonial and postcolonial judicial culture which encouraged upholding and applying the law even, at times, in the face of some resistance from popular political leaders. In this context, it is perhaps no accident that the citizenry regard the courts, despite their undoubted deficiencies, as among the state institutions to which they attach most respect.[44] A second factor is somewhat paradoxical. It is the authoritarian structure of the political parties, their traditionally deep roots amongst the masses and the popular following of the party leader. Each of these has meant that even if drug money took over a significant section of a party's base or bought influence over some MPs, its impact on the system as a whole could be contained so long as the party leader was not corrupted. To whatever extent that there has been linkage between party and drug don, it is the party that has more controlled the latter rather than the other way around. Of course, it is apparent that both these elements of civic culture and political structure are changing but, hitherto, they have been significant in insulating Jamaica's democracy against greater damage from the drugs industry.

Other more policy-related factors, by and large not specific to Jamaica, have also been of relevance to this issue. One such has been the huge challenge of matching the transnational capability of the drug gangs without adding to the country's democratic deficit, without subordinating Jamaica's democratic authorities to unaccountable sites of external power. In meeting this challenge, the main policy line has been to shape the country's international relations in a manner which resists the imposition of one-sided obligations on Jamaica and seeks reciprocity with other countries in order to extend the capacity of the Jamaican state vis-à-vis transnational drug criminals. This approach has had to confront many obstacles in the policy environment, not least of all the immense asymmetries of power particularly vis-à-vis the United States and the strength of what Dominguez has called "small islandist"[45] ideology which continues to hamstring regional collaboration amongst Anglophone Caribbean states. Put bluntly, the need has been how to avoid or, at least, reduce American domination whilst accepting "the need to strengthen international cooperation" and recognizing the obvious fact that "eradication of illicit traffic is a collective responsibility of all states".[46]

The record of the cooperation between the American and Caribbean, specifically Jamaican, authorities, is well documented in the annual International Narcotics Control Strategy Reports of the State Department.[47] At the same time, there appears to have been a definite tendency on the part of the United States to dictate to Caribbean governments on the appropriate methods and techniques of the anti-narcotics struggle. So much so that the chairman of the Ninth 1988 Conference of CARICOM Heads of Government, Antigua's Prime Minister Vere Bird wrote to President Reagan on behalf of the Conference, expressing concern at, among other things, "attempts to extend domestic United States authority into neighbouring countries of the region without regard for their sovereignty and independent legal systems of those countries".[48] These attempts took the form, in particular, of 'hot pursuit' interdiction and seizure of suspected drug traffickers within CARICOM territorial waters. In this context, the West Indian Commission Report recorded that "Caribbean governments have been subject to more than a little coercion by US agencies".[49]

Two related questions immediately arise in assessing the consequences for regional democracy of this reality. One is whether the degree of coercion is such as to pass beyond cooperation into a subordinate relationship. The second, obviously closely connected, question is whether the outcome of the relationship focused on anti-narcotics matters is such as to reflect, in some measure, the uncoerced will of the elected governments in the region. To the extent that outcomes, especially of a legally binding character, do not reflect the public interest as interpreted by the elected government but by some external, unaccountable authority, then obviously to that extent democracy is undermined. CARICOM states, including Jamaica, have clearly had a continuing concern on this issue. So much so that the Fifth Special Meeting of the Conference of Heads of Government, convened in December 1996, mainly on the instigation of Jamaica, while reaffirming "commitment . . . to strengthen cooperation with the United States" on anti-narcotics matters, nevertheless "rejected any threat or suggestion of coercive measures as a means of securing compliance with pre-determined policies".[50]

The matter of "coercive measures" to secure "compliance with pre-determined policies" arose most sharply in the context of negotiations between the United States and the CARICOM states towards concluding anti-narcotics maritime agreements in the region. The United States put forward a draft treaty through which, in essence, each CARICOM signatory would provide blanket, once and for all, authority to US anti-narcotics agencies to enter the signatory's territorial waters and, in some instances, air space in 'hot pursuit' without need for specific authorization. Nine CARICOM states between 1995 and 1996 signed on the dotted line, albeit with varying degrees of willingness. (See Table 4.3.) In contrast, the governments of Jamaica and Barbados, whilst recognizing the necessity for new maritime anti-narcotics arrangements, nevertheless objected to certain aspects of the American draft and, consequently, entered into relatively prolonged negotiations with the United States.[51]

It was in the course of these discussions that the question of Jamaica being "decertified" as a country cooperating with the United States anti-narcotics programme was raised.[52] Decertification, of course, implied the possibility of harsh punitive consequences for Jamaica under American law and therefore opened the issue of how far relations with the United States in the anti-drug struggle reflected international cooperation or superpower coercion. In Jamaica itself, the government as well as the opposition parties and the major elements of civil society took the position that any Shiprider Agreement should, in the final analysis, reflect not only American positions but also, in some measure, the concerns of Jamaica's democratically elected government. Ultimately, the agreement arrived at differed in significant respects from the American draft (accepted by other CARICOM states) and clearly reflected, in part, proposals from the Jamaican government.[53] To that extent, the achievement of this agreement demonstrated that attempts to cope with the transnational power of the illegal drug networks in international arrangements need not simply express super-hegemony. The Jamaican case suggests that such arrangements are compatible with showing regard for the interests of small states as interpreted by their democratically elected governments, thereby giving expression to, rather than negating, the significance of democracy in such circumstances.

A similar issue arises in relation to the obligations imposed on individual states by international, hemispheric, or regional treaties on drug trafficking and illegal narcotics. The 1998 UN Vienna Convention, for example, requires ratifying states to comply with a number of provisions normally demanding domestic legislation. Amongst these are provisions to criminalize "money-laundering", relax "bank secrecy", facilitate asset forfeiture or property seizure, require "extradition" and "mutual legal assistance" arrangements among states. Two concerns are of importance to us here. One is the extent to which this treaty took into account, at least to some minimum extent, the interests and concerns of all states especially, from our perspective, those with democratically elected administrations as against those acquiescing to superpower pressure. The second is the degree to which individual states have a real (as against formal or nominal) option not to accede to the Convention to the extent that its requirements diverge from their specific interests. On this latter score, it is worthy of note that successive Jamaican governments delayed ratification of the 1988 convention until December 1995 without any discernible punitive consequences.

At the regional and hemispheric levels, in some contrast with the global, recent developments offer the possibility of helping to sustain (by multilateral means) rather than constrain the effectiveness of democracy in smaller states. One such is the OAS Santiago Commitment and Resolution on Representative Democracy approved in 1991.[54] On the specific anti-narcotics front, the Plan of Action endorsed by the US-Caribbean Summit in May 1997 took into account major concerns of the Jamaican government. Primary amongst these is the development of an "Arms Trafficking Control Regime for the Carib-bean"[55] to which the plan commits itself. Moreover, the document acknow-ledges that "the United States has been a significant country of origin for firearms illegally diverted to other nations" and, on this basis, incorporates a "pledge" by the United States, as well as by other regional states, "to cooperate in . . . examining the adequacy of existing legislation to combat the illegal . . . traffic in arms, ammunition . . ."[56] Moreover, the plan commits the signatories "to work towards the early adoption of an international agreement against the illicit manufacturing and trafficking in arms . . ."[57] These are issues, in the main, put on the table by the Jamaican government but they particularly reflect a major area of anxiety of the Jamaican public.

In this context, much more significant but obviously related to the Plan of Action was the convention agreed on by the OAS within six months of the US-Caribbean Summit. The Convention Against Illicit Manufacturing and Trafficking in Firearms, Ammunitions, Explosives[58] commits the US to take action to prevent gun-smuggling out of the US, to provide training, informa-tion and access to technical equipment to strengthen the capabilities of other states to deal effectively with illegal arms trafficking. The terms of the convention are very explicit. Article IV requires member states, including the United States, to "adopt the necessary legislative or other measures to establish as criminal offences under their domestic law the illicit . . . trafficking in firearms, ammunitions and explosives".[59] Article X, in addition, requires the adoption of "such measures as may be necessary to detect and prevent illicit trafficking in firearms" and, as importantly, ensure "strengthening controls at export points".[60] Towards the end, appropriate training, technology and equipment are to be made available and a consultative committee, constituted by representatives of member states, set up to monitor implementation. Clearly, if ratified and put into effect, this convention, which regards itself as "a precedent for the international community", represents an extension rather than a contradiction of the power of Jamaica's democracy (and that of the other signatory states) in the struggle against the international narcotics industry.

The Domestic Anti-Narcotics Agenda

On the more specifically domestic front, a number of items, at various stages of discussion and implementation, have appeared on the anti-narcotics agenda. On their fate, in significant measure, rests the strength or otherwise of the resistance of the Jamaican body politic to the illicit narcotics disease. Amongst the more important of these are programmes for inner-city rehabilitation.[61] These programmes involve investment in inner-city economic projects, skill training and character building for young people, the creation of employment and self-employment opportunities, the provision of support for sports and cultural activities and anti-narcotics education. Much of the success of these efforts depends on the capacity of the communities to develop sustainable organizations on a non-partisan basis and to accept significant responsibility for community development programmes, with appropriate assistance from government, the private sector and international agencies.

The success of this process is closely linked to efforts to reform the criminal justice system at both the local and national levels. At the former level, existing mechanisms to identify, discipline or otherwise bring to justice police who abuse citizens' rights or who are linked to the narcotics industry need to be strengthened. In the inner-city communities, "the police were perceived as corrupt . . . involved in illegal activities . . .[and] there were widespread accusations that the police colluded with local dons . . ."[62] The reversal of the realities underlying these perceptions is critical to the anti-narcotics struggle at the community level, not least of all because of the community perception that the police are not only a part of the problem but also an essential part of the solution. For this second role to be realized, the citizens themselves need to be facilitated in fulfilment of more effective 'oversight' functions possibly by way of the community consultative committees in relation to the police; conversely, "community policing" needs to show itself more effective in apprehending the drug dealers and in building neighbourhood watches and police youth clubs.

In the rural areas, the programmes of alternative crop and income substitution need to be strengthened in the main marijuana producing areas. In at least one such area, South West St Ann, an agricultural rehabilitation project, begun in 1988 with funding from the European Community, has been successful in providing alternative income-earning activity for ganja farmers.[63] A new grant proposal, "Alternative Systems for an Illegal Crop", which would improve the lives of thousands of ganja farmers in a range of rural parishes needs to be pursued urgently. While earnings from substituted crops are not as high as those from cannabis cultivation, the removal of the risk factor in the context of aggressive ganja eradication programmes has obviously made substitution attractive to farmers. Hence the need for more of these programmes.

At the national level, one important imperative is the strengthening of the criminal justice system. In this context, the passage of anti-corruption legislation, now before parliament, is a significant milestone in that process. As significant will be measures to ensure, specifically in relation to corruption, an effective investigative capability and sophisticated prosecutorial competence especially in the context of increasingly complex narcotics-connected white-collar crime. The ability of the state to secure convictions, the willingness of the judiciary to impose appropriately severe sentences and the application of the law regarding asset forfeiture to the big fish[64] (and not just the small fry) in narcotics-related cases would go some way to strengthen and restore damaged confidence in the rule of the law.

One other connected matter is of importance to this fundamental underpinning of democratic order. That is the major role of drug-related detentions and arrests in overloading the courts and in strengthening the perception that the justice system is unfair as well as class discriminatory. Amongst the narcotics-related matters, offences connected to marijuana take great preponderance over those related to cocaine and other illicit drugs. (See Table 4.4.) In 1996, for example, seven times as many locals and foreigners were arrested for ganja than for cocaine. In the first five months of 1997, the ratio was even greater. It can hardly be denied that the far greater prevalence of ganja offences and amongst these, the high incidence of the charge of simple possession, the increasingly militant resentment of the citizenry at these arrests and the consequent disproportionate pressure on the justice system have been concerns bringing the issue of decriminalization of marijuana for personal use back on the Jamaican public agenda.

Other compelling reasons for advocacy of this option have suggested themselves. One is a Jamaican historical and cultural context in which the possession and use of marijuana for personal purposes has deep roots. So much so that one of the more recent ethnographic studies found that a plurality of the population considered alcohol and cigarettes more harmful than ganja and the majority was in support of the latter.[65] Needless to say, popular attitudes make a sharp distinction and draw a definite line between ganja on the one hand and cocaine on the other. Cocaine is regarded in almost entirely negative terms and, correspondingly, the coke-head or coke addict is considered an outcast compared to the ganja user.[66] There is, of course, much pharmacological support for distinguishing these two substances and, therefore, some scientific basis for treating them differently in the legal system. In any event, democracy requires that where there is such widespread divergence between law and popular culture, as well as behaviour, the former should be subjected to the most thorough review. The more so in Jamaican circumstances where marijuana criminalization constitutes so considerable a source of pressure on the justice system as well as of aggrievement on the part of disadvantaged social groups.

It is perhaps necessary to note that the 1988 UN Convention on Illegal Narcotics does not in and of itself require Jamaica or any other state to convict or punish citizens for the possession of marijuana. Article 3 of the convention allows for states to determine when drug cases are "of minor nature" and, in those circumstances, to make provision for "alternatives to conviction or punishment". Such alternatives, according to the convention, may include measures for education, rehabilitation or social reintegration "as well as, when the offender is a drug abuser, treatment and aftercare". Such options are being actively explored and, in cases, actually applied in a number of countries of the European Union as well as in some American states. There is undoubtedly a strong case, given the specifics of Jamaica, to decriminalize the possession of ganja for personal use, treat the issue as a public health matter[67] reduce the pressure on the justice system and, thereby, contribute to improving the quality of democracy.

More generally, within recent years the overall climate for consideration of a more flexible approach to illicit drugs and, in particular, marijuana use has undoubtedly become more favourable.[68] There is a growing consensus that the 'war on drugs' is being lost and that the appropriateness of the very concept of 'war' needs to be reconsidered. Against this backdrop, "in the 1990s the trend toward decriminalization of cannabis has accelerated in Europe".[69] Initiated in the Netherlands in 1976 and continued subsequently (despite some pressures from other European states), the Dutch approach of decriminalizing soft drugs whilst increasing penalties for hard drugs such as heroin has been emulated by Spain and, more cautiously, Germany. Outside Europe, cannabis has been decriminalized in parts of Australia and, in Canada "a recent poll found that 51 percent of Canadians favour decriminalizing marijuana".[70] Even from within the law enforcement community, as important a figure as the secretary general of Interpol was quoted as declaring himself "totally against legalization, but in favour of decriminalization for the user".[71]

In the United States, where official support for an undifferentiated war against drugs has traditionally been strongest, signs of a less generalized opposition to decriminalization are apparent. In 1996 voters in California passed Proposition 215 which legalized the medical use of marijuana and the Arizona electorate approved by two to one not only decriminalization of marijuana for medical use but also mandated treatment rather than jail for the non-violent drug offender's first two offences. One consideration driving review of incarceration policies in the United States has been similar to the situation in Jamaica – the overloading of jails by marijuana possession offenders. In 1996, 85 percent of the 641,642 people arrested for marijuana in the United States were held for "possession, not sale, of the drug".[72] "From Baltimore to Arizona, California to Oklahoma, state and local officials dealing with overcrowded prisons, clogged court dockets, and a seemingly unending stream of youthful drug offenders, are beginning to look for alternative ways of dealing with the drug problem."[73]

There can be no question that this search "for alternative ways" is now impacting on the policy community at the national and global levels. One indication of this was an open letter to the secretary general of the United Nations on the occasion of the 1998 Special General Assembly Session of the UNO on the illicit narcotics issue. The letter affirmed the belief of the signatories that "global war on drugs is now causing more harm than drug abuse itself".[74] The letter argued that in the name of the drug war:

In many parts of the world . . . Human rights are violated, environmental assaults perpetrated and prisons inundated with hundreds of drug law violators. Scarce resources better expended on health, education and economic development are squandered on even more expensive interdiction efforts.[75]

It concluded by calling on the UN secretary general to "initiate a truly open and honest dialogue regarding the future of global drug control policies – one in which fear, prejudice and future prohibitions yield to common sense, science, public health, and human rights". Amongst the 500 prominent personalities who signed the letter were former UN secretary general, Javier Perez de Cuellar, former US secretary of state, George Shultz, leading scholars from the American and international academic community as well as signifi-cant figures from the public health and law enforcement fraternities. Within this group was Colonel Trevor McMillan, former commissioner of police of Jamaica. In reducing the negative impact of drugs on Jamaican democracy, there can hardly be a greater priority than the consideration of decriminalizing marijuana for personal use.

More broadly, we may conclude that how Jamaican elites and the mass public deal with the issue of illicit drugs has significant implications for democratic renewal. On one level, the development of alternative sources of income and livelihood is vital for the inner-city youth and rural farmers – the sectors most vulnerable to production, consumption and trafficking of illicit drugs. In this regard, as well as in matters of interdiction and law enforcement, transnational collaboration amongst governments and NGOs is essential. But such relations have the potential of either augmenting or diminishing the institutional capability of the Jamaican state, depending on whether they are marked by consensual or hegemonic relations particularly with the US. Finally, the extent of damage from corruption, an important measure of the quality of democracy, and in this case drug related, shall to a large degree depend upon the effectiveness of anti-corruption safeguards put in place and on how much public support they attract.

5

Civil Society:
Between Decline
and Renewal

Civil Society and Democracy

It was suggested in chapter 1 that the character of civil society has a great deal
to do with the quality of democracy. It is precisely around this question that
there has been within recent years a revival of discussion of "civil society"[1] and
continuing debate about the relationship between civil society, social cohesion
and democratic renewal. In Jamaica, the concern with civil society has grown,
somewhat paradoxically, in part out of acute frustration with anything but civil
relations in everyday life;[2] in part, out of continuing alienation of a significant
body of Jamaicans from competitive party politics; in part, out of the turn of
many to non-political forms as one way of transcending partisan divisiveness
and of advancing common goals. How strong are these non-political groups
and this civic tendency? How are they to relate to politics and politics to them?
How far does civil society itself reflect rather than transcend social divisions?
How can this non-partisan sphere be assisted to develop in a manner which
helps to strengthen social cohesion and to build democratic renewal? These are
questions very much on the Jamaican national agenda.

Elsewhere, the questions are somewhat different as the issue of civil society
has come to the fore not so much out of concern to overcome "political
tribalism" and social disarray. Rather it has come from two quite different
sources. First, from the role played by the rise of civic associations and social
groups of various types in the resistance to authoritarianism and in the

transition to democracy in previously communist, one-party and military regimes throughout Eastern Europe, Latin America and sub-Saharan Africa.[3] Secondly, and from the opposite direction, the concern has been with the apparent decline of civic associations in mature democracies such as the United States and the role played by this decline in undermining civic engagement, levels of social trust and the quality of democracy itself. This concern has led to a policy preoccupation with the revival of voluntarism in the United States,[4] a concern not dissimilar to the anxiety in Jamaica to strengthen civic associations and invigorate civil society.

Against this background, we take the term *civil society* to refer not only to non-political voluntary associations occupying the space between the state and the market. We take it, as well, to refer to networks and relationships which may or may not crystallize into groups but which nevertheless connect individuals together in some non-coercive, reciprocally purposive manner. It is of some importance for our purposes to regard networks and relationships, and not just groups, as component elements of civil society. This is so because many such networks and relations, do in fact, serve to connect people together in pursuit of common designs and, especially in Third World contexts, very often do not develop into formal groups. To exclude them from the purview of civil society on this ground would undoubtedly and unjustifiably narrow the concept and its application. With this qualification, Schmitter's more comprehensive working definition of civil society is appropriate as:

a set or system of self-organized intermediate groups [that]

1) are relatively independent of both public authorities and private units of production, that is, firms and family;

2) are capable of deliberating about and taking collective actions in defence/promotion of their interest or passion

3) but do not seek to replace either state agents or private (re) producers or to accept responsibility for governing the polity as a whole;

4) but do agree to act within pre-established rules of a 'civil' or legal nature . . .[5]

Some observations are appropriate in relation to this definition. First, this understanding, correctly in my view, places political parties as well as private sector corporations beyond the sphere of civil society. By the same token, the positioning of other groups such as trade unions or inner-city corner gangs vis-à-vis civil society would vary according to their specific features in different contexts. Secondly, the groups which constitute civil society need not be totally autonomous but only "relatively independent" of either the government or the private sector. Indeed, very often support for voluntary effort from the government and from the private sector can provide a well-needed 'kick start' or 'helping hand' without necessarily compromising the independence of the civic association. Thirdly, Schmitter's notion that the group must act within "pre-established rules of a 'civil' or legal nature . . .", while generally acceptable, ought not to be interpreted too rigidly or taken too literally. One reason is that in authoritarian systems, groups which properly form vital elements of civil society often are compelled to behave in very 'uncivil', even illegal, ways. Less obviously, in 'electoral' democracies, particularly in Third World contexts, large segments of the urban population often survive in the informal economy and operate in informal network associations of street vendors, squatters and corner gangs. The activities of these groupings sometimes skirt the boundaries of civil and lawful behaviour.[6] Yet much would be lost by excluding them from the bounds of civil society on this ground alone as such groups provide important, sometimes the only, opportunities for popular expression of significant interests and, at the same time, channels for "grass roots" demands for the deepening of democratic governance.

Similarly, whether civil society promotes or undermines democracy can hardly be assumed. This must depend on the characteristics of the actual associations and networks themselves – are they relatively democratic in their internal structures? Do they embody and help sustain or, alternatively, undermine exclusivistic and unequal relations based on class, geography, sex, race, colour or ethnicity? Does their collective presence discourage and resist authoritarianism as well as facilitate citizen involvement in or influence on decision-making? These are questions the answers to which will vary with time and place. Hence, to that extent, will also vary the role of civil society in the democratic process. As such, "the conclusion we draw . . . is neither to romanticize civil society as an ideal sphere of freedom and association . . . nor to dismiss civil society as a theoretically and politically redundant concept".[7] Rather, "civil society" should be "scrutinized and evaluated according to the quality of its potential contribution"[8] and its real role in the process of governance.

In this regard, a number of tendencies have been observed globally in relation to this role and to the character of civil society within recent times. One such tendency has been a steady but marked decline in associational life of various types and, along with this, a decline in the stock of "social capital", of citizen cooperation and reciprocal relationships, particularly in the United States.[9] This, it is argued, has undermined an important foundation of American democracy. At the other end of the spectrum, particularly in states developing out of one or another type of authoritarian rule, the emergence of voluntary groups of all sorts played an important role in the transitions to democracy as well as in the consolidation of new regimes. In this context "a revitalization of the civil society can easily be detected: its associational texture is now richer".[10] But even here the character of these bodies is not uniform; "It includes a motley array of very different voluntary associations and institutions alongside others which are of a clearly neo-tribal nature, often based on ethnic, communal belief or other affinities . . ."[11]

This somewhat complex picture of civil societies in different countries, playing both negative and positive roles, depending on the context, has given rise to a number of alternative analyses. One such relates the decline of civil society in the United States to the growth of modern 'individuating' technologies (particularly television), the changing characteristics of the labour force, in particular the integration of women, and, interestingly, the hegemony of an 'each-man-for-himself' neoliberal spirit and ethos.[12] Another perspective distinguishes between 'elite-challenging' and 'elite-directed' forms of activity and, by implication, of organization. Within this framework, across a wide band of nations, much evidence suggests that in established as well as emergent democracies, elite-challenging associations are on the rise whilst elite-directed activity is on the decline.[13] This appears especially to be the case in relation to the Third World. Here, a massive proliferation of action-oriented groups has been observed. Invariably these bring together disadvantaged sectors at local, regional and even national levels for the main purpose of protesting against some deprivation and of demanding redress of grievances of one sort or another. "It would seem", as one scholar has commented, "that the 1990s are characterized by something new: the tendency to reject power imposed without consultation or responsibility and to demand a fair share of resources for all".[14]

The Trade Unions

In the Jamaican context, this tendency led to popular social upheaval in the late 1930s which gave birth to trade unions in the 1940s, among the more important elements of civil society. The trade unions, and the political parties to which they are related, helped to undermine colonial authoritarianism and to promote the transition to modern democracy. Thus, the trade union movement, historically, arose not so much as a 'special' or 'sectional interest' but as the fundamental base of an emerging 'national interest' in the achievement of decolonization and the attainment of democratic statehood.[15] During the pre-independence period, the trade unions contributed to reducing autocratic rule at the workplace, helped to enhance upward social mobility for the black working class, improved levels of real income for unionized sectors and their dependents and brought the interests of labour to bear on national decision-making. During those years, adversarialism with its armoury of weapons, most notably the strike, was central to working class progress, and to the strengthening of civil society as a force for expanding democracy. This adversarial culture arose and became consolidated in the trade unions primarily as a means of overcoming strong resistance to unionization and of winning what workers regarded as adequate wage increases as well as improved benefits from a conservative economic elite. Such tactics could produce positive results in the context of an expanding economy, protected markets relatively insensitive to cost and quality considerations and a political elite relatively favourably disposed towards the unions.[16]

In postcolonial Jamaica of the 1970s and 1980s, and even more so in the radically changed global as well as national environment of the 1990s, circumstances would combine to modify both the strength and the role of trade unions as a vital element of civil society. In the first place, after peaking in the 1970s, trade union membership as a percentage of the labour force steadily declined into the 1990s. Similarly, the financial base of the unions weakened, in many years reflecting deficits as dues income had difficulty in keeping up with increasing levels of expenditure. (See Figures 5.1[a] and 5.1[b].) Strikes and militant industrial actions fell off as workers and unions came to regard them as both less effective and appropriate. The factors contributing to the decline in union strength in Jamaica are not dissimilar from contributing circumstances elsewhere.[17] One such has been the changing character of the labour force – the decline in employment levels in traditional centres of unionism such as export agriculture, domestic manufacturing, public utilities and public administration.[18] At the same time, there has been a significant growth in those segments of the labour force which were more difficult to organize using traditional methods. Among them are self-employment, employment in micro-enterprises (both primarily in the 'informal economy'), low wage employment in export processing zones and white-collar employment in the service economy alongside continued high levels of unemployment and underemployment. In sum, these tendencies in the Jamaican economy, linked to an increasingly competitive global environment, to economic liberalization and to the conditions of IMF–World Bank loans reduced the proportion of relatively easily unionized sectors and helped shift the balance of power against the trade unions.

Even so, the tendency to decline was not uniform but somewhat differentiated as between the more elite-directed and elite-challenging unions. Membership fell off in unions historically associated with, and, to a lesser extent, organizationally affiliated to, the parties which alternated in government in the pre- and postcolonial period. On the other hand, unions without such connections and professing independence of politics, in fact, experienced membership growth. Similarly, in the case of the most important of these, the UAWU, financial surpluses appeared to be more the norm than in the traditional unions. More often than not, the advances of independent unionism were at the expense of the 'political' unions. While this often reflected a level of interunion competition which could be regarded as undesirable in the context of the more intense pressure on labour in the 1990s, the fact is that the turn towards a unionism less affiliated to the established parties reflected a strong and widespread impulse within the working class.[19] The workers wished their unions free of loyalty to governing parties increasingly subordinated to domestic and international elites, thereby becoming better able to take independent positions based on the merits of the particular issue. In a sense, Jamaican labour was signalling to the trade unions the desire that they disconnect from governing coalitions in which, after the 1980s, they were at best junior partners, and resume a more independent role in expanding democratic influences on the state, particularly in the area of economic decision-making.

This renewed role was encouraged by growing tendencies towards joint action and organizational collaboration despite continued rivalries within the labour movement. The establishment of the Joint Trade Union Research and Development Centre (JTURDC) and the formation of the Jamaica Confederation of Trade Unions (JCFTU) reflected and carried forward these unifying tendencies, as did increasing contacts between unions in these centres on the one hand and those outside on the other. Nevertheless, there can be no question that during the 1990s the balance of power in the political economy shifted against the Jamaican trade unions and they became a less significant factor in civil society.

There were many consequences that resulted, at least in part, from this shift. For much of the decade 1986 to 1997, real wages of unionized workers lagged behind the rate of inflation and there appeared to be a redistribution of income from labour to capital.[20] Despite defensive actions by the unions, violations of the national labour code and labour legislation by elements of capital were more determined and dramatic.[21] Not surprisingly, support for unions remained strong among the traditional working class even as that segment of the labour force contracted and the impulse to collective organization became more apparent amongst some sections of white-collar workers. The fact is, however, that the regard for unions as important elements in national life fell in the eyes of the Jamaican people.[22] Overall, these developments undermined the quality of Jamaican democracy for a number of reasons. Reflecting in part the weakening of the unions vis-à-vis capital, civil society declined as a force for equality. Social and income gaps widened; poverty levels rose to include not only the unemployed and underemployed but also a layer of 'working poor'. Partly because of these factors, violent crime rose.[23] Perceptions of politics as contributory and the state as ineffective grew. This in turn strengthened dissatisfaction with Jamaican democracy and tendencies to reject not just the old order but any order at all.

For this trend to be reversed, one important requirement is the renewal and revitalization of the trade unions as important elements of civil society. For this to happen, the trade unions need to become more effective in upholding the interests of their members and of the wider society in the changed conditions of economic liberalization and globalization. This requires more independent and united action in defence of the traditional rights to freedom of association, free collective bargaining and job security. At the same time, the unions need to go beyond such legitimate concerns and break with a past of relative indifference to competitive performance and work to raise overall levels of productivity. This must mean a new quality effort to reduce adversarial relations and build mutually beneficial partnerships with capital in the productive process. Failure to successfully pursue these goals and continuation of the old adversarialism (which brought gains prior to globalization in an era of protectionism) will almost certainly have negative consequences for the economy and the working class, resulting in increased production costs, reduced competitiveness, accelerated plant closures (or redundancies) and worsening of the investment climate in a world in which capital enjoys unprecedented mobility. The increased recognition of these realities is encouraging a new approach in the trade union leadership – one which seeks information-sharing, consultation, dialogue and employee involvement with management in place of employee subordination, authoritarian workplace governance and union management confrontation. This recognition, whilst by no means universal in the leadership of the labour movement and even less so amongst the rank and file, is undoubtedly growing.[24] On another level, the union leadership is demonstrating renewed understanding of the link between the national and transnational in determining the worker's fate. Hence union representatives are invariably present in national delegations discussing issues with IMF teams. Moreover regional and international collaboration among worker organizations is being strengthened.

On the side of capital and management, alongside some resurgence of old anti-union attitudes cloaked in the new imperatives of labour market flexibility, there is growing recognition of the need for a less adversarial and more collaborative approach to labour. This tendency has been driven primarily by the new competitive environment brought on by trade liberalization and globalization in which the keeping and expansion of market share dictates cost reduction, increased efficiency as well as improved quality in ways difficult to achieve without labour's cooperation. Hence the customary exclusion of the trade unions and employees from managerial domains, traditionally defined, is giving way initially to limited information sharing, then to greater transparency regarding cost structure, comparative performance indicators and other aspects of the productive process relevant to the market position of the firm and its product. The concern of management that workers "buy into" and "take part ownership" of the drive to greater productivity and competitiveness is undoubtedly encouraging new levels of information-sharing and consultation at the workplace. While as yet limited this trend, if developed, has considerable potential to undermine the pervasive lack of management communication with labour and the associated sense of mutual disrespect – a critical underlying reason in Jamaica of "why workers won't work".[25]

In this regard, the government's approach to labour market reform and to the renewal of trade unions as vital elements in civil society has left much to be desired. In the first place, the interim report of the Labour Market Reform Committee[26] mentions the importance of employee involvement but fails to give it the central position it deserves in any enlightened transformation of Jamaica's industrial relations system. More significantly, in its attempt to develop a 'social partnership' between the private sector, the trade unions and itself, the government adopted a national rather than sectoral or 'firm-specific' approach. This reflected, at least in part, a failure to grasp the extent of the lack of communication and the depth of distrust at the various points of production and that bridges would first have to be built at these levels before a national accord would become feasible. As a consequence, talks toward a national social partnership floundered at the very same time that possibilities toward accords at lower levels were beginning to bear fruit.

Perhaps the most important of these was the Memorandum of Understanding[27] initialled in May 1998 (and signed in July 1998) between the Bauxite-Alumina corporations, the government and the trade unions representing labour in the sector. In the Bauxite-Alumina Memorandum, the unions expressed support for "an efficient industrial disputes resolution process . . . without recourse to strike [and] . . . go-slows" and committed to "refrain from engaging in rivalry . . . detrimental to the stability of the industry". The companies for their part affirmed recognition "that employee involvement and acceptance will enhance the process" of increasing labour productivity and expressed its commitment "to achieving industry best practices . . . in information-sharing, [and] employee involvement" in the interest of improving the international competitiveness of the Jamaican industry. A similar landmark memorandum was signed in November 1998, after two and a half months of consultation, between the unions representing workers in the banana industry and the Jamaica Producers Group who are responsible for 70 percent of Jamaica's banana production. In important plants in other sectors, particularly manufacturing, practical arrangements for employee involvement as well as jointly designed and administered productivity incentive schemes reflect the early beginnings of a new, more collaborative, partnership between management and union in place of the old adversarial relationship.[28]

To the extent that the unions marry this approach to the continued defence of traditional rights of freedom of association and free collective bargaining, it should raise their effectiveness in playing a role in ensuring not only job security but also employment creation and investment attraction. This combined with greater trade union unity, democratization of internal structures, technological modernization and rank and file education will place the trade unions in a better position not only to represent their members. They could also become a more effective lobby at national and international levels for policies and programmes aimed at achieving economic growth whilst redressing widening socioeconomic gaps. The development of this less traditional, more inclusive, collaborative and democratic approach would no doubt strengthen the trade unions as elements of civil society as well as enhance the role of civil society in Jamaica's democratic renewal.

The Churches

Like the trade unions, but even more so, the Church has deep roots in Jamaican history and is a major element of civil society. During slavery, it served as a support to the system of enslavement while also being a significant force in the movement for abolition and emancipation. In post-emancipation colonial Jamaica, the Church served as a critical institution of "free Jamaica". To one degree or another, the various Christian denominations reflected and promoted economic self-reliance in 'free villages', black self-esteem, Church-sponsored schools and Christian values – albeit with colonial overtones throughout Jamaica society. In the century and a quarter between emancipation and independence, the Church in the community, rural and urban, was a centre of social intercourse, philanthropic activity and voluntary organization.

Again, not unlike the trade unions, the churches had a differentiated relationship to the Jamaican authority structure. Among the traditional or 'historic' churches, the Anglicans, the Roman Catholics and, to a lesser extent, the Methodists drew their main membership from the state as well as socio-economic elites and the racial minorities. Generally, they were to one degree or another close to the establishment and supportive of the status quo. The Baptists were much more closely associated with the black majority and disadvantaged classes. Despite the differing positions, the Christian Bible and religion provided both ideology and symbolism for grass roots resistance to oppressive colonial conditions and for anticipation of a better life in some future "promised land". In the popular revolt of the late 1930s, for example, Christian hymns like "Onward, Christian Soldiers" were main theme songs for the workers and unemployed in the strikes, protest marches and demonstrations which rocked the island and initiated the process of decolonization.[29] During this period, the churches also helped to develop important mass institutions including burial societies and credit unions. In the postcolonial state, in the developing culture of the dispossessed, Christian religion provided the most enduring and effective metaphors. "Babylon" was the popular designation of an increasingly inequitable and unjust Jamaica;[30] "Pharaoh", "Little David", "Moses", "Joshua", were some of the biblical names attached to various political leaders. With this legacy, the churches as a whole, unlike the trade unions, have shown little sign of membership decline as a proportion of the Jamaican population. Moreover, the public continues to regard the Church as an institution of the highest importance, second only in significance to the mass media.[31]

Within this general overall pattern, the experience of the various denominations has, however, been quite different. In particular, the 50 years between the mid 1940s and the mid 1990s has seen an initial steady and then, more recently, phenomenal growth of the fundamentalist denominations and a decline, in both relative and absolute terms, of the historic churches. In 1943, census data showed the Church of God as second to last amongst the seven denominations into which the population was grouped. At that time the Anglicans and the Baptists had respectively eight and seven times the membership of the Church of God. By 1960, the Church of God had risen to third in the ranks and two decades later was number one. By 1991, the membership of the Church of God and the Seventh Day Adventists far exceeded that of all other churches combined.[32] Data obtained from churches themselves tend to confirm the trends revealed in the Census reports.[33] In the ten year period leading up to the mid 1990s, while membership figures for the Anglican, Baptist, Roman Catholic, and United Churches remained near constant, the Seventh Day Adventists increased by 51 percent over the same period. The membership in the latter in the mid nineties surpassed that of the Anglicans, Baptists and Roman Catholics combined. (See Table 5.1; Figure 5.2.) In terms of financial strength, the picture appeared no different.

While these trends appear similar to developments elsewhere, it remains unclear what implications, if any, they hold for the role of the Church in civil society. Two decades ago, during the ideological polarization of the 1970s, the growth of fundamentalism reflected and strengthened rejection of socialism, promoted anti-statism, and pro-market conservatism amongst the people. The fact that on the other hand the traditional churches, and in particular their leadership, maintained a sympathy for centre-left, social democratic tendencies meant that they reflected, more than bridged, the prevailing political divisions. To that extent, they helped to maintain the competitiveness of Jamaican politics but at the expense of being caught up in the acute, even violent contestation which damaged the quality of the country's democracy.

In the post-Cold War consensus on neoliberal economic and social policy, the Church has been either silent or relatively ineffective as a national force on the main issues of the day. No growth, high inflation, widening income gaps, increasing crime, growing corruption, a decline in social order and high levels of poverty have initially accompanied the turn from statism to economic liberalization. The churches, and in particular the fundamentalist denominations, have been critical of the materialism of the new dispensation, calling for a renewal of spiritual values and seeking to strengthen welfare activity at the level of individual parishes and congregations. But by and large, apart from a continuing traditional opposition to the introduction of casino gambling, the church has either been silent or ineffective on issues of democratic renewal at the national level. The one, or perhaps the most notable, exception to this rule has been on the question of electoral reform.

In the late 1980s and 1990s, the democratic character of Jamaican elections deteriorated. The persistence of violence and intimidation in political campaigns and on election day; the erosion of political rights and civil liberties in so-called garrison constituencies and communities; corrupt abuse of election administration and the ineffectiveness of the justice system in righting electoral malpractices – all these contributed to growing alienation from politics amongst widening sectors of the electorate. They also spurred elements within the Church, particularly the leadership of the Roman Catholics, to take the initiative to deal with the decline and to help strengthen the democratic character of Jamaican elections. These efforts first took definite organizational form prior to the 1993 general elections. At that time, the Catholic Church was able to organize about 200 persons – mainly from the ranks of its own clerics and laity – to monitor the elections in a few polling divisions of a handful of urban garrison constituencies.[34] The effort attracted no significant support inside or outside the Catholic Church; there was neither national organization nor international linkages. At best, it added to the documentation of gross irregularities in garrison constituencies but was clearly a token gesture with little deterrent value. But the 1993 initiative marked a new beginning of Church activism on electoral reform, the short-run futility of which clearly fuelled resolve rather than discouragement on the matter of dealing with electoral malpractices.

Against this background, the run-up to the general election due constitutionally by March 1998 was a different kettle of fish, revealing considerable possibilities as well as some limits on the role of the Church in civil society as a force for democratic renewal. In early 1997, the Roman Catholic Archbishop sought to convene a group on the question of improving the quality of Jamaican elections. From the very inception of this initiative, however, the leadership of the Church went outside its own ranks and sought systematically to interest other denominations as well as prominent public personalities in coming together to form an organization intended to eradicate electoral irregularities and to restore genuinely democratic elections in Jamaica. From the outset, linkages with INGOs and government agencies in the democracy-promoting global community were contemplated and initiated. The end result was the formation, within six months, of CAFFE.[35]

By the 18 December 1997 elections, this body was able to bring together on its directorate the leadership of traditional and fundamentalist churches alongside persons of considerable credibility in Jamaican civil society. Its field organization included but reached beyond a strong clerical core and CAFFE enlisted ten times as many volunteers in 1997 as in the 1993 effort. The organization raised over J$6 million dollars from local and international private and public sector sources in six months. Despite considerable controversy and some difficulty, CAFFE nevertheless won endorsement from all sections of the Jamaican media, the state and each of the three parties competing in the elections. In the end, the presence and role of CAFFE monitors was universally acknow-ledged to have contributed in no small measure to the reduction in electoral irregularities, particularly the relative non-violence, in the 1997 elections.

This experience does suggest the potential of the Church for playing a more decisive role in Jamaica's democratic renewal. But it also suggests that such a role requires resolute leadership in the face of inevitable setbacks and, even more so, inter-denominational collaboration as well as determined outreach to civil society, including sectors which are not overtly religious. "Strong private sector support, local and . . . foreign"[36] is essential but insufficient. It would appear that to fulfil this role the Church would have to free itself somewhat from the more strident anti-government, anti-politics of some tendencies in civil society and to demonstrate willingness to work with political parties as well as state agencies on a reform agenda. Cooperation with, without subordination to, the international 'democracy-promoting' community would also appear to be essential. Even so, with the best organizational tactics, and even greater effort at mobilizing congregations than was seen in the 1997 general elections, the decline in public spiritedness and voluntarism and the corresponding growth of individualism and demoralization which is now accompanying neoliberalism in Jamaica will set definite limits on even Church-led mobilization for democratic renewal.

Voluntary Associations

The extent of these limits and, more so, the degree of decline in civil society and associational life is a matter of some dispute. On the one hand, there is the view "that the decline in volunteerism is part of a much wider picture in which, almost inexorably, a whole collapse of civil society is taking place in Jamaica".[37] There is from this perspective "an all-class crisis, a point of historical decline", "a terminal decline", "the breakdown of civil society in Jamaica". A less pessimistic but related view which upholds some prospect for "democratic renewal" nevertheless sees Jamaica "careening on the edge of an abyss".[38]

At the same time, a quite different perspective sees "an increasing number of non-political community groups . . . emerging from across the country" and regards this as possibly "the best thing that has happened to Jamaica since Independence".[39] These groups are interesting themselves in local issues relating to education, drug abuse, the environment, improved infrastructure. In this context, even the pessimist view concedes "the relative success of the Neighbourhood Watch Programme in which citizens participate voluntarily".[40] More generally, "communities are going ahead and electing non-political community councils . . . a deepened form of participatory democracy."

The question, therefore, arises: Are volunteerism, associational life and civil society in Jamaica in the midst of "terminal decline" or on the eve of a "new beginning"? In my view, these perspectives and the processes to which they refer are not so mutually exclusive as might initially appear as there are elements of truth in both views. The fact is that civil society and associational life are undergoing both processes of decay and renewal simultaneously. In regard to the former, there is much truth in the observations that:

everyday personal . . . life in . . . Jamaica . . . is becoming more volatile and unpredictable, ever more coarse, ever more directionless . . . That the common bond among ourselves as citizens is becoming weaker and weaker . . . that simple politeness and civility are perceived to be a fatal display of weakness . . . this pervasive sense that Jamaica is not a moral, but only a geographical, expression is at the root of the crisis of volunteerism in Jamaica today.[41]

But is it not also true that the very acuteness of all-pervasive incivility and the increasing sense of its potentially terminal character are generating a growing collective self-interest in renewal?

Without some appreciation of the strength of this impulse and the opportunity which deepening crisis is presenting, it is difficult, if not impossible, to explain important indicators of renewal in civil society. More to the point, it is hard to understand why acts of regeneration taking place within recent months did not occur, despite effort, but a few years ago. I have in mind two such: the establishment and consolidation of CAFFE between September and December 1997 and the negotiation and signing of a "social partnership" in the important bauxite-alumina sector in the first half of 1998. In each case, earlier efforts had failed; in each case – the 'stillborn' CAFFE of 1993 and the sterile social partnership dialogue of 1995–97 – the general context and the principal actors in the failure were essentially the same as brought subsequent success. The critical difference between later success and earlier failure was the deepening crisis, the increased awareness of crisis, and the more fertile ground which this presented for skilled leadership to bear fruit.

More broadly, I believe similar circumstances are now at work in helping to slow the decline of voluntary associations and even to lead to what in Jamaican circumstances appear to be impressive rates of formation of new civic groups. Over the past five years, for example, Neighbourhood Watches have been formed at the rate of two to three per month; the total number of such groups has grown by almost 50 percent during this time. In terms of the youth, the number of Police Youth Clubs has more than doubled since 1993;[42] 4H Clubs have grown by almost 25 percent[43] and Youth Clubs affiliated to the Government Social Development Commission by approximately 15 percent[44] (the latter since 1990–91). While data are not very reliable, there appear to be approximately 2,000 community-based organizations spread in every parish across the country. (See Table 5.2.) This does not include the large number of individual churches from each of which significant community networks radiate.

The argument here is not that these groups constitute a burgeoning or even healthier civil society. Nor is it that these associations do not reflect rather than bridge 'spatial segregation' amongst the different classes and localities. It is even less in dispute that the development of the voluntary spirit and the growth of civic groups at various levels is urgently in need of an appropriate national vision as well as carefully crafted national programmes and policies. What is being contested is the idea that 'terminal decline' describes the current state of associational life in Jamaica. On the contrary, it is being argued that renewal, albeit in extremely trying circumstances, is (or, at least, has the near potential to be) as much a feature of civil society as is decline. Moreover, the processes of renewal which are evident are taking place in civil society are taking place not in isolation from government but with appropriate support from the state. This suggests that while subordination to politics and government on the one hand and to the private sector on the other are the death of civil society, carefully designed cooperation with both is often the source of survival and beneficial growth.

This general rule would appear to be even more applicable, on another level, to associations and networks concerned with sports and culture, particularly music, which have become increasingly important elements of Jamaican civil society. In this respect, it needs to be remembered that Jamaicans have for some time regarded the country's sporting and cultural achievements,[45] not its political nor economic progress, as those aspects of national life since independence of which they can be most proud. These sentiments, particularly in respect to track athletics and soccer, have been in recent times vigorously reinforced by the significant achievements of national teams at the 1997 Atlanta Olympics and in the "Road to France" World Cup elimination rounds.[46] Soccer clubs and associations, competitions and leagues, at the community and national levels have attracted a growing following and support. By and large, these activities help to reduce individualism and negativism, facilitate the building of self-esteem and the team approach amongst youth, generate points of bonding amongst the different classes and colours – qualities of significance to the renewal and sustainability of Jamaican democracy. Indeed, the occasion in late 1997 of Jamaica qualifying for the World Cup in France, the first English-speaking Caribbean team ever so to do, and the creditable performance of the team during the tournament, saw affirmation of national identity and outpourings of positive feelings about Jamaica such as had not been since the country's independence 35 years ago.

More generally, the success of the national soccer team appeared to underline some of the factors important to the development of civil society in Jamaica. One is the necessity for collaborative, not subordinate, relations between civic bodies on the one hand and the government as well as the private sector on the other. Secondly, the Road to France experience brought out the need, the benefits and the possibility of bridging the social divisions of Jamaican society in a process whereby each class and colour is encouraged to bring its particular talents to the table and consciously seeks to overcome historical inequalities and disrespect of each for the other.[47] Thirdly, the success of the team demonstrated the importance of civic bodies building moral values and inculcating patriotic sentiment but in a manner which actively subordinates national narrow-mindedness. This can happen at two levels: first, in reaching out and forging links of equality with the overseas Jamaican, the 'Jamaican diaspora';[48] secondly, in building relations in the international community, which, at some cost, allow access to the most modern expertise, technologies and methods.[49]

The situation regarding music is somewhat more complex. On the one hand, there can be little doubt that important networks and relationships have developed particularly among inner city youth around the production, marketing, presentation, and consumption of Jamaican popular music. The crews that form around the more prominent artists or DJs, the followers of the various sound systems or sets, the regulars at the many dance halls – all bring together youths and constitute significant elements of civil society in contemporary Jamaican conditions. The critical question is: What is their role and character? Do they foster helpful cooperative relations and healthy competition, thereby helping to build social capital in these sectors? Or do they provide yet another arena facilitating violence within and among communities, rendering the fostering of community trust and organization-building that more difficult? More likely, is it a mixture of both negative and positive tendencies in the popular music phenomenon and its organizational aspects? These are questions on which little or no research has been done and which are in urgent need of probing. This is especially true as "in many poor urban communities, the dance hall was the central institution for young people . . . [a] point of convergence out of which other institutions, both good and bad, emanate . . ."[50]

On balance, civil society in Jamaica appears to be renewing itself even as it experiences the tendency to decline and, as yet, is producing no significant discernible improvement in civic conduct. A major role in fostering the development of this contradictory tendency has been played by sections of the mass media. These, particularly the radio talk shows, have reflected and promoted critiques – both constructive and destructive – of the operations of political as well as economic institutions. Listenership, viewership and readership of an increasingly diverse Jamaican media has grown in the 1990s (see Tables 5.3[a] and [b]) and, alongside this growth, a utilization of the media as a means of unconventional participation by civil society in meeting its own diverse needs. Making representations through a talk show against some abuse of authority, violation of rights, deterioration in community services, or, alternatively, citizens calling for some modification of policy or practice, for help from the appropriate authorities to accomplish some common purpose or for the change of some institution or individual – use of the media in these ways by civil society has become more important, and perhaps more effective, than conventional representations to the politician or to the boss.

The growth of the media has therefore facilitated the development of civil society as a check on the abuse of power by placing in the hand of interested publics a means of power which it would otherwise not have had and which in earlier years was not available. Negatively, the media have helped to discredit government, and, to a lesser extent, the private corporate sector, often without concern for alternatives, thereby fostering tendencies to alienation and anarchy. On occasion, the media directly encourage the formation and development of civic associations and popular organizations independent of establishment institutions. Indeed, in some sense the radio audience and the listener-participant networks around the more prominent talk shows – *Independent Talk, Perkins on Line, Action Line, Breakfast Club* – have become not only vehicles for the development of civil society but components of civil society itself. It remains true, however, that these as well as other elements of Jamaican civil society at this stage more constitute negative constraints on the abuse of power rather than positive avenues for institutionalizing citizen involvement in decision-making and hence democratization. This deficiency is perhaps as much a reflection of weakness in popular political culture as of inadequacies in the institutional structures of governance at the level of the state and of the firm.

In relation to popular political culture, it is quite clear that a large proportion of the people now believe that their democratic rights are more effectively secured on a day-to-day basis by direct action, for example in the form of street protests, rather than by using conventional channels of representation to members of Parliament, or ministers of government.[51] There appears to be, however, a significant gap between the high incidence of protests of one form or another and the far less frequent formation of enduring grass roots organizations. This in turn gives mass impact on authority structures and processes an episodic (more than a lasting) character compared to that of more elite social strata. One reason for this hiatus between spontaneous action and group formation is, no doubt, the apparent unresponsiveness of the powers to established associations of the grass roots. A strengthening of the role and responsibilities of local government authorities and provision for meaningful empowerment of community groups within a reformed local government system would undoubtedly provide some incentive for building and sustaining civic associations.

In this regard, the Local Government Reform Programme[52] initiated in 1992 offers some positive prospects. Under this programme, the parish councils are resuming responsibility for the maintenance of drains and gullies, over 900 minor water supplies, and 13,000 kilometers of parochial roads out of a total island network of 18,000. Of perhaps greater significance is the provision for sources of local government funding relatively autonomous of central government. Finally, to the extent that the proposed parish advisory councils bring together representatives of bona fide community groups as well as of agencies that provide vital community services, then this should go some way to better achieving goals of citizen empowerment through "maximum participation".[53]

6

Conclusion: Global Reforms and the Jamaican Agenda

In general, the reform of government and politics in democratic states only became a central preoccupation during the 1990s. Prior to this, calls for the strengthening of democracy fell largely on deaf ears or, at least, on ears attuned to little else but the primacy of the struggle against communism. Reform proposals were, therefore, regarded as secondary, or worse, associated exclusively with leftist critiques of democratic systems. As such, they drew support from socialist and social democratic constituencies in Europe and left liberal circles in the United States. Outside these spheres, mainstream media and the mass publics in the West showed little interest in reform projects, particularly in the 1980s, caught up as they were in the fight against "the evil empire" or indifferent towards politics and politicians of all stripes.

It was the fall of the Berlin Wall (1989), the dissolution of the Soviet Union (1991) and the ending of the Cold War which, in retrospect, were to signal important changes in the prospects of democracy and the concern for democratic reforms. In the East, the transition from communism (by definition) multiplied the number of 'electoral' democracies. Elsewhere, in Africa, Latin America and, to a lesser extent, Asia, one-party rule, military regimes and other forms of authoritarianism gave way to governments elected in more or less fair and free elections. But a significant paradox accompanied the conclusion of this 'third wave of democratization'. At the very moment that people around the newly democratizing world were celebrating the fall of autocracy, the mass public and strategic elites in 'first' and 'second wave' democracies were becoming increasingly critical of their own democracies, political institutions and politicians. The pervasive evidence and widespread exposure of corruption in public life was the main catalyst of this new anxiety in mature democracies. The offering and the taking of bribes or the buying and selling of influence, in one or another form, was revealed as widespread and, in many cases, institutionalized in the newly victorious 'free world'. Italy became exposed and stood out as the most extreme example. Between 1992 and the end of 1994, nearly half of the membership of Italy's two chambers of parliament and 2,500 politicians and businessmen were under criminal investigation on various charges of corruption. Long-standing connections between successive postwar Italian Christian Democratic governments and prime ministers on the one hand and the Mafia on the other were confirmed in a series of dramatic judicial hearings. In other European first wave democracies, less pervasive but nevertheless disconcerting graft and corruption were exposed. In France, for example, by the end of October 1994, one ex-minister was in jail, another had been forced to resign, at least five others were under investigation in relation to corruption allegations and 29 members or ex-members of parliament had been charged or already convicted for various illegalities. In Spain and Britain, the latter the most venerable of parliamentary democracies, cases of corruption and of questionable ethics stained the institutions of government and further damaged the reputations of politicians.

Outside Europe, important leaders and significant figures in the world of established democracy also fell victim to corruption. The chairman of the House Ways and Means Committee of the US Congress and pillar of the Democratic Party, Dan Rostenkowski, had to serve time in federal prison; so too an associate attorney general, Webster Hubbell, in the Clinton administration, both having been found guilty of corruption charges. In Venezuela, one of the more long-standing democracies in Latin America, and Brazil, newly in transition from military rule, previously popular presidents Carlos Andres Perez and Fernando Callor de Mello were impeached in 1992 and in 1993 respectively. Colombian President Ernesto Samper narrowly avoided a similar fate arising out of credible allegations of accepting millions of dollars of drug money for his 1994 election campaign. In India, the world's largest democracy, the government of Prime Minister Rao fell under the weight of charges of corruption against the prime minister himself and some of his most senior ministers. By the mid 1990s, there was hardly a democracy in which corruption had not placed the credibility of political leadership on the line and the reform of democratic institutions on the agenda.

Important changes in the political landscape of the early 1990s obviously had much to do with this new development. The demise of communism facilitated the exposure of unethical or even illegal conduct in democracies (such as corrupt links with the Mafia) which might have been previously ignored, underplayed or excused in the name of the struggle of the 'free world' against communist totalitarianism. In any event, with no credible systemic challenge, the risk of 'washing one's dirty linen in public' either disappeared or was significantly reduced. In addition, at least three other factors appeared to encourage corrupt behaviour.[1] One was the increased need on the part of politicians and parties to raise large sums of money as the cost of election campaigns in democracies skyrocketed relative to party membership contributions. A second was the increased incentive for the private sector in an age of varying degrees of economic liberalization and deregulation to influence state elites to utilize the state power in the interest of one or another of the elements in the business community. Finally, the triumph of the market seemed to have carried with it a weakening of traditional values and a corresponding rise of an unethical, self-interested materialism.

Whether it was, in fact, that the incidence of corruption grew or whether it was the exposure of corruption that increased is not so important for our purposes. What is significant is that the recurring charges, the revelations, the resignations and the convictions of political personalities for corruption fuelled a deepening cynicism in mass publics towards established political leadership and political institutions across a wide band of democratic states. Opinion surveys confirmed the growing belief amongst electorates that politicians were corrupt and that governments could not be trusted. Interestingly, the legitimacy of democracy as a system appeared not to be a question; rather it was the performance of democracies which produced varying but significant levels of dissatisfaction.

Changes in the character of electorates also contributed to the pervasive discontent. Rising levels of education; more access to information; better living standards; greater social mobility; increased self-confidence; changing values – all combined to reduce historic gaps between leaders and led, weaken traditional deference to authority and loosened long-standing loyalty to established parties. All in all, there was developing a greater capacity amongst voters to be critical and an enhanced inclination to be independent. Pre-existing tendencies to alienation from politics and to dissatisfaction with democracy were therefore accelerated rather than initiated by corruption-related scandals.

Alienation and dissatisfaction were compounded by the apparent inability of prevailing democratic forms to allow greater citizen control over decisions affecting everyday life. The development or the decline of local communities, individual workplaces or natural environments seemed more determined by distant governments in capital cities, bureaucrats in unaccountable authorities or big corporations beholden to anonymous shareholders. In Europe, the transformation of the European Community into the European Union and the closer advance to some form of transnational federalism appeared to widen rather than narrow the distance between legislatures over which electors could exercise some periodic control on the one hand and, on the other, sites of real and more powerful executive authority over whose decisions the people had little say. The democratic deficit, particularly in relation to smaller states, was aggravated by the real power of transnational capital and the apparent erosion of the ability of democratic governments to deal with growing socioeconomic inequality and weakened welfare systems.

The expectations of democracy varied, depending on whether the value orientations in the particular political culture were more liberal-individualistic or more social-communitarian. But everywhere, to one degree or another, expectations were less than fulfilled in the democracies of the early 1990s. This led to at least three consequences. One was a general tendency to reduced levels of participation in 'elite-directed' politics. For example, membership in traditional political parties declined; electoral turn-out, already low, fell off further; respect for established authorities eroded. At the same time, however, these developments did not signal political apathy. On the contrary, a second tendency took shape: there was marked growth in non-traditional political participation.[2] The use of petitions instead of votes, the effort to form non-political civic organizations, the willingness to back non-political personalities for public office, the inclination toward mechanisms of direct democracy alongside or as superior devices to representative government – all in one way or another reflected the fact that dissatisfaction with democracy's performance was energizing innovation as much as producing alienation. This underlying impulse provided the basis for the third development – a re-engineering of institutions and the search for reform among mature and established democracies in the mid 1990s.

Dimensions of Reform

Not surprisingly, given the significant role of public disquiet at political corruption in stimulating concern for reform, much thinking focused on more effectively regulating money in politics. Two levels attracted attention – first, the funding of candidates, parties and election campaigns; secondly, the personal finances of members of legislatures and executives.

In relation to party and campaign finance, much debate centres around three dimensions of reforms. The first relates to limits on the sources and amounts of donations; the second to transparency, as in declaring the sources and amounts of contributions to parties and candidates; and the third to public or state funding of political parties. By and large, the mature democracies, with the notable exception of Great Britain, made provision for all three elements. (See Tables 6.1[a] and [b].) Developments in the 1990s, however, placed on the agenda of these countries the question of the adequacy of public funding and the issue of more stringent regulation of private financing of political parties and election campaigns. In the United States, for example, a task force[3] of political scientists in examining the complex issue of campaign finance reform proposed to ban private contributions to political parties entirely, that is, 'soft money' (as distinct from individual candidates) and to extend state contributions from presidential campaigns to congressional elections. In Britain, similarly, Prime Minister Blair declared willingness to break with tradition and readiness "to consider . . . proposals for state funding of political parties . . . [and] to publish names and amounts"[4] of contributions to political parties from private donors.

On another level, that of the personal finances of parliamentarians, legislators and members of the executive, regulations sought to deter and to detect corruption.[5] Elected representatives were required to sign registers of interests. In some instances, such registers were open to the public and in Italy and the USA the representative was required at the same time to declare the monetary value of such interests. Most importantly, some countries obliged the politician to specify any gifts received above a certain value. The general direction of the reform agenda, however, went well beyond anti-corruption measures which understandably provided so much of its initial and continuing impetus.

One broad dimension the agenda incorporated was of interest in processes of direct democracy. In that context, more frequent use of the referendum as a device of decision-making was apparent. The average annual number of referendums in first world countries increased dramatically in the second half of the 1980s compared to the decade of the 1960s. Moreover, in Europe the first three years of the 1990s saw the average number of referendums per year double compared to the decade of the 1980s.[6] Decisions on fundamental issues such as proposals for change in territorial boundaries of the state, the nature of the political regime (Chile 1988; South Africa 1992), the type of democratic system (Brazil 1993), the character of the electoral arrangements (New Zealand 1992, 1993) were increasingly taken by referendum. The inclination to put policy questions to the people also grew. Most significantly, in a mature democracy like the United States where there is no constitutional provision for the use of referendums nationally, opinion polls nevertheless indicated a majority in favour of the use of national referendums. Similarly, in Britain where the politically elite traditionally opposed the referendums as a decision-making device, "public support for referendums is high". In fact, in 1995, "77 percent favoured a 'referendum system whereby certain issues are put to the people to decide by popular vote' as compared to only 19 percent favouring a system whereby 'Parliament should decide all important issues'."[7]

It is hard to overestimate the significance of the referendum as an indicator of one important basis and direction of democratic reform into the millennium. For one reason, the growth of public support for its usage is a clear signal of the extent of distrust of politicians and of political parties. Secondly, its more frequent employment in determining challenging issues has helped to enhance the legitimacy of national decisions taken in this manner. At the same time, contrary to the expectations of its opponents, the referendum has not produced a tyranny of the majority nor the negation of representative government. Rather it has been, on balance, an important supplement to indirect democracy and a vital element on the agenda of reform.

So much so is this the case that it has impacted on the growing concern regarding the democratic deficit in the international sphere. To be sure, the puzzle remains largely unresolved of how to make transnational organizations more accountable, in democratic terms, the more their authority intrudes through increasingly permeable national boundaries. One idea is to transnationalize and increasingly empower democratic institutions by, for example, creating or strengthening regional parliamentary bodies. Another is to use transnational referendums to decide transnational issues, thereby providing "new vehicles for democratic expression at the national level that also provide national democratic access to supranational decision-making".[8] Of course, such usage may very well now appear remote in the context of a resurgence of particularistic 'identity politics', of caution over ceding territorially bounded popular sovereignty and of interstate asymmetries of power. Nevertheless, the transnational referendum as one component of a more 'cosmopolitan' democracy was justifiably an item for serious consideration on the reform agenda towards the century's end.

Other aspects of that agenda have moved beyond consideration to action and are producing more or less definite trends in relation to institutional design. One fundamental area relates to choices and changes as between parliamentary and presidential systems of democracy. In terms of initial choice, it is apparent that countries in transition from authoritarian regimes have opted, in the main, for new constitutions in the presidential or semi-presidential rather than the parliamentary mould. At the same time, in established or resumed democracies, discussion has been considerable of the strengths and weaknesses of these two basic competing models although action in the direction of overall system change has been minimal. Indeed, there appears to have been no instance of any existing presidential system changing to the parliamentary alternative or vice versa. In Brazil, which was among those which came closest to such a change, nationwide debate led to a national referendum in 1992 on the issue of changing the country's presidential system for a parliamentary type constitution. By a margin of two to one, undoubtedly influenced by the successful impeachment of President Callor under the presidential constitution, the electors voted to retain that system. Despite the considerable discussion, not least of all amongst academics, on the respective merits of parliamentary and presidential systems no state has changed from one to the other, leading one scholar to describe existing constitutions as "renegotiation proof".[9]

Not so, however, has been the experience regarding the design and operation of institutions within each prevailing system. Within executives, for example, particularly in the parliamentary system, one definite trend has been away from single-party Cabinets. The tendency to coalition governments and power-sharing at the executive level has grown. Legislatures have become less arenas for two-party dominance and more for multiparty representation as the base of long-established parties narrowed and new political organizations emerged with some popular support. This tendency was facilitated by significant changes in electoral systems among the areas of more important reforms instituted in established democracies during the 1990s. There the main trend has been away from the pure type of either proportional representation or the first-past-the-post system: the tendency remains towards designs which combine elements of each in a way which preserves the advantages and reduces the disadvantages of the pure types. In this regard, Germany's mixed electoral system has become influential as a model; the shifts to hybrid electoral arrangements in Italy and New Zealand during the 1990s are an indicator of the direction of changes being considered elsewhere.

This line of attempting to 'get the best of both worlds' rather than totally throwing out one pure type for another is evident in much of the prevailing approach to democratic renewal. At the system level, for example, attention is shifting from wholesale change from presidentialism to parliamentarian or vice versa. More thought is being given to so redesigning institutional rules and structuring incentives within each system in ways which borrow elements from the alternative system and which allow reduction in the negatives of the existing order. Hence, current consideration in Latin America of engrafting procedures on existing institutions that could facilitate the development of Congressional parties disciplined enough to provide presidents with working majorities but not so beholden to the executive as to dilute legislative checks and balances. Conversely, in parliamentary systems, mechanisms are being considered, in some cases already being tested, of utilizing presidential devices to make executives more authoritative in the context of shifting, and sometimes short-lived, coalition-based legislative majorities. One such mechanism is direct election of the prime minister as has been recently adopted in Israeli parliamentary system. Another device to strengthen the separation between legislature and executive, thereby reducing executive dominance of parliament in Westminster-type systems, is to require that elected representatives once appointed to the Cabinet, must give up their parliamentary seats, as is the case in New Zealand.

The main point here is not so much the specifics of the particular mechanism. More important, is a reform methodology which is flexible, selectively inclusive and synthesizing rather than rigid, exclusivistic and purist. Since each democratic system and each institutional subset has by the end of the twentieth century displayed both strengths and weaknesses, selective redesign rather than wholesale retention or rejection to maximize advantages and minimize disadvantages in relation to concrete contexts appears to be the more productive way to proceed. This need not amount to incrementalism since cumulative re-engineering can and does produce qualitative change. The aggregative approach to transformation leads to discussion of one other dimension of the philosophy of democratic reform: consensualism rather than majoritarianism.

As the terms imply, consensualism seeks the broadest agreement; majoritarianism is satisfied with majority endorsement in all aspects of democratic governance. In the former the winner shares all, the loser gets much; in the latter the winner takes all, the loser gets nothing. Hence the competitive stakes in majoritarian systems tend to be much higher and of a different quality from those in consensual democracies; leaders and followers, parties and party activists, elections and legislatures are more partisan and adversarial, even confrontational, in the former than in the latter. In this context, two circumstances towards the end of the century combined to breathe new life into consensualism and to undermine the attractiveness of the majoritarian approach. One was widespread public dissatisfaction with partisan politicking amongst established parties, which often appeared to put party advantage above public interest. A second was the role of race, ethnicity, religion, language, region, and so on in forming politically relevant exclusivistic identities and in fomenting reciprocal distrust among majority and minority groups. In either case, winner-take-all majoritarianism tended to reduce the possibility of 'give and take' and aggravate problems of democratic governance; conversely, consensualism, reflected in power-sharing institutions and consociational arrangements, offered real opportunity to reduce divisiveness and increase democratic legitimacy.

In advancing or impeding reform, in raising or lowering the quality of democracy, the "enormous importance of leadership"[10] has been appropriately acknowledged. This is not to deny the role of institutions in shaping leadership as well as in enabling or constraining leadership action. What it is to suggest is that prevailing conditions near the century's end allow leadership with the requisite qualities to play an exceptional role in enhancing or eroding democracy. Amongst the favourable prevailing conditions are, not least of all, the relatively high levels of education, information, skill and confidence of today's citizens, preparing a potential 'followership' of considerable problem solving, self-directing capability once such can be brought together with appropriate leadership. The leadership has to base itself on an influence more than an authority (or worse, authoritarian) relationship with followers; on persuasion more than directive; on inspiration more than charisma; on stimulating more than stifling feedback; on valuing more than vanquishing diversity. Moreover, in relation to competitors and adversaries, such leadership needs to commend rather than condemn constructive opposition; show respect rather than arrogance; work for compromise rather than confrontation; most of all, build institutions and processes of collaboration and cooperation rather than of exclusion and rejection.

Elements of Jamaica's Reform Agenda

Within this global context, reform in Jamaica has displayed both similarities to and differences from the overall pattern. In the first place, as elsewhere, a new quality concern for change begun to express itself in the early 1990s. Here too, the ending of the Cold War had an important influence though not so much in exposing political corruption for financial gain amongst the elite. Rather, the ending of the Cold War reduced ideological policy divergence in Jamaica's politics and strengthened pressures towards 'across the board' adoption of neoliberal economic and social policies. The IMF and the World Bank were confirmed as major conduits of this pressure; the radical left (though not without continuing influence on reform processes) dissolved organizationally in the new consensus and the politics of the country converged toward the centre of the political spectrum.

This post-Cold War dispensation contributed, as it did elsewhere, to a growing alienation from traditional Jamaican politics and to a renewal of impulses to reform the country's democracy. In the first place, the end of ideological polarization in Jamaica removed any conceivable philosophical rationalization by any of the competing political parties for waging war against one another. To the extent that the two sides were proposing and implementing much the same by way of programme and policy, why should electoral competition mean physical confrontations? Political violence then had no excuse grounded, with whatever degree of justification, in Cold War circumstances, whether in the defence of freedom against communism or in the protection of the people against imperialism. By the end of the 1980s and early 1990s, political violence lost any such high-sounding association and became progressively more senseless to more and more Jamaicans and, as such, perhaps the single most important reason for withdrawal from traditional politics. Post-Cold War political violence, therefore played in Jamaica much the same role as post-Cold War political corruption played elsewhere in diminishing the quality of political life, aggravating discontent with the working of democracy and stimulating processes of reform.

In Jamaica, this violence had become connected to a variety of other electoral irregularities and to a confrontationist style of political competition. Provocative marches and motorcades; inflammatory campaign speeches and mass meetings; intimidation of political opponents and electoral officials; ballot stuffing and over-voting; partisan manipulation of the police – these were but some of the concerns which by the 1990s, especially in urban areas, had developed to dangerous proportions in the country's body politic. Underpinning this deformation of electoral competition into political warfare was the extremism of the Jamaican case of winner-take-all majoritarianism. To the activists and supporters of the winning party would go almost exclusively the spoils of office: government contracts, employment opportunities, job promotion, housing, land allocations. To the losing party would go little or nothing and often victimization and dispossession of benefits earlier obtained when the losing party had held office. Thus, clientistic relations provided strong material foundations for traditional party loyalism and the spoils system fuelled historically high fanaticism amongst party activists.

Given these dynamics, the failure of the Jamaican economy to grow and the contraction of the state along with the resources available to it would have serious implications for the performance of Jamaican democracy. The more so as the absence of growth and the weakening of the state was accompanied by widening socioeconomic gaps between rich and poor. For the political parties and party leadership, this situation meant more difficulty in sustaining party activists and significant fall off in party loyalists. For the most disadvantaged, particularly the unemployed youth, lack of opportunity and increasing iniquity meant growing frustration, anger and resentment as well as openness to drugs, crime and violence. For a growing proportion of citizens, the political tribalism and economic nonperformance of the system meant a turning away from traditional politics and a search for new beginnings. This turning away, particularly amongst civic-minded elements in the middle strata, gave rise to the formation of anti-political groups, not dissimilar to formations elsewhere. Thus, the New Beginning Movement and the Constitutional Reform Network emerged as two manifestations of the desire for a new political order and contributed to the impulse for change. Amongst the masses, alienation took more aggressive forms of representation for redress through street protests on the one hand and media talk shows on the other. However divergent the forms, the underlying messages were in large measure the same. Jamaican democracy was in need of renewal; with varying degrees of consciousness, a reform agenda was being elaborated as the millennium drew closer.

Item 1 on this agenda was not dissimilar from an increasing preoccupation in so many other democracies: How could the growing distance between the people and their representatives be reduced and how could the representatives be made more accountable to the people? In Jamaica, dealing with this issue clearly related to correcting deficiencies and deformities which had developed over time in winner-take-all politics. By the mid 1990s, political leaders and activists were more preoccupied with gaining or retaining the spoils of office than with representing the interests of the people. To that extent, the situation called for a redesign of institutions to require or facilitate a sharing of spoils, to strengthen checks and balances on power-holders as well as to encourage popular participation in all aspects of governance.

In this context, consensus soon emerged on a number of points: that the executive power was too concentrated; the legislature too subordinate; that the award of public contracts and the disposal of public assets should be more effectively insulated from partisan political influence and considerations; that, similarly, sensitive areas of state power, such as the operational direction of the police and the administration of elections, should be removed from partisan direction and control. The rate of implementation of the agreed reforms was, however, uneven. At one end, was the extreme sluggishness in putting into effect "a series of far-reaching recommendations"[11] to change the system of awarding public sector contracts. At the other end, by way of contrast, was the relative speed in amending the law to remove the commissioner of police from the operational control of the political directorate. Beyond such important implementation issues, there remain critical policy differences on other vital questions, equally hotly disputed in other countries undergoing reform, on whether a parliamentary or presidential system and on whether a weak or strong local government would better moderate the winner-take-all politics in Jamaican circumstances.

Item 2 on the agenda of democratic renewal is more peculiarly Jamaican. It is the need for electoral reform so as to significantly reduce irregularities and malpractice in the electoral process. Most of all, the priority is to eliminate garrison communities and garrison constituencies in which democracy is all but dead and one party dominance is maintained by force and fraud. This is acknowledged as requiring the most concerted effort by the state, the private sector, and civil society, both Jamaican and international, in dismantling this apparently unique Jamaican phenomenon. Even more so is the necessity to mobilize social and political will as there has developed significant agreement on what needs to be done to dismantle the garrisons. Not least amongst the agreed measures are the steps necessary to end "the distribution of 'scarce benefits' along political lines"[12] and to empower community-based organizations. Nevertheless, it is clear that sectors with a vested interest in the perpetuation of political tribalism are impeding the implementation of the necessary reforms. Whilst this particular reform is more or less specific to Jamaica, enhancement of the democratic character of Jamaican elections also raises a more general issue – the need to combine the existing winner-take-all, first-past-the-post electoral system with some element of proportional representation. Admittedly, the first-past-the-post electoral system has outdone itself in Jamaica in producing its much touted advantage – legislatures with majority party representation, single-party cabinets and, consequently, stable government. There can be no question, however, that this has been at the cost of generating, to an equally extreme degree, its acknowledged disadvantage in Jamaica – disproportionate legislative representation of the majority, under-representation of the opposition, nonrepresentation of minority opinion and, most of all, encouragement of adversarial politics. As the millennium approaches, these disadvantages have come to balance, even outweigh, the positives of an exclusively first-past-the-post system. This situation, in Jamaica as elsewhere, calls not for a turn to pure proportionalism but for a mix of electoral systems with the objective of reducing winner-take-all tendencies and of achieving both governmental stability and legislative fairness in electoral outcomes. Failure to develop a combination suited to Jamaican circumstances is going to continue to compromise the extent to which legislative outcomes contribute to democratic renewal.

Item 3 on the Jamaican agenda, is perhaps, among the most common and problematic preoccupations of democratic reform processes as the millennium approaches. It is the question of campaign finance reform and the broader issues of regulating the power of special interests and reducing the level of political corruption. The Jamaican experience is placing alongside the traditional arguments against public financing of political parties compelling consideration for developing an appropriate system of public subsidy, either in cash or kind. The alternative, in the prevailing exclusively market system, is for special interests to have greater opportunity to exercise inordinate influence on political parties and on public policy. The danger of widescale influence-buying and influence-selling threatens Jamaica's democracy and calls for a carefully crafted anticorruption regime. Such a regime would have at its core principles of transparency and accountability as well as effective mechanisms of investigation and enforcement. No doubt such a framework would upgrade existing integrity legislation for parliamentarians as well as for public officials. It should also require the registration of political parties and their adherence to certain internal norms of democratic governance.

Item 4 on Jamaica's agenda is also a universal preoccupation: improved protection of human rights and significant reform in the criminal justice system. Credible complaints against police carrying out extra-judicial killings and beatings, arbitrary arrests and detentions, especially of youth in inner-city communities, continue. While there has been some effort to investigate and punish offending members of the security forces, existing measures are far from adequate, breed widespread hostility to the police and bring the rule of law into disrepute. Prison and jail conditions remain poor and overcrowded; the judicial process slow and overburdened; some laws, particularly in relation to marijuana possession, oppressive, and sentencing policy class-discriminatory. The improvement in the quality of democracy requires these deficiencies in the justice system to be more urgently remedied. Moreover, given the serious blemishes in the country's human rights record and the strength of popular feeling on human rights issues, the enhancement of Jamaica's democracy would seem to require that no government take any policy decision with possibilities of diminishing the enjoyment of human rights in Jamaica without first ascertaining the popular will. In this context, the proposal to withdraw the Jamaican courts from the jurisdiction of the Judicial Committee of the Privy Council should be subject to popular referendum.

In this regard, finally, the issue of the people playing a more direct role in decision-making, for much the same reason as elsewhere, has also been put on the agenda of democratic renewal in Jamaica. The coming referendum to determine the basic structure of government and, thereby, resolve political differences in the political elite is a positive step. The use of the referendum should be extended, however, to allow the electorate to decide fundamental policy relating to important national or international issues. Moreover, provision should be made, with appropriate safeguards against abuse, for the people to enjoy the right of recall of elected representatives and the power to legislate by petition leading to referendum. This trend toward more participatory democracy should find its fullest expression in the processes and institutions of local government. The ongoing Local Government Reform Programme in Jamaica explicitly embraces this participative principle[13] and has the potential, especially if implemented on a consensual basis, of significantly contributing to democratic renewal.

Democratizing Foreign Relations and Changing Leadership Requirements

As the millennium draws near, the growing intensity of Jamaica's foreign relations reflects the increasing importance of such relations to smaller nations and the need for any agenda of democratic renewal to embrace this sphere. Any number of domestic issues have an external dimension and, conversely, external arrangements have internal implications. Tackling the high levels of

crime, for example, unavoidably raises the question of international cooperation to deal more effectively with transnational criminal organizations operating in Jamaica, the deportation of convicted Jamaican criminals from the
United States to Jamaica, extradition from Jamaica, and so on. In the economy,
the growth of national production, income and employment increasingly and
unavoidably involve the extent and quality of relations with transnational
corporations, multilateral institutions, and overseas Jamaicans. Hence the
multiplication of relations by Jamaica and other similar states with IGOs and
INGOs as well as the growing number of external agreements, and arrangements to which the country is a party. Any agenda of democratic renewal must
involve the democratization of such relations. This is as much a philosophical
imperative to enhance the popular legitimacy of such arrangements as it is a
practical necessity to make them effective. For example, a transnational corpo-
ration which requires production costs to be reduced, industrial action to be
minimized, and product quality to be enhanced in order to sustain or to expand
production is not likely to achieve such results without democratizing employer-
employee relations. Similarly, the domestic legitimacy as well as the effectiveness
of international agreements relating to sustaining the environment, fighting crime,
stabilizing the economy, attracting investment, expanding exports, developing
sports and so on can go so far and no further without reducing the democratic
deficit in relation to such arrangements.

Hence, democratic renewal in respect of the external relations of Jamaica
and the smaller states requires a new approach. There must be continuing
dialogue and consultation with the people by private and public sector
authorities on such matters. In this process, the mass media have a critical rule
to play in two-way communication and information flows. Moreover, the
institutions of civil society have a special responsibility to develop linkages with
their counterparts elsewhere and to facilitate popular influence on the nation's
external relations. A corollary of this has to be support by government as well
as by NGOs for greater transparency, representativeness and accountability in
the institutions of regional and international governance, particularly in the
UN system.

In advancing this agenda, one of several critical challenges lies in overcoming
insularity. Practical experience as well as public education shall have to
demonstrate that coping more effectively with local and national problems is
not impeded but enhanced by a certain quality of cooperative transnational
relations. Doing well in World Cup soccer as much as reaping benefits from
the global economy requires transforming old and developing new partner-

ships with the external world. These new ties entail not the abandonment of national or of class identity but reworking such identity to incorporate the best of global society. Identifying, learning from and applying 'best practice' from the world of sport, politics, electoral reform or economic production must mean retention of the positive in the national at the same time as shedding the negative and adding value from the transnational.

Amongst the negatives is a small-island mentality which too often sees only or primarily threats rather than opportunities in closer ties with the outside world. Unless this mentality with its extremes of smugness and self-deprecation is more successfully combated, benefits from and contributions to the strengthening of ties with overseas Jamaicans or deepening of the regional integration movement are inevitably reduced. In this context, the inexorable growth of external relations and the increasing intrusion of the foreign into the domestic will tend to constrain rather than renew democracy.

In general, tackling these pressing and complex issues on the reform agenda more successfully is, in present circumstances, largely dependent on the quality of leadership, primarily but far from exclusively, in the political sphere. Experience is also confirming the need for a new kind of leadership in the economic marketplace and in civil society as well. In politics, no longer is charisma appropriate in that too often at the same time as it motivates and mobilizes it also incapacitates and subordinates followers in dependence on the leader. Much less needed is technocratic managerialism which, whilst competent, leaves little room for disagreement, diversity and initiative – in a word, democracy, especially from below. At the workplace, no longer is authoritarianism – whether open or disguised in paternalism – effective, as it carries relations of subordination and attitudes of disrespect incompatible with eliciting the efficiency, quality and productivity levels which now are more than ever both necessary and possible. In civil society, no longer is traditional leadership – based primarily on light skin colour or on middle income, higher formal education, maleness and middle age – going to be able to rebuild organizations in decline or to develop and sustain new civic groups so long as such leadership continues to subordinate or stifle the initiative of blacks, youth and women, particularly from the disadvantaged and less educated sectors.

On the contrary, the leadership that is required *at all levels*, but especially in national politics, must be of a different quality. Perhaps above all else, such leadership must encourage a followership which is informed, educated, active, diverse, independent, self-directed, and self-organized in ways that are largely incompatible with charismatic, managerialist, authoritarian or paternalistic leadership. In this sense, Joseph Rost is right when he comments that in "the post-industrial model", the word 'followers' has a new meaning: "followers are active agents in the leadership relationship, not passive recipients of the leader's influence".[14] Moreover, leadership must be consciously consensual, seeking to build bridges and negotiate compromises, rather than majoritarian in orientation and insensitive to minorities. In so doing, leadership of the new type cannot neglect the empowerment of the majority whilst seeking to power-share with minorities – whether political or ethnic – not only as a temporary expedient but as an enduring appreciation of their permanent place and valued contribution to society. This is never an easy endeavor (as the course of the negotiated settlements and continuing challenges in South Africa and Ireland graphically illustrate) but it is especially complex in Jamaica. At the minimum, such leadership has to develop an attitude of respect for 'the other sides', resist recrimination and victimization, promote meaningful dialogue and continuing consultation in crafting and sustaining institutions which facilitate majority upliftment and, at the same time, minority partnership.

Since so much depends, in Jamaica and elsewhere, on this calibre of leadership, it is of no little significance that elements of it have become recently apparent in the political, economic and civic spheres. The fact is that prevailing conditions and existing circumstances no longer breed nor encourage (as much as they used to) charisma or managerialism, paternalism or authoritarianism. It is the emerging elements of the new that are likely to be more dynamic than the remnants of the old. In this regard, the signals from both the economic and political market place play a big part in this process of discrediting outdated and archaic leadership. But in the meantime, it has to be acknowledged that adversarialism and majoritarianism, authoritarianism and confrontationalism do live on and often dominate prevailing leadership culture and behaviour. The success of democratic renewal and the raising of the quality of Jamaica's democracy into the millennium depend in no small measure on how quickly the negatives of the old can be made to give way to new, twenty-first century leadership. In this sense, Jamaica is not far different from other established democracies undergoing varying degrees of crisis.

Conclusions

In the Jamaican case, the crisis presents an opportunity for twenty-first century leadership to make a difference in halting the decline and in raising the quality of democracy in terms of the indicators which we have been utilizing.

Political participation: As we have seen, electoral turnout has fallen significantly and, more importantly, the balance between conventional and non-conventional forms of political participation has shifted dramatically in favour of the latter. The call-ins to the talk shows, the street demonstrations and the road blocks pose the danger of an authoritarian backlash from the state and other elites. At the same time they present a golden opportunity for genuinely democratic leadership to shift the balance of forces against preserving grossly inadequate channels of popular representation and in favour of meaningful reforms facilitating popular empowerment. For a new quality democracy to prevail over incipient authoritarianism and potential anarchy, a greater urgency and more radical content is required in ongoing processes of restructuring, particularly in local government and in workplace governance. One enduring imperative driving the latter process, it is worth noting, is the necessity in the interest of global competitiveness to reduce worker alienation and to empower labour in the production process.

Political contestation: Jamaican democracy has been severely impaired by a degree of partisanship that has too often passed from healthy competition into political warfare. This analysis suggested, however, that the pressure of growing national revulsion against political violence and 'tribalism' as well as timely monitoring of the 1997 elections by the global democratic community has within recent times been opening up greater possibilities for change. Within the established parties, and even more so outside of these parties, tendencies toward political peace and away from tribal war are growing. To consolidate such tendencies, however, is going to require a strengthening of inclusivistic leadership and a redesign of governmental institutions away from winner-take-all politics. In such a redesign, made possible by the development of some consensus on the need to restructure government, pending constitutional and political reform offers some chance to move from a majoritarian to more consensual democracy. Such a transformation would, if carried out appropriately, make room at the table for all viable tendencies in the political system and in civil society. Here again, the depth of the overall crisis is providing compelling argument for a more national government, even on a temporary basis, and for less destructive forms of political contestation.

Civil society: After a period of some decline, the analysis suggests that signs of revival are apparent in important segments of civil society. This revival is by no means strong, nor as yet irreversible, but is quite apparent in the Church, communities, and even in the labour movement. This incipient renewal of associational life harbours strong antipolitical tendencies, is suspicious of the private sector and wants to develop as an independent force. Its potential for raising the quality of democracy is real, however, to the extent that its development as a partner, and not as a surrogate to the state as well as the private sector, is facilitated. Towards that end, leadership needs to steer the various groups towards becoming vehicles of popular empowerment, not least of all in their own internal life.

The degree of corruption: The analysis suggests that a major blot in the quality of Jamaican democracy is growing corruption, despite the relative failure to date of illicit drugs to take significant control of state elites. Excessive influence of 'special interests' from the private sector and the transnational community on the Jamaican government and political parties were, with good cause, perceived to real threats to the integrity of democratic governance. The national mood is such that it provides a popular base for thoroughgoing anticorruption measures in terms of new legislation, institutions and processes of transparency in the fight against corruption. In this regard, the imperatives of renewal raise the possibility and the necessity of greater openness in the finances of political parties, declaration of sources of funds, and appropriately designed provisions for public support of bonafide party activity.

Outcomes of state policy and attitudes to government: Outcomes of state policy in the 1980s and 1990s have been skewed towards the elites and neglectful of the popular masses. In the criminal justice system, biases against the disadvantaged, particularly the inner-city youth, have severely scarred Jamaican democracy and narrowed the popular base of the established authority system. The democratization of the authorities and the redress of the inequities in the outcomes of state policies are both indispensable to reducing popular alienation and turning public attitudes in a healthy direction. Overall, therefore, it can be concluded that the Jamaican experience suggests that the renewal of democracy is not only necessary but possible going into the next millennium. To realize that possibility, inherent in deepening crisis, requires a new synergy between radical democratic leadership and participative followership in coming to grips with the multidimensional challenge of raising the quality of democracy. Put starkly, the alternative to deepening democracy in this way is growing anarchy and its invariable backlash of rising authoritarianism.

Appendix

Tables

Figures

Table 2.1   Jamaica General Election Candidates

Year	Female	Male	Total	% Female
1989	15	109	124	12.1
1993	12	118	130	9.2
1997	30	178	208	14.2

Source: Reports, Director of Elections, Jamaica.

Table 2.2(a): Jamaican General Election 1997 Results

Population	2,595,275
Total electors	1,182,294
Total voting	780,982
% turnout	66.06
Total voting JLP	303,595
% voting JLP	38.87
Total voting PNP	433,046
% voting PNP	55.45
Total voting NDM	36,737
% voting NDM	4.71
Independent candidates	885
% independent candidates	.011
Rejected ballots	6,719
% rejected ballots	.86

Percentage Voted – Jamaican General Elections

Year	Percentage
1944	55.1
1949	63.8
1955	63.9
1959	65.3
1962	72.3
1967	81.5
1972	78.2
1976	86.1
1983	28.9
1989	77.6
1993	66.7

Members	Elected
PNP	51[1]
JLP	9[1]
NDM	Nil
Independent	Nil

[1] Arising from the re-taking of the poll in West Central St Andrew on 26 March 1998 and subsequently on 30 June 1998, the PNP lost and the JLP gained this seat. The final result was therefore PNP 50, JLP 10 members elected.

Source: Director of Elections, Electoral Office of Jamaica (by fax, 15 Oct. 1998).

Table 2.2(b): Average Turnout in Free Elections to the Lower House in
38 Countries, 1960–1995 (in percentages)

Australia[a] (14)	95	Costa Rica[a] (8)	81
Malta[a] (6)	94	Norway[a] (9)	81
Austria[a] (9)	92	Israel[a] (9)	80
Belgium[a,b] (12)	91	Portugal[a,b] (9)	79
Italy[a,b] (9)	90	Finland[a] (10)	78
Luxembourg[a,b] (7)	90	Canada[a] (11)	76
Iceland[a,b] (10)	89	France[a,b] (9)	76
New Zealand[a] (12)	88	United Kingdom[a,b] (9)	75
Denmark[a,b] (14)	87	Ireland[a,b] (11)	74
Venezuela[a] (7)	85	Spain[a,b] (6)	73
Bulgaria[b] (2)	80	Japan[a] (12)	71
Germany[a,b] (9)	86	Estonia[b] (2)	69
Sweden[a] (14)	86	Hungary[b] (2)	66
Greece[a,b] (10)	86	Jamaica (7)	64
Lithuania[b] (1)	86	Russia[b] (2)	61
Latvia[b] (1)	86	India[a] (6)	58
Czech Republic[b] (2)	85	United States[a,b] (9)	54
Brazil[a] (3)	83	Switzerland[a] (8)	54
Netherlands[a,b] (7)	83	Poland[b] (2)	51

Source: Adapted from LeDuc et al., *Comparing,* 218 and *Voter Turnout from 1945 to 1997: A Global Report on Political Participation* (Stockholm: International Institute for Democracy and Electoral Assistance, 1997), 69.

Note: Numbers in parentheses are the number of elections included in each average. For the United States, only 'on year' congressional elections are included (i.e., elections held in conjunction with presidential elections). US midterm elections do not respond to the same forces as elections elsewhere, because executive power is not as stake. For the Netherlands, the series starts in 1968, after the abolition of compulsory voting there.

a.   Included in country-level analysis (29 countries).

b.   Included in individual-level analysis. Romania (86 percent turnout) is included in these analyses (for a total of 22 countries), but it does not qualify as a democracy according to established criteria.

Table 2.3: Jamaica – Number of Roadblocks

1986	1987	1988	1989	1990	1991	1992	1993	1994	1995	1996	1997
23	29	31	31	42	42	45	29	173	202	185	207

*important to note that data source changed in 1993

Figure 2.1: Jamaica – Number of Roadblocks

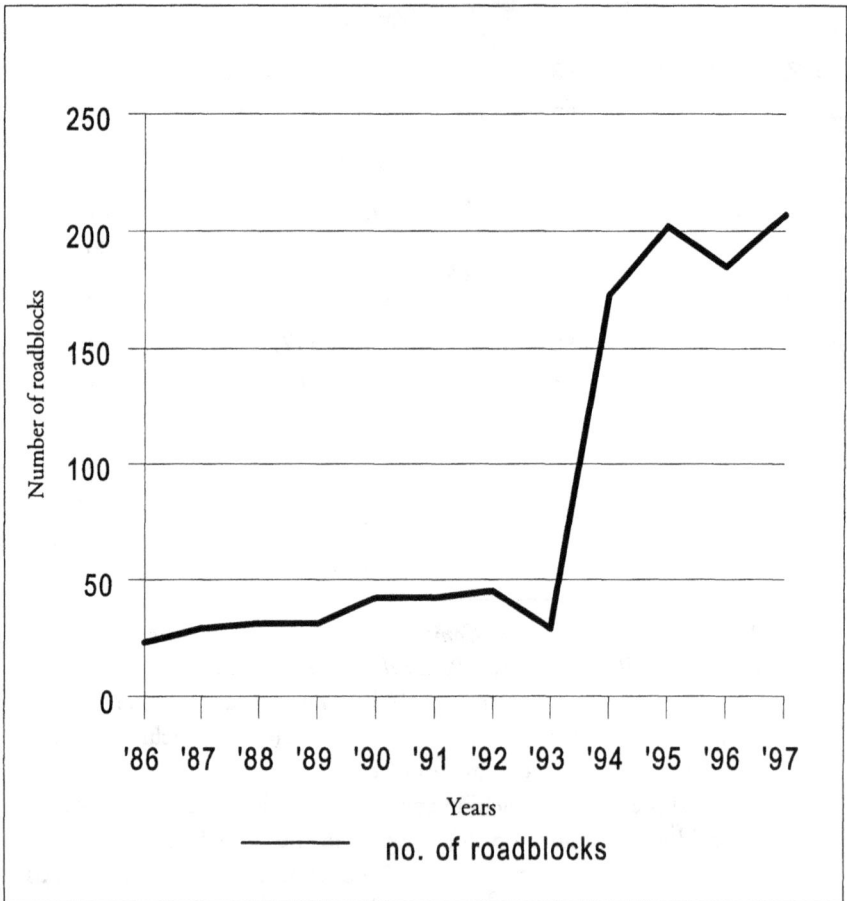

Source: Daily Gleaner, Police Information Center, Jamaica Constabulary Force.

Table 2.4:   Jamaica General Elections 1955–1997: Disproportionality between Percentage of Ballots Cast and Seats Won

Election	Winning Party			Losing Party		
	% seats	% votes	surplus	% seats	% votes	deficit
1955[1]	56.3 (P)	50.5	+5.8	43.8 (J)	39	+ 4.8
1959	64.4 (P)	54.8	+9.6	35.6 (J)	44.3	- 8.7
1962	57.8 (J)	50.0	+7.8	42.2 (P)	48.6	- 6.4
1967	62.2 (J)	50.7	+11.5	37.8 (P)	49.1	-11.3
1972	69.8 (P)	56.4	+13.4	30.2 (J)	43.4	-13.2
1976	78.3 (P)	56.8	+21.5	21.7 (J)	43.2	-21.5
1980	85.0 (J)	58.9	+26.1	15.0 (P)	41.1	-26.1
1983[2]	100.0 (J)	89.7	+10.3	–	–	–
1989	75.0 (P)	56.6	+18.4	25.0 (J)	43.3	-18.3
1993	86.7 (P)	61.3	+25.4	13.3 (J)	38.1	-24.8
1997	83.3 (P)	55.4	+27.9	16.7 (J)	38.9	-22.2

P = PNP   J = JLP

1. In the 1955 general election Independent candidates won no seats but received 10.5 percent of accepted ballots cast. The losing party, the JLP, therefore got a lower percentage of ballots cast as well as a higher proportion of seats won than would be the case in subsequent elections in which there was no significant percentage of non-PNP, non-JLP vote.

2. The 1983 General Election was not contested by the PNP; hence the losing party got no seats and no votes.

Source: Constructed from Director of Elections, Electoral Office of Jamaica (fax, 15 October, 1998).

Table 3.1: Levels of Satisfaction with Democracy

Question: "On the whole are you very satisfied, fairly satisfied, not very satisfied
or not at all satisfied with the way democracy is developing in (your country)?"

Very and Fairly Satisfied %	Countries	No. of cases
83.5	Denmark	975
81.8	Luxembourg	466
69.4	Ireland	932
66.5	West Germany	981
64.5	The Netherlands	1,009
64.0	United States	1,000
62.0	Canada	1,000
61.0	Albania	893
57.6	Belgium	990
57.3	France	972
56.6	Uruguay	1,209
53.1	Northern Ireland	288
51.0	Great Britain	989
50.8	Argentina	1,194
50.5	Poland	989
48.5	Croatia	955
46.6	Portugal	955
45.5	Czech Republic	1,029
43.9	Georgia	1,015
43.8	Peru	1,226
39.2	East Germany	1,000
37.1	Macedonia	902
36.7	Slovenia	1,111
36.7	Romania	1,107
36.7	Estonia	940
36.2	Venezuela	1,200
35.5	Jamaica	1,258
34.0	Spain	947
33.0	Chile	1,240
31.6	Greece	964
30.3	Brazil	1,078
28.2	Paraguay	584
27.9	Latvia	1,054
26.2	Slovak Republic	1,044
25.4	Italia	982

Table continues

Table 3.1 *continued*

Very and Fairly Satisfied %	Countries	No. of cases
23.5	Lithuania	934
22.2	Mexico	1,199
20.0	Hungary	969
17.5	Armenia	913
14.6	Ukraine	1,132
12.8	Belarus	1,001
12.0	Bulgaria	1,013
6.0	Russia	1,135

Source: *Governance and Democratic Development in Latin American and the Caribbean* (UNDP, 1996), 24. (Data on Jamaica inserted from Stephen Rodriques, "The Jamaica political culture: a theoretical and empirical exploration", MPhil, Department of Government, UWI, 1997, 75.)

Table 4.1:   Narcotics and Democracy

Category	Country Rating		
	Free	Partly Free	Not Free
Major Drug-Producing / Drug Transit Center	Aruba, Bahamas, Belize Bolivia, Jamaica, Panama Venezuela	Brazil, Colombia, Dominican Republic, Ecuador, Guatemala, Haiti, Mexico, Paraguay, Peru	
Major Money Laundering Center	Aruba, Bahamas, Panama, Cayman Island Costa Rica, Netherlands Antilles, Uruguay United States	Brazil, Colombia, Dominican Republic, Mexico, Paraguay, Peru, Antigua-Barbuda	

Source: Compiled from International Narcotics Control Strategy Report 1998 (Washington DC: Department of State, United States Government, 1998); *Freedom in the World: The Annual Survey of Political Rights and Civil Liberties, 1996–1997* (New Brunswick and London: Transaction Publishers, 1997), 579–81.

Table 4.2:   Cases per Resident Magistrate

Criminal and civil totals minus St Andrew

	1989	1990	1991	1992	1993	1994	1995	1996
Total no. of cases	124,685	173,139	171,114	186,187	197,013	189,702	219,572	251,304
No. of RMs	36	36	37	37	37	37	37	37
Avg. cases per RM	3,462	4,809	4,625	5,032	5,325	5,127	5,934	6,792

Figure 4.1:   Cases per Resident Magistrate

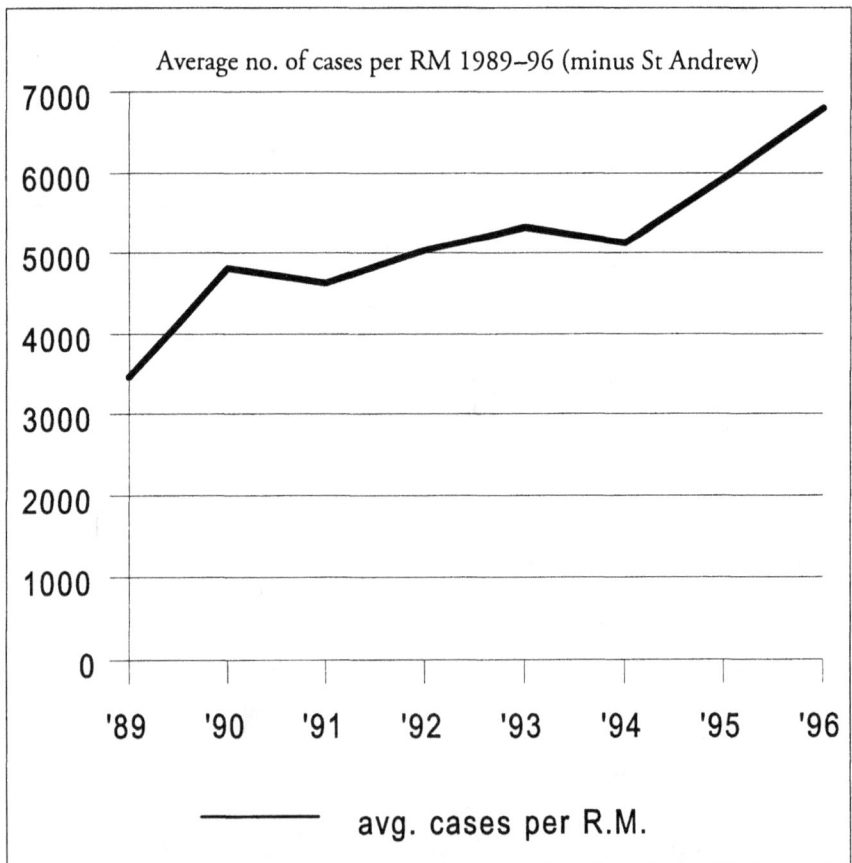

Average no. of cases per RM 1989–96 (minus St Andrew)

avg. cases per R.M.

Source: Court files, 1989–96.

Table 4.3:   US-Caribbean Bilateral Interdiction Agreements

Country	Entry to Investigate	Order to Land	Overflight	Pursuit	Ship Boarding	Ship Riding
Antigua-Barbuda	X	X	X	X	X	X
Bahamas			X			X
Barbados	–	–	–	–	–	–
Belize	X			X	X	X
Dominica	X			X	X	X
Dominican Republic	X			X	X	X
Grenada	X			X	X	X
Guyana			X			
Haiti	X			X		
Jamaica	–	–	–	–	–	–
Netherlands Antilles	X		X	X		X
St Kitts-Nevis	X	X	X	X	X	X
St Lucia	X	X	X	X	X	X
St Vincent & Grenadines	X			X	X	X
Trinidad & Tobago	X	X	X	X	X	X
Turks & Caicos Islands						X
United Kingdom					X	X

Source: US Department of State, December 1996; Ivelaw Lloyd Griffith, *Drugs and Security in the Caribbean: Sovereignty Under Seige* (University Park: Pennsylvania State University Press, 1997), 214.

Table 4.4:   Arrests Made for Ganja and Cocaine

| Year | Arrests Local | | | | Arrests Foreigners | | | |
| | Ganja | | Cocaine | | Ganja | | Cocaine | |
	Male	Female	Male	Female	Male	Female	Male	Female
1992	445	131	133	50	151	149	16	27
1993	2,352	1,450	1,310	705	552	302	130	112
1994	939	195	148	83	183	94	10	15
1995	3,679	321	249	99	203	148	52	52
1996	2,415	230	251	106	130	88	24	15
1997	2,629	246	202	69	90	47	37	54
Totals	12,468	2,573	2,293	1,112	1,309	828	269	275

Source: Compiled from Jamaica Constabulary Force, Narcotics Division Data.

Figure 5.1(a):   Total Union Membership 1986–1996

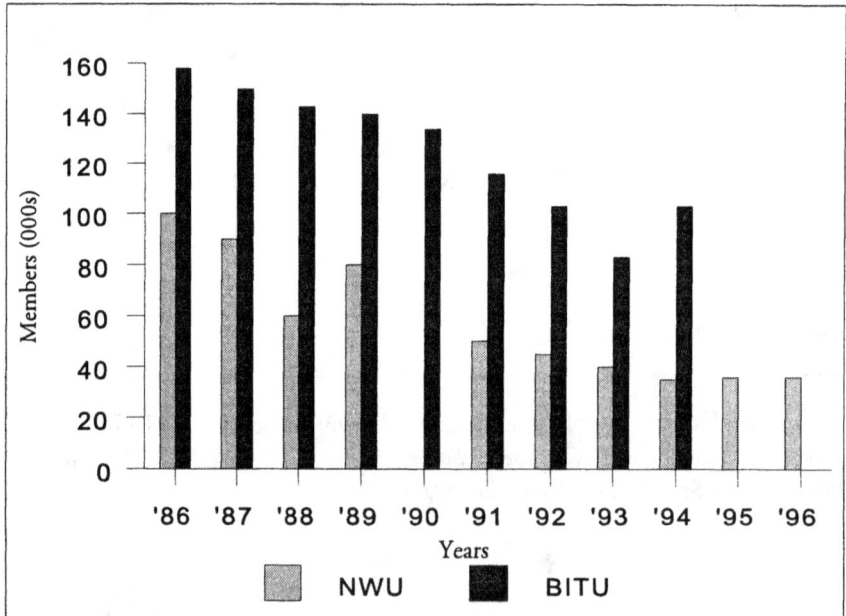

Source: Annual Returns, Registrar General's Department

Figure 5.1(b): Trade Union Surplus/Deficit 1986–1996

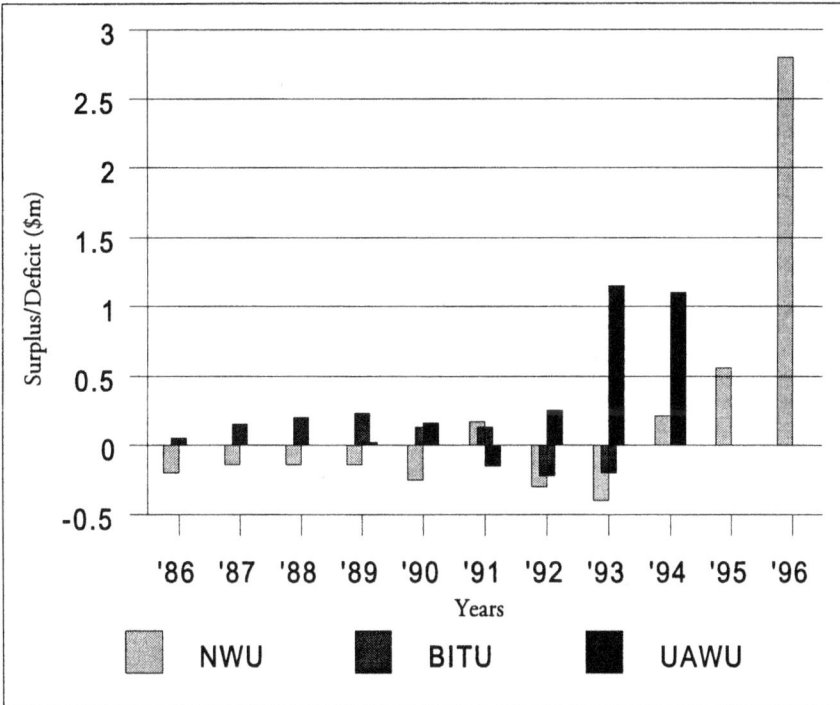

Source: Annual Returns, Registrar General's Department.

Table 5.1:   Church Membership

	1986	1987	1988	1989	1990	1991	1992	1993	1994	1995
Seventh Day	–	–	130,853	136,640	141,993	148,340	153,314	158,982	164,046	172,006
Anglican	38,572	38,213	35,989	32,011	36,185	37,123	36,614	34,741	32,620	
Baptist							38,825	42,802	36,7778	37,107
United	14,032	14,205	14,078	13,755	11,982					13,399

Source: Files, individual denominations.

Figure 5.2:   Church Membership

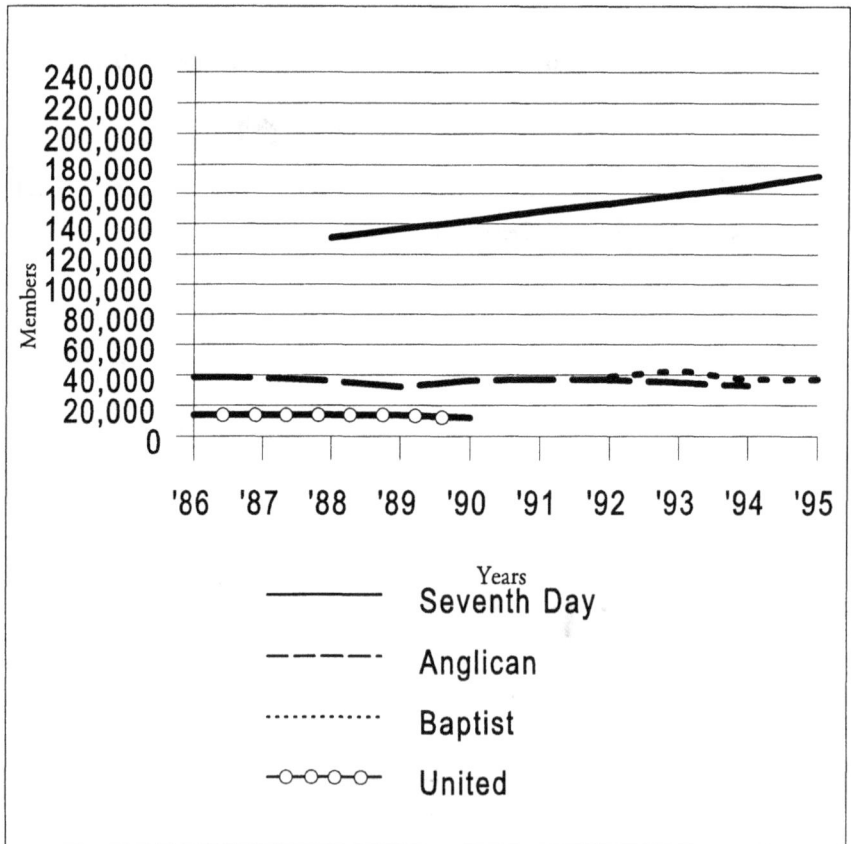

Table 5.2: Community Based Organizations

	Up to 1993	1994	1995	1996	1997	1988 1 Jan–31 Mar.	Total
Police Youth Clubs	104	+8	+11	+36	+35	+22	216 +181[1] / 397

[1]These 181 police youth clubs have been formed and are being sensitized for launch.

	1987/88	1990	1991	1992	1993	1994	1995	1996	1997	1988 1 Jan–31 Mar.	Total
Neighbourhood Watches	27	+110	+104	+73	+34	+35	+32	+29	+28	+7	479 +157[2] / 636

[2]These 157 Neighbourhood Watches have been formed and are being sensitized for launch.

		1985/86	1986/87	1988/89	1989/90	1990/91	1992/93	1994/95	1995/96	1996/97
4H Clubs	N	300	421	296	537	291	442	445	392	581
	M	27,692	35,836		33,004	16,693	25,805	29,389	20,745	36,043
Youth Clubs	N				596	615			986	727
SDC	M				23,922	25,860				

Note: N = number; M = membership
Source: Jamaica Constabulary Force, Community Relations Division; 4H Clubs; Social Development Commission.

Table 5.3 (a):   Democracy in Jamaica, Jamaican Media Profile – Selected Talk Shows

('000s)	1989		1990		1991		1992		1993		1994		1995		1996	
	A	TA	A	TA	A	TA	A	TA	A	TA	A	TA	A	TA	A	TA
Public Eye	111	517	98	488	91	578	93	718	82	935	45	638	57	798	48	800
Hotline	239	425	235	414	225	586	248	718	359	915	303	570	261	816	277	795
Breakfast Club									50	842	93	986	110	1054	68	906
Straight Talk			41	508	108	588	206	736	122	955	172	856	136	802	167	811
Independent Talk													52	1054	35	906
Total	349	943	375	1410	424	1751	546	2172	612	3647	613	3050	616	4524	595	4218
Average	175	471	125	470	141	584	182	724	153	912	153	762	123	905	119	844
Potential	1295		1346		1399				1651	1624.5	1755		1751		1763	

A: average

TA: total average

Source: Jamaica Media Survey.

Table 5.3 (b): Democracy in Jamaica
Jamaican Media Profile, 1987–1996

Radio

	1987	1988	1989	1990	1991	1992	1993	1994	1995	1996
No. of Radios	1,373,577	1,448,122	1,481,000	1,549,240	1,639,500	1,685,500	1,856,000	1,873,300	1,914,000	1,929,000
Potential Audience	1,232,931	1,241,150	1,295,000	1,346,510	1,399,000	1,624,500	1,651,000	1,755,000	1,751,000	1,763,000
No. of Radio Stations	5	5	5	5	7	7	9	9	9	9

Television

	1987	1988	1989	1990	1991	1992	1993	1994	1995	1996
No. of Televisions			484,000	500,630	527,000	545,000	699,000	719,000	744,000	773,000
Potential Audience	859,000	878,000	894,000	821,043		984,500	1,120,000	1,215,000	1,210,000	1,194,000
No. of Stations	1	1	1	1	1	1	2	2	2	2

Readership

	1987	1988	1989	1990	1991	1992	1993	1994	1995	1996
Newspaper Readership (*Daily Gleaner*)	341,000	366,000		360,000	382,000			415,000	417,000	419,000

Set Count

	1987	1988	1989	1990	1991	1992	1993	1994	1995	1996
No. of videos	151,000	161,000	170,050	211,476	211,000	235,000	294,000	303,000	311,000	316,000
No. of satellites	6,700	13,200	13,650	17,845	21,005	25,000	34,000	42,000	44,000	46,000
Cable								62,000	115,000	137,000

Source: Jamaica Media Survey.

Table 6.1(a) Public Subsidies to Parties and Candidates

| Country | Recipient | Direct Subsidies | | | Specific Grants or Services | Indirect Subsidies |
		Interval	Basis	Eligibility		
Australia	Candidates, parties	Per vote		At least 4% of vote. Must be registered with electoral commission.	Transportation, encouragement of voting, broadcasting	
Austria	Parties, parliamentary groups		Per vote		Billposting, broadcasting, printing ballots, party foundations, press and publications, women's and youth organizations, education and information	
Belgium	No direct subsidies	N/A	N/A	N/A	Broadcasting, encouragement of voting	
Canada	Candidates, parliamentary groups	Election	Per vote	Candidate: 15% of votes in an electoral district. Party: must spend at least 10% of limit.	Broadcasting, encouragement of voting	Tax credits
Denmark	Parliamentary groups	Annual	Per seat		Broadcasting, press and publications, women's and youth organizations	

Table continues

Table 6.1(a) *continued*

| Country | Recipient | Direct Subsidies | | | Specific Grants or Services | Indirect Subsidies |
		Interval	Basis	Eligibility		
Finland	Parties	Annual	Per seat		Billposting, broadcasting, press and publications, women's and youth organizations	
France	Presidential candidates	Election			Billposting, broadcasting, printing ballots, press and publications	Kickbacks of deputy salaries
Germany	Parties	Election	Per vote	0.5% of votes for national party lists, of candidates or 105 of first votes cast in a constituency if no regional list has been accepted	Broadcasting, subsidies to party foundations	Tax deductions
Greece	Parties	Election	Equal distribution of 10% of flat rate, then per vote. If coalition, amount divided by agreement among parties involved.	Participated in last election and got at least 3% of votes. Has a list of candidates in at least 2/3 of the electoral districts. If a coalition: received at 5%–6% of votes depending on coalition status.		
India	No direct subsidies	N/A	N/A	N/A	Broadcasting (by agreement)	

Table continues

Table 6.1(a) *continued*

| Country | Recipient | Direct Subsidies | | | Specific Grants or Services | Indirect Subsidies |
		Interval	Basis	Eligibility		
Ireland	No direct subsidies	N/A	N/A	N/A	Broadcasting	
Israel	Party groups	Annual, every election	Per seat	Had at least 1 MP in last parliament. Recognized as a group by Knesset Committee. Named representatives to deal with finances.	Broadcasting, encouragement of voting, transportation	
Italy	Parties, parliamentary group	Annual, every election	Per vote	Parties presenting candidate lists in more than 2/3 of constituencies and obtaining no less than 300,000 votes or 2% of total amount of votes.	Broadcasting (according to guidelines of Parliamentary Committee), women's and youth organizations, education and information	Kickbacks of deputy salaries
Japan	Candidates	Every election			Transportation, publication, broadcasting, advertising, use of public halls, financing of election bulletins on candidates	Tax benefits
Mexico	Candidates	Annual, every election	Per vote	Party should obtain more than 1.5% of the total ballot.	Broadcasting	Tax exemptions

Table continues

Table 6.1(a) *continued*

Country	Recipient	Direct Subsidies			Specific Grants or Services	Indirect Subsidies
		Interval	Basis	Eligibility		
Netherlands	No direct subsidies	N/A	N/A	N/A	Broadcasting, encouragement of voting, party foundations women's and youth organizations	Tax deductions
Norway	Parties, parliamentary groups	Annual	Per seat		Broadcasting, nomination costs	
Poland	No direct subsidies	N/A	N/A	N/A	Broadcasting, use of public halls, printing and mailing, encouragement of the vote	Limited tax exemptions for political parties
Spain	Parties	Annual every election	Per vote	Party must have won at least one parliamentary seat (which requires at least 3% of the national vote).	Broadcasting, free space for posters, use of public hall, reduced postal rate for campaign mail	
Sweden	Parties, parliamentary groups	Annual	Per seat, per vote	Party support: obtained at least 2.5% of votes in last two elections. Basic support: party obtained over 4% of the votes. Supplementary support: based on number of parliamentary seats won by each party.	Publication, encouragement of voting, broadcasting, women's and youth organizations	

Table continues

Table 6.1(a) *continued*

| Country | Recipient | Direct Subsidies | | | Specific Grants or Services | Indirect Subsidies |
		Interval	Basis	Eligibility		
Switzerland	No direct subsidies	N/A	N/A	N/A		
Taiwan	Candidates		Per vote	Candidate should receive at least ¾ of the number of votes needed to be elected to their constituency.	Publication, encouragement of voting	Tax benefits
Thailand	No direct subsidies	N/A	N/A	N/A	Broadcasting, encouragement of voting	Tax benefits
Turkey	Parties	Annual	Per vote	Party must have obtained 7% of votes in last parliamentary election.	Broadcasting, encouragement of voting	Tax benefits
United Kingdom	Parliamentary groups	Annual			Publications, mailing broadcasting, free use of public halls	Gifts to parties exempt from inheritance tax
United States	Candidates in presidential primaries and election	Election	Matching grant in primary, fixed sum in election from funds earmarked by taxpayers		Nomination costs, mailing; most states pay for voter registration and ballots	Tax credits, tax deductions

Table continues

Table 6.1(a) *continued*

Country	Recipient	Direct Subsidies			Specific Grants or Services	Indirect Subsidies
		Interval	Basis	Eligibility		
Venezuela	Parties	Election	Per vote		Broadcasting, election advertising	

Source: Lawrence LeDuc, Richard G. Niemi, Pippa Norris, eds., *Comparing Democracies: Elections and Voting in Global Perspective* (Thousand Oaks, London, New Delhi: Sage Publications 1997) 38-41.

Table 6.1(b) Statutory Control of Campaign Finances

Country	Reporting				Disclosure	Audit of Reports	Publicity	Limits on Contribution	Limits on Expenditures
	Interval	By	To	Of					
Australia	Every campaign	Candidate	Electoral commission	Expenditures	Details of expenditures, amount of contributions and donor's identity	Yes, if public funding sought	Public inspection	No	No
Austria	Annual and prior to every campaign	Parties	Government auditors	Expenditures	Details of income, sources, ands expenditures	Yes	Annual public tatements		
Canada	Annual and every campaign	Candidate and party	Chief electoral officer	Contributions and expenses	Amounts of contributions, donor's identity, details of expenditures	Yes	Public inspection, daily press, reports to legislature	No	On total amount and by segment spent by candidates and parties
Germany	Annual and every campaign	Party	Speaker of the federal diet	Contributions, expenditures, assets, total campaign expenditures	Amount of contributions, donor's identity	Yes		No	No, but implicit because grants have to be matched by party's private income
Greece	Annual and every campaign	Candidate and party	President of parliament and minister interior	Contributions and balance sheets, campaign expenditures	For donations greater than 200,000 drachmas, identity of contributor	Yes	Published in Athens newspaper	No	No

Table continues

Table 6.1(b) *continued*

Country	Interval	By	Reporting To	Of	Disclosure	Audit of Reports	Publicity	Limits on Contribution	Limits on Expenditures
India	Every campaign	Candidate	District election officer	Election expenditures	Any corporate donations	No	Public inspection	Yes	On total amount spent by candidates
Israel	Annual and every campaign	Party group	State comptroller	Financial accounts	Amount of contributions, details of expenditures	Yes	State comptrollers report can be made public, report to legislature	On amount and source	On total amount spent by candidates and limits on parties relating to Government funding
Italy	Annual and every campaign	Party	Minister or speaker of legislature	Contributions and expenses	Amount of contributions and donor's identity	Yes	Daily press, reports to legislature	No	No
Japan	Annual	Treasurer of political organization	Minister of Home Affairs or local Election Management Commission	Contributions and expenses	Amount, date, and source of contributions	Yes	Public inspection, published in official gazette	On amount and source	On total amount and by segment
Mexico	Every campaign	Political campaign	General Council of the Federal Electoral Institute	Irregularities in other parties' finances	Contribution	Yes	Secretariat of Government informed of violations of law	Forbidden from abroad	
Netherlands	No reporting	N/A	N/A	N/A	N/A	N/A	N/A		

Table continues

Table 6.1(b) *continued*

Country	Reporting					Audit of Reports	Publicity	Limits on Contribution	Limits on Expenditures
	Interval	By	To	Of	Disclosure				
Poland	Every campaign	Minister of Finance (parliamentary and local elections); presidential candidates campaign (presidential election)	Public; Chair of State Electoral Committee	Report on expenditure funded from state budget; reports of expenditures	Sources of contributions		Public inspection	On sources	By segment
Spain	Every campaign	Parties	Election Commission	Contributions and expenses	Revenue and expenditures	No	Public Inspection	On amount and sources	On amount pent in each district
Sweden	Not mandatory	N/A	N/A	N/A	N/A	N/A	N/A	No	No
Taiwan	Every campaign	Candidates	Electoral Commission	Contributions and expenses		Yes		On amount and source	On total amount
Thailand	No reporting	N/A	N/A	N/A	N/A	N/A	N/A	On sources	On total amount
Turkey	Annual	Parties	Constitutional Court and Attorney-General	Financial statements	Any expenditure over 5,000 lira, contributions	Yes	Announcement of Constitutional Court decisions	On amount and source	No

Table continues

Table 6.1(b) *continued*

| Country | Reporting | | | | Disclosure | Audit of Reports | Publicity | Limits on Contribution | Limits on Expenditures |
	Interval	By	To	Of					
United Kingdom	Every campaign	Candidate	Returning Officers	Contributions and expenses	Details of expenditures, contribution from corporations and trade unions	No	Public inspection, sreport to legislature	No	On total amount spent by candidates
United States	Annual and every campaign	Candidate, party, political committee	Federal Election Commission	Contributions, expenditures	Amount of expenditure, donor's identity, details of expenditures	Yes	Public inspection, reports to legislature	On amount and source	On total amount if candidate accepts public funds

Source: LeDuc et al., *Comparing Democracies*, 42-44

Notes

Chapter 1

1. One indication of the volume of this literature is suggested by the fact that a keyword DEMOCRACY search of the Harvard On Line Library Information Service (HOLLIS) for the five years ending in 1997 produced almost 3,000 books, not to mention journal articles and other scholarly publications.
2. Robert D. Kaplan, "Was democracy just a moment?", *Atlantic Monthly* (December 1997): 55–80.
3. Ricardo Hausman, "Will volatility kill democracy?", *Foreign Policy*, no. 108 (Fall 1997): 54–67.
4. Fareed Zakaria, "The rise of illiberal democracy?", *Foreign Affairs* 76, no. 6 (November/December 1997): 22–43.
5. Jacques Attali, "The clash of western civilization: the limits of the market and democracy", *Foreign Policy*, no. 107 (Summer 1997): 54–64.
6. Arend Lijphart, "Unequal participation: democracy's unresolved dilemma", *American Political Science Review* 91, no. 1 (March 1997): 1–4.
7. Cf. e.g., Karen L. Remmer, "New theoretical perspectives on democratization", *Comparative Politics* 28,

no. 1 (October 1995): 103–22; Henry S. Rowen, "The tide underneath the 'Third Wave' ", *Journal of Democracy* (January 1995): 52–64.
8. Cf. e.g., Samuel P. Huntington, "Democracy for the long haul", in *Consolidating the Third Wave Democracies: Themes and Perspectives*, edited by Larry Diamond et al. (Baltimore and London: Johns Hopkins University Press, 1997); Marc F. Plattner and Carl Gershman, "Democracy gets a bum rap", *The Wall Street Journal*, 26 January 1998; Marc F. Plattner, "Liberalism and democracy", *Foreign Affairs* 77, no. 2 (March/April 1998): 171–80.
9. Cf. e.g., Ian Budge, "Direct democracy: setting appropriate terms of debate", in *Prospects for Democracy*, edited by David Held (Stanford: Stanford University Press, 1993), 154.
10. The reference to 'first', 'second' and 'third waves' of democratization is taken from Huntington's usage (1991: 16). The first wave, 1828–1928, produced the established democracies; the second wave lasted from 1943 to 1962 and post-colonial democracies such as India

and Jamaica; the third wave began in 1974.

11. Carl Stone, *Class, State and Democracy in Jamaica* (New York, Praeger Press, 1986), 187.

12. Carlene J. Edie, "Jamaica: clientelism, dependency and democratic stability", in *Democracy in the Caribbean: Myths and Realities*, edited by Carlene J. Edie (Westport, CT: Praeger Publishers, 1994).

13. Plattner, "Liberalism and democracy", 177.

14. Jeff Haynes, *Democracy and Civil Society in the Third World* (Cambridge: Polity Press, 1997).

15. Ibid., 81.

16. Ibid., 82.

17. Ibid., 85–86.

18. Cited in Larry Diamond, "Is the third wave over?", *Journal of Democracy* 7, no. 3 (July 1996): 20–37.

19. Cited in Frank Cunningham, *Democratic Theory and Socialism* (Cambridge and New York: Cambridge University Press, 1987), ch. 3.

20. Raymond Duncan Gastil, "The Comparative Survey of Freedom: experiences and suggestions", in *On Measuring Democracy: Its Consequences and Concomitants*, edited by Alex Inkeles (New Brunswick and London: Transaction Publishers, 1993), 36.

21. Samuel P. Huntington, *The Third Wave: Democratization in the Late Twentieth Century* (Norman and London: University of Oklahoma Press, 1991), 7.

22. Ibid., 6.

23. Cf. e.g., Diamond, "Is the third wave over?", 21–22.

24. Ibid.

25. Cf. Abe Lowenthal, "Battling the undertow in Latin America", in *Consolidating the Third Wave Democracies: Themes and Perspectives*, edited by Larry Diamond, et al. (Baltimore and London: Johns Hopkins University Press, 1997), 62.

26. Larry Diamond, "Democracy in Latin America: degrees, illusions and directions for consolidation", in *Beyond Sovereignty: Collectively Defending Democracy in the Americas*, edited by Tom Farer (Baltimore and London: Johns Hopkins University Press, 1996). Horizontal accountability refers to the extent to which the executive is responsive to the legislature and the judiciary. Vertical accountability refers to the degree of responsiveness of the executive to civil society.

27. "Latin American barometer 1996", in *Governance and Democratic Development in Latin American and the Caribbean*, United Nations Development Programme (n.d., c. 1997), 34.

28. Stephen Anthony Rodriques, "The Jamaican political culture: a theoretical and empirical exploration" (MPhil thesis, Department of Government, UWI, Mona 1996), 145.

29. Cf., e.g., Samuel Huntington in *Consolidating the Third Wave Democracies: Themes and Perspectives*, edited by Larry Diamond et al. (Baltimore and London: Johns Hopkins University Press, 1997), 10.

30. *Freedom in the World – the Annual Survey of Political Rights and Civil Liberties*, 1996–1997 (New Brunswick and London: Transaction Publishers 1997), 572–85.

31. Kenneth A. Bollen, "Political democracy: conceptual and measurement traps", in *On Measuring Democracy: Its Consequences and Constraints*, edited by Alex Inkeles (New Brunswick and London: Transaction Publishers 1993), 10.

32. Michael Coppedge and Wolfgang H. Reinicke, "Measuring polyarchy", in *On Measuring Democracy: Its Consequences and Concomitants*, edited by Alex Inkeles (New Brunswick and London: Transaction Publishers, 1993), 63–66.

33. Tatu Vanhanen, *Prospects of Democracy: A Study of 172 Countries* (London and New York: Routledge, 1997), 86–87.

34. Keith Jaggers and Tedd Robert Gurr, "Polity III: regime type and political authority" (Inter-university Consortium for Political and Social Research, Ann Arbor, MI, 1996), cited in *World Development Report 1997: The State in a Changing World* (New York: Oxford University Press 1997), 112.

35. Diamond, "Democracy in Latin America", 57.

36. I accept James Rosenau's usage that by "democratic deficit . . . is meant the absence of procedures and institutions to hold the UN its agencies and NGOs accountable for their actions". James N. Rosenau,

Along the Domestic-Foreign Frontier: Exploring Governance in a Turbulent World (Cambridge: Cambridge University Press, 1997), 335. See also Susan Strange, "The erosion of the state", *Current History* (November 1997): 366.

37. Rosenau argues convincingly that "the world is not so much a system dominated by states and national governments as a congerie of spheres of authority (SOAs) . . . SOAs are, in effect, the analytic units of the new ontology". Rosenau, *Along the Domestic-Foreign Frontier*, 39.

38. Vanhanen, *Prospects of Democracy*, 161.

39. Raymond Duncan Gastil, "The Comparative Survey of Freedom: experiences and suggestions", in *On Measuring Democracy: Its Consequences and Concomitants*, edited by Alex Inkeles (New Brunswick and London: Transaction Publishers, 1993), 30.

40. *Freedom in the World 1997*, 573.

41. David Beetham, "Key principles and indices for a democratic audit", in *Defining and Measuring Democracy*, edited by David Beetham (London: Sage Publications, 1994), 38.

42. Vanhanen, *Prospects of Democracy*, 161.

43. Rosenau, *Along the Domestic-Foreign Frontier*, 115.

44. Ibid., 43.

45. David Held, *Democracy and the Global Order: From the Modern*

State to Cosmopolitan Governance (Stanford: Stanford University Press, 1995), 108.

46. Rosenau, *Along the Domestic-Foreign Frontier*, 150.

47. Held, *Democracy and the Global Order*, 99–135; Strange, "The erosion of the state", 368; Claude Ake, "Dangerous liasons: the interface of globalization and democracy", in *Democracy's Victory and Crisis*, edited by Axel Hadenius (Cambridge: Cambridge University Press, 1997), 287; Phillipe C. Schmitter, "Exploring the problematic triumph of liberal democracy and concluding with a modest proposal for improving its international impact", in Hadenius, ibid., 300.

48. Rosenau, *Along the Domestic-Foreign Frontier*, 410.

49. In fact this network of transnational ties has developed so rapidly that the Jamaican Ministry of Foreign Affairs itself is even now facing something of a challenge in tracking down all the IGOs to which the country belongs and the treaties to which it is a signatory. [Personal interview 1997.]

50. Between 1980 and 1991, successive Jamaican governments entered into approximately 40 agreements with the IMF and the IBRD; cf. Anthony Bogues, *The Limit of Political Sovereignty: A Review of the Jamaican Experience* (Kingston: Friedrick Ebert Stiftung, 1994).

51. This very comprehensive anti-narcotics Convention requires of ratifying states the passage and enforcement of legislation on a wide range of issues in-cluding often controversial measures to deal with extradition, money laundering, etc. See also Dorith Grant-Wilson, "Globalization, structural adjustment and democracy in Jamaica", in *Democracy and Human Rights in the Caribbean*, edited by I.L. Griffith and B.N. Sedoc-Dahlberg (Boulder: Westview Press, 1997), 193–211.

52. See Jane Harrigan, "Jamaica", in *Aid and Power: The World Bank and Policy-based Lending Vol. 2: Case Studies*, edited by Paul Mosley, Jane Harrigan, and John Toye (London and New York: Routledge, 1991), 331, 334. This study certainly indicates that Jamaica did, on occasion, extract concessions from the IMF. Recent successfully concluded negotiations with the United States on a maritime anti-narcotics agreement (the so-called Shiprider Agreement) also demonstrated the possibility of meaningful give and take in bargaining even with the hegemonic power.

53. Held, *Democracy and the Global Order;* Schmitter, "Exploring the problematic triumph".

54. Ibid.

55. Susan Strange, *The Retreat of the State: The Diffusion of Power in the World Economy* (Cambridge: Cambridge University Press, 1996), 198.

56. Rosenau, *Along the Domestic-Foreign Frontier*, 410.

57. Ralph Nader and Lori Wallach, "GATT, NAFTA and the subversion of the democratic process", in *The Case Against the Global Economy*, edited by Jerry Mander and Edward

Goldsmith (San Francisco: Sierra Books, 1996), 104.

58. Strange, *The Retreat of the State*, 197.

59. Louis W. Pauly, *Who Elected the Bankers? Surveillance and Control in the World Economy* (Ithaca and London: Cornell University Press, 1997), 140.

60. Juan J. Linz and Alfred Stepan, "Toward consolidated democracies", in *Consolidating the Third Wave Democracies: Themes and Perspectives*, edited by Larry Diamond et al. (Baltimore and London: Johns Hopkins University Press, 1997), 15.

61. Ibid.

62. Cf., e.g., Surjit Bhalla, "Freedom and economic growth: a virtuous cycle?", in *Democracy's Victory and Crisis*, edited by Axel Hadenius (Cambridge: Cambridge University Press, 1997), 228; Larry Diamond, *Political Culture and Democracy in Developing Countries* (Boulder: Lynne Reiner, 1993), 245.

63. *World Development Report* 1997, 149.

64. Ibid.

65. Adam Przeworski and Fernando Limongi, "Democracy and development", in *Democracy's Victory and Crisis*, edited by Axel Hadenius (Cambridge: Cambridge University Press, 1997), 178.

66. Adam Przeworski and Fernando Limongi, "What makes democracies endure?", in *Consolidating the Third Wave Democracies: Themes*

and Perspectives, edited by Larry Diamond et al. (Baltimore and London: Johns Hopkins University Press, 1997), 303.

67. Carl Stone, *Class, State and Democracy*, 188–89.

68. In the literature, the distinction is most clearly expressed by Linz and Stepan, "Toward consolidated democracies", 16, 30, but somewhat blurred by Diamond, "Democracy in Latin America".

69. Linz and Steppan, "Toward consolidated democracies", 16.

70. Juan J. Linz, "Some thoughts on the victory and future of democracy", in *Democracy's Victory and Crisis*, edited by Axel Hadenius (Cambridge: Cambridge University Press, 1997), 418.

71. The important distinction is made by Ronald Inglehart, "Postmaterialist values and the erosion of institutional authority", in *Why People Don't Trust Government*, edited by Joseph S. Nye, Jr., Philip D. Zelikow, and David C. King, (Cambridge: Harvard University Press, 1997), 233–36.

72. Within the considerable body of work that has appeared in recent times on 'civil society', special attention should be paid to the analyses which avoid idealizing the concept and its role in democracy. Cf. e.g. Haynes, *Democracy and Civil Society*, 170; *Civil Society: Democratic Perspectives*, edited by Robert Fine and Shirin Rai (London, Portland: Frank Cass, 1997), 2; Lawrence

Whitehead, "Bowling in the Bronx: the uncivil interstices between civil and political society", in Fine and Rai, ibid., 106; Salvador Giner, "Civil society and its future", in *Civil Society: Theory, History, Comparison,* edited by John A. Hall (Cambridge: Cambridge University Press, 1997), 321.

73. Larry Diamond , "Promoting democracy in the 1990s: actors, instruments and issues", in *Democracy's Victory and Crisis,* edited by Axel Hadenius (Cambridge: Cambridge University Press, 1997), 359.

74. P.C. Schmitter, "Exploring the problematic triumph of liberal democracy and concluding with a modest proposal for improving its international impact", in *Democracy's Victory and Crisis,* edited by Axel Hadenius (Cambridge: Cambridge University Press, 1997), 297.

75. Robert Putnam, "Bowling alone: America's declining social capital", *Journal of Democracy* 6, no. 1 (January 1995): 77.

76. *The State of Disunion: 1996 Survey of American Political Culture,* The Postmodernity Project Executive Summary (Charlottesville: The Post-modernity Project, 1996), 5.

77. Nye, *Why People Don't Trust Government,* 279.

78. Diamond, "Promoting democracy", 359.

Chapter 2

1. *The 1997 General Elections in Jamaica: The Establishment of CAFFE and Its*

Role in the Electoral Process, edited by Alfred Sangster and Lloyd Barnett (Kingston: CAFFE, 1998), 7 (hereinafter referred to as CAFFE Report); The Carter Center *The Observation of the 1997 Jamaican Elections* (Atlanta: The Carter Center, 1998), 13, 37 (hereinafter referred to as Carter Report).

2. Carter Report, 49.

3. Douglas W. Payne, *The 1997 Jamaican Elections: Post-Election Report,* Western Hemisphere Election Study Series 16, Study 1 (Washington, DC: CSIS Americas Program, 1998), 1.

4. *Report of the Duffus Commission of the Enquiry into the 1986 Local Government Elections* (Kingston: Government Printing Office, 1987), 6.

5. Ibid., 8.

6. Carter Report, 15.

7. *Report of the National Committee on Political Tribalism,* 23 July 1997, cited in CAFFE Report, 16.

8. *Sunday Herald,* 4 April 1993.

9. *Jamaica Herald,* 3 April 1993.

10. Stone Poll, *Daily Gleaner,* 17 March 1994.

11. *Daily Gleaner,* 4 May 1993.

12. *Electoral Advisory Committee Interim Report Part II: Recommendations for Legal Reform,* 24 April 1996 (Kingston, Jamaica), 2–12; CAFFE Report, 11, 15; Electoral Advisory Committee, *Report to Parliament on Electoral Reform,* 13 August 1997.

13. Electoral Advisory Committee, *Report To Parliament,* 26.

14. Jorgen Elklit and Palle Svensson, "What makes elections free and fair?",

Journal of Democracy 8, no. 3 (July 1997): 33.

15. Neil Nevitte and Santiago A. Canton, "The role of domestic observers", *Journal of Democracy* 8, no. 3 (July 1997): 59.

16. Cf. e.g. Conference on Security and Cooperation in Europe: Document of the Copenhagen Meeting of the Conference on the Human Dimension (CSCE, 1990), sec. 1, par. 8.

17. Carter Report, 8.

18. "General Elections 1993: Report of the Ombudsman for Political Matters", mimeo.

19. National opinion polls reveal the dramatic growth of the 'uncommitted' segment of the Jamaican electorate from an average of under 20% in election years during the 1970s and 1980s to well over 40% in the 1990s; cf. Stephen Rodriques, "The Jamaican political culture: a theoretical and empirical exploration" (MPhil, Department of Government, UWI, Mona, 1996), 117; also National Democratic Movement, *A Winnable Alternative* (Kingston: NDM, 1997), 2.

20. CAFFE Report, 27, 44.

21. Joseph S. Nye, Jr., et al., *Why People Don't Trust Government* (Cambridge: Harvard University Press, 1997), 233; Also cf. Paul R. Abramson and Ronald Inglehart, "Comparing European publics", *American Political Science Review* 92, no. 1 (March 1988): 186, 190.

22. For some indication of the process of give and take as well as the contending arguments, cf. Carter Report, 18–19, 82–83; Electoral Advisory Committee, *Report to Parliament on Electoral Reform*, 13 August 1997, 3–11. National opinion surveys on this issue suggested a fairly even balance on views for and against inviting international observers at a point in the debate when Prime Minister Patterson had expressed opposition to such an invitation (September 1997 Stone Poll [mimeo in author's possession]). For an insightful discussion of the pros and cons of international versus domestic observations cf. Nevitte and Canton, "The role of domestic observers"; also Thomas Carothers, "The observers observed", *Journal of Democracy* 8, no. 55 (July 1997): 17–31.

23. CAFFE Report, 37.

24. Ibid., 44.

25. Carter Report, 25.

26. CAFFE Report, 45; Carter Report, 33.

27. Carter Report, 25.

28. Ibid., 34–35.

29. CAFFE Report, 45.

30. Stone Poll.

31. Pippa Norris, "Legislative recruitment", in *Comparing Democracies: Elections and Voting in Global Perspective,* edited by Lawrence LeDuc, Richard G. Niemi, Pippa Norris (Thousand Oaks, Calif.: Sage, 1996), 186.

32. Carl Stone, *Democracy and Clientelism in Jamaica* (New Brunswick

and London: Transaction Books, 1980); Maxine Henry-Wilson, "The status of the Jamaican woman, 1962 to the present", in *Jamaica in Independence: Essays on the Early Years*, edited by Rex Nettleford (Kingston and London: Heinemann Caribbean and James Currey, 1989).

33. Norris, "Legislative recruitment", 212–14.

34. Personal interviews by the author with the General Secretary and Treasurer respectively of the PNP and the JLP (January 1998). Much of what follows is based partly on these interviews.

35. David M. Farrell, "Campaign strategies and tactics", in *Comparing Democracies: Elections and Voting in Global Perspective*, edited by Lawrence LeDuc, et al. (Thousand Oaks, Calif.: Sage, 1996), 171–75. The counter-position of capital intensive" to "labour intensive" campaigns can be overdrawn, even in the United States. See, for example, the extent to which the high AFL-CIO expenditure was combined with high volunteer mobilization in securing the defeat of Proposition 226 in the California State Elections of 2 June 1998. *Wall Street Journal*, Thursday, 4 June 1998.

36. At the high point of Jamaican electoral participation in the early 1970s, levels of grass-roots activism were significantly higher than in mature democracies like Britain and the United States. Cf. Carl Stone *Electoral Behaviour and Public Opinion in Jamaica* (Kingston: ISER, 1974), 47.

37. Edward Seaga, Foreword to *A Statement on the Irregularities of Jamaica's General Elections*, 18 December 1997 (Kingston: Jamaica Labour Party, 1998), 1.

38. Cf. Richard S. Katz, "Party organizations and finance", in *Comparing Democracies: Elections and Voting in Global Perspective*, edited by Lawrence LeDuc et al. (Thousand Oaks, Calif.: Sage, 1996), 107–33.

39. The matter was raised in Parliament by a member of the governing PNP prior to the 1997 elections.

40. This information is largely based on the January 1998 discussion with the PNP and JLP officials referred to in Note 34.

41. Hopeton Dunn, "The PNP won the advertising campaign too", *Sunday Observer*, 21 December 1997. Also cf. CAFFE report, 30–31.

42. Cf. the results of the Anderson Polls conducted from 26 September to 6 October and the Stone Polls conducted on 23 August, 24 ff. These were published in the *Daily Gleaner* and *Observer* newspapers respectively.

43. Helmut Norpoth, "The economy", in *Comparing Democracies: Elections and Voting in Global Perspective*, edited by Lawrence LeDuc et al. (Thousand Oaks, Calif.: Sage, 1996), 317.

44. Carl Stone *Politics versus Economics: The 1989 Elections in Jamaica* (Kingston: Heinemann, 1989), x.

45. Ian McAllister, "Leaders", in *Comparing Democracies: Elections and Voting in Global Perspective*, edited by

Lawrence LeDuc et al. (Thousand Oaks, Calif.: Sage, 1996), 294.

46. Arend Lijphart, "Unequal participation: democracy's unresolved dilemma", *American Political Science Review* 91, no. 1 (March 1997): 6.

47. Mark N. Franklin, "Electoral participation", in *Comparing Democracies: Elections and Voting in Global Perspective*, edited by Lawrence LeDuc et al. (Thousand Oaks, Calif.: Sage, 1996), 231, in reference to one reason for low turnout in the United States.

48. This refers to the large and growing proportion of electorates who have abandoned historic "alignments", primarily based on party, and have become "independent" or "uncommitted" to any traditional party. For an interesting review of this phenomenon, cf. Russel J. Dalton, "Political cleavages, issues, and electoral change", in *Comparing Democracies: Elections and Voting in Global Perspective*, edited by Lawrence LeDuc et al. (Thousand Oaks, Calif.: Sage, 1996), 319–42.

49. Franklin, "Electoral participation", 232.

50. Arend Lijphart, "Unequal participation", 1.

51. Ibid.

52. Juan J. Linz, "Some thoughts on the victory and future of democracy", in *Democracy's Victory and Crisis*, edited by Axel Hadenius (Cambridge: Cambridge University Press, 1997), 416–17.

53. For manifestation of this phenomenon in the recent politics of the hemisphere, cf. Douglas W. Payne, *Storm Watch: Democracy in the Western Hemisphere into the Next Century*, Policy Papers on the Americas 9, Study 3 (Washington, DC: CSIS Americas Program, 1998), 4–8.

54. Cf. NDM, *1997 Manifesto of the NDM* (Kingston: Gleaner Co., 1997).

55. There is a great deal of literature on different types of electoral systems and their effects. For two comprehensive reviews of recent writing on this subject, cf. David M. Farrell, *Comparing Electoral Systems* (London: Prentice Hall/Harvester Wheatsheaf, 1997), Andre Blais et al., "Electoral systems", in *Comparing Democracies: Elections and Voting in Global Perspective*, edited by Lawrence LeDuc et al.

56. Vernon Bogdanor, *Power and the People: a Guide to Electoral Constitutional Reform* (London: Victor Gollancz, 1997), 53.

57. Stone, *Politics versus Economics*, 109, 114.

58. This disproportionality tends to accompany first-past-the post electoral systems and has been particularly marked throughout the Anglophone Caribbean; cf. Patrick A.M. Emmanuel, *Governance and Democracy in the Commonwealth Caribbean: An Introduction* (Barbados: ISER, 1993), 43–44.

59. Cf. Table 1.4 in LeDuc et al., *Comparing Democracies*, 20–37.

60. Peter Mair, "Party systems and structures of competition", in *Company Democracies: Elections and Voting in Global Perspective*, edited by Lawrence Le Duc et al. (Thousand Oaks, Calif: Sage, 1996), 104.

61. Ibid., 105.

62. CAFFE Report, Appendix 5.2, 130–33.

63. The constituency of West Central St Andrew changed hands from the JLP to the PNP on the re-run of the election.

64. Carter Report, 46.

Chapter 3

1. Following their election in 1995 and 1996, respectively, both Prime Minister Owen Arthur of Barbados and Prime Minister Basdeo Panday of Trinidad and Tobago placed the issue of constitutional and electoral reform on their national agendas.

2. *Time for Action: Report of the West Indian Commission* (Black Rock, Barbados: International Development Options, 1992).

3. Mark P. Jones, "A guide to the electoral systems of the Americas: an update", *Electoral Studies* 16, no. 1 (March 1997): 13–15; Scott Mainwaring and Matthew Soberg Shugart, *Presidentialism and Democracy in Latin America* (Cambridge: Cambridge University Press, 1997), 2.

4. There can be little doubt that "campaign finance reform" and the larger question of money in politics is probably the most important issue in American politics. Yet "true reform will remain elusive", even though "a New York Times/CBS poll found that 90 per cent of Americans wanted finance reform". Gil Troy, "Money and politics: the oldest connection", *Wilson Quarterly* (Summer 1997): 32.

5. For a comprehensive discussion of the main issues of constitutional reform in Britain cf. Vernon Bogdanor, *Power and the People: A Guide to Constitutional Reform* (London: Victor Gollancz, 1997).

6. *Comparing Democracies: Elections and Voting in Global Perspective*, edited by Lawrence LeDuc, Richard G. Niemi, Pippa Norris (Thousand Oaks, Calif.: Sage, 1996), 2–3; Axel Hadenuis, ed., *Democracy's Victory and Crisis* (Cambridge: Cambridge University Press, 1997), 2–3; Erik Olin Wright, ed., *Associations and Democracy* (London, New York: Verso, 1995), 3.

7. LeDuc et al., *Comparing Democracies*, 6.

8. J.G. March and J.P. Olsen, "The new institutionalism: organizational factors in political life", *American Political Science Review* 78 (1984): 734–49; R.A.W. Rhodes, "The institutional approach", in *Theory and Methods in Political Science*, edited by David Marsh and Gerry Stoken (London: Macmillan, 1995).

9. Stephen Anthony Rodriques, "The Jamaican political culture: a theoretical and empirical exploration" (MPhil thesis, Department of Government, UWI, Mona, 1996), 64, 152.

10. Ibid., 67, 145.

11. Ibid., 105.

12. Ibid., 104.

13. Cf. Table 1, "Levels of satisfaction with democracy", in *Government and Democratic Development in Latin American and the Caribbean* (UNDP, n.d., c. 1996), 24.

14. Trevor Munroe, "Caribbean democracy: decay or renewal?", in *Constructing Democratic Governance*, edited by Jorge I. Dominguez and Abraham I. Lowenthal (Baltimore and London: Johns Hopkins University Press, 1996), 104–17; Carl Stone, "Power, policy and politics in independent Jamaica", in *Jamaica in Independence: Essays on the Early Years*, edited by Rex Nettleford (Kingston and London: Heinemann Caribbean and James Currey, 1989).

15. For data relating to some of these conditions, cf. e.g. *Jamaica: Survey of Living Conditions 1996* (Kingston: Statistical Institute of Jamaica and Planning Institute of Jamaica, 1997). This report "describes living conditions in Jamaica in 1996 particular and from 1989 to 1996 in general", xiii.

16. United Nations Development Program, *Human Development Report* 1995 (New York and Oxford: Oxford University Press, 1995); *Aid and Power: The World Bank and Policy-based Lending*, vol. 2, *Case Studies*, edited by Paul Moseley, Jane Harrigan and John Toye (London and New York: Routledge, 1991), 311.

17. *Report of the Committee to Examine Ways of Strengthening the Roles and Performance of Parliamentarians*, Appointed by the Prime Minister on 14 June 1990, Ministry Paper No. 11, 1991. (Hereinafter called the Stone Committee Report.)

18. Stone Committee Report, 23.

19. Rodriguez, *Jamaican Political Culture*, 108.

20. Stone Committee Report.

21. *Final Report of the Joint Select Committee of the Houses of Parliament on Constitutional and Electoral Reform*, Gordon House, 31 May 1995, 5. (Hereinafter called the Joint Select Committee Report.) Subsequent page references are given in the text in parentheses.

22. In the five years between 1989 and 1993, the average annual number of parliamentary questions asked in the 60-member House of Representatives was 11.

23. For extensive review and discussion of the right to recall, cf. Joseph Zimmermann, *The Recall: Tribunal of the People* (Westport: Praeger, 1997).

24. Ibid., 92.

25. Stone Committee Report, 51, 56. It should be noted that while opinion polls in the United States have consistently shown a majority in favour of the application of the right of recall at the federal government level, this proposal has not been accepted.

26. Cf. David Butler and Austin Renney, eds., *Referendums around*

the World: The Growing Use of Direct Democracy (Washington: American Enterprise Institute, 1994), Table 1-1 (p. 5) and Appendix A, 265–95. Also, John T. Rourke, Richard Hiskes and Cyrus Ernesto Zirakzakeh, *Direct Democracy and International Politics: Deciding International Issues Through Referendums* (Boulder and London: Lynne Reiner, 1992), 4–5.

27. Hiskes, et al., *Direct Democracy*, 5
28. Butler, et al., *Referendums around the World*, chapter 7.
29. Kris W. Kobach, "Switzerland", in *Referendums around the World: The Growing Use of Direct Democracy*, edited by David Butler and Austin Renney (Washington: American Enterprise Institute, 1994), 98.
30. Bogdanor, *Power and the People*, 120–21.
31. For an important and well-documented discussion of these circumstances, cf., e.g. *Economist*, 21 December 1996, "Survey: full democracy".
32. Butler, et al., *Referendums around the World*, 3.
33. Helena Catt, "The other democratic experiment: New Zealand's experience with citizens initiated referendum", *Political Science* 48, no. 1 (July 1996): 42.
34. David B. Magleby, "Direct legislation in the American states", in *Referendums around the World: The Growing Use of Direct Democracy*, edited by David Butler and Austin Renney (Washington: American Enterprise Institute, 1994), 250. For

recent contributions to the continuing debate on the appropriateness of mechanisms of direct democracy and their use in the United States, cf. "Ballots boom, but is it good government?", *Christian Science Monitor*, 20 May 1998; "Will politicians take the initiative?", *Wall Street Journal*, 1 June 1998; "Direct democracy: lex populi", *Economist*, 30 May–5 June 1998, 26, 31.

35. Magleby, "Direct legislation"; *Economist*, "Survey: full democracy".
36. Cf. Stone Committee Report and Joint Select Committee Report.
37. Cf. Stone Poll.
38. Amongst the more important publications in this debate are Mainwaring and Shugart, *Presidentialism and Democracy*; Juan T. Linz and Arturo Valenzuela, eds., *The Failure of Presidential Democracy: The Case of Latin America* (Baltimore: Johns Hopkins University Press, 1994); Matthew S. Shugart and John M. Carey, *Presidents and Assemblies: Constitutional Design and Electoral Dynamics* (Cambridge: Cambridge University Press, 1992); Arend Lijphart, ed., *Parliamentary versus Presidential Government* (Oxford: Oxford Univeristy Press, 1992); Kurt von Mettenheim, ed., *Presidential Institutions and Democratic Politics: Comparing Regional and National Contexts* (Baltimore and London: Johns Hopkins Univeristy Press, 1997).
39. NDM, *1997 Manifesto of the NDM* (Kingston: Gleaner Co., 1997), 9–10.

40. Cf.,e.g. Trevor Munroe "Constitutional reform", *Sunday Gleaner*, April, May 1994.

41. Cf. Von Mettenheim, *Presidential Institutions*, 237–46.

42. Cf. Mainwaring and Shugart, *Presidentialism and Democracy*, 394–437.

43. Cf. Charles O. Jones, "The American presidency: a separationist perspective", in *Presidential Institutions and Democratic Politics: Comparing Regional and National Contexts*, edited by Kurt von Mettenheim (Baltimore and London: Johns Hopkins Univeristy Press, 1997), 19–44.

44. Arend Lijphart *Democracy in Plural Societies* (New Haven: Yale, 1977); Arend Lijphart, "Constitutional choices for new democracies", in *The Global Resurgence of Democracy*, edited by L. Diamond and M.F. Plattner (Baltimore: Johns Hopkins University Press, 1993); 146–58; also Arend Lijphart, "The puzzle of Indian democracy: a consociational interpretation", *American Political Science Review* 90, no. 2 (June 1996): 258–68.

45. Mark Jones, "Assuring the public's understanding of constitutional reform: evidence from Argentina", *Political Behaviour* 18, no. 1 (1996): 25, 26.

46. Cf., e.g., Mainwaring and Shugart, *Presidential Institutions*, 3.

Chapter 4

1. Anthony P. Maingot, *The United States and the Caribbean* (London: Macmillan, 1994), 156.

2. West Indian Commission, *Time for Action: Report of the West Indian Commission* (Black Rock, Barbados: International Development Options, 1992), 343, 351, 352.

3. *United Nations Convention against Illicit Traffic in Narcotic Drugs and Psychotropic Substances 1988.* (Hereinafter referred to as the UN 1998 Vienna Convention.)

4. United Nations International Drug Control Programme, *World Drug Report* (Oxford: Oxford University Press, 1997), 124.

5. The perception of the US throwing its weight around on anti-narcotic issues is widespread. The annual requirement of US law that the US President certify or decertify states depending on the US assessment of their anti-narcotics policies is a major source of hemispheric friction and is currently under review in order to develop a process more compatible with reciprocal recognition of national sovereignty. In addition, the activity of US enforcement agencies on foreign soil, often without the knowledge of "friendly" governments, are occasions for "extraordinary diplomatic uproar". In relation to Mexico-US relations, cf. e.g. "US drug sting riles Mexico, imperiling future cooperation", *New York Times*, 11 June 1998. For

opinion on the broader issue of certification, cf. e.g. "Has the time passed for US drug sanctions?", *Wall Street Journal*, 24 February 1998; "Drugs, Latin America and the United States", *Economist*, 7 February 1998.

6. National Defense University, Institute for National Strategic Studies, *1997 Strategic Assessment: Flashpoints and Force Structure* (Washington, DC: National Defense University, 1997).

7. Ivelaw Lloyd Griffith, *Drugs and Security in the Caribbean: Sovereignty under Siege* (Pennsylvania: Pennsylvania State University Press, 1997), 88.

8. Caribbean/United States Summit, Partnership for Prosperity and Security in the Caribbean, Bridgetown, Barbados, 10 May 1997, 8.

9. National Defense University, *1997 Strategic Assessment*, 205.

10. United Nations International Drug Control Programme, *World Drug Report*, 143.

11. Ibid.

12. National Defense University, *1997 Strategic Assessment*, 205.

13. Ibid.

14. Faye V. Harrison, "Drug trafficking in world capitalism: a perspective on Jamaican posses in the US", *Social Justice* 16 (Winter 1989): 123, cited in Bernard Headley, *The Jamaican Crime Scene: A Perspective* (Washington, DC: Howard University Press), 31.

15. United Nations International Drug Control Programme, *World Drug Report*, 9.

16. Ibid., 18.

17. P. Williams and C. Florez, "Transnational criminal organizations and drug trafficking", *Bulletin on Narcotics* (United Nations International Drug Control Programme) 46, no. 2 (1994): 11.

18. National Defense University, *1997 Strategic Assessment*, 199.

19. Anthony Harriott, "The changing social organization of crime and criminals in Jamaica", *Caribbean Quarterly* 42, nos. 2–3 (June–September 1996): 75.

20. Ibid.

21. Ibid., 74.

22. Ibid., 75.

23. "Drug consumption and distribution in Jamaica: a national ethnographic study", Executive Summary prepared by Melanie Dreher, Solores Shapiro and Ann Stoddard, 1997 (mimeo), 97.

24. National Defense University, *1997 Strategic Assessment*, 201.

25. United Nations International Drug Control Programme, *World Drug Report*, 133–34.

26. Excerpts from Intelligence Report. Commissioner of Police, Jamaica, *Sunday Gleaner*, 2 October 1994, 8A.

27. Harriott, "Changing social organization", 72.

28. Ibid., 77.

29. Ibid.

30. Edward Seaga in an interview on "The Breakfast Club", KLAS FM 89, 28 September 1994 (published in the *Herald* [Jamaica], 30 September 1994).

31. *Daily Gleaner*, 20 October 1994, 1.

32. Cf. e.g. The Jamaica Constabulary Force, *Annual Report 1996*, 9; *Annual Report 1995*, 10–11.

33. Harriott, "Changing social organization", Table 4.

34. Trinidad and Tobago, Ministry of National Security, *Final Report for the Government of Trinidad and Tobago on Investigations . . . in Respect of Allegations . . . About Corruption in the Trinidad and Tobago Police Service*, cited in Ivelaw L. Griffiths, *Drugs and Security*, 163; and *Trinidad Guardian*, 1 December 1993, 9–10.

35. US Department of State, *Country Reports on Human Rights Practices for 1997* (Washington, DC: Department of State, 1998), mimeo section on Jamaica, 1–2. (Hereinafter referred to as State Department Report 1997.)

36. US Department of State, *Country Reports on Human Rights Practices for 1995* (Washington, DC: Department of State, 1996).

37. Harriott, "Changing social organization", 69.

38. Caroline Moser and Jeremy Holland, *Urban Poverty and Violence in Jamaica*, World Bank Latin American and Caribbean Studies (Washington, DC: World Bank, 1997), 1.

39. Cf. Jamaica Constabulary Force Crime Review Period 1 January 1997 to 31 December 1997 vs 1 January 1996 to 31 December 1996 (mimeo from Commissioner of Police, 11 February 1998).

40. State Department Report 1997, 2.

41. Ibid.; Planning Institute of Jamaica, *Economic and Social Survey: Jamaica, 1997* (Kingston: PIOJ, 1998), chapter 23, Table 23, 8; cf. also the latest in a number of official reports that identify prison overcrowding as "the root of the problem" in Jamaica's prisons, "Report Board of Enquiry into disturbances at the Tower Street Adult Correctional Centre and the St Catherine Adult Correctional Centre between 20th–23rd August 1997", 14 (mimeo).

42. Douglas W. Payne, *Storm Watch: Democracy in the Western Hemisphere into the Next Century*, Policy Papers on the Americas, CSIS Americas Program (Washington, DC: CSIS, 1998), 7.

43. Claire Sterling, *Thieves' World* (New York: Simon and Schuster, 1994), 21, quoted in Ivelaw L. Griffith, *Drugs and Security*, 166.

44. Stephen Anthony Rodriques, "The Jamaican political culture: a theoretical and empirical exploration" (MPhil thesis, University of the West Indies, Mona, 1996), 109.

45. Jorge I. Dominguez, "The powers, the pirates, and international norms and institutions in the American Mediterranean", in *From Pirates to Drug Lords: The Post-Cold War Caribbean Security Environment*, edited by, Michael C. Desch, Jorge I. Dominguez, and Andres Serbin (Albany: State University of New York Press, 1998), 82–84.

46. UN 1998 Vienna Convention.

47. "Ten years of Jamaican-US cooperation", mimeo.

48. West Indian Commission, *Time for Action*, 348.

49. Ibid., 338.

50. Summary of Conclusions of the Fifth Special Meeting of the Conference of Heads of Governments held in Barbados, 16 December 1996.

51. Trevor Munroe, "Cooperation and conflict dynamics in the US-Caribbean drug connection", in *The Political Economy of Drugs in the Caribbean*, edited by Ivelaw Griffiths (London: Macmillian, forthcoming).

52. Edward Seaga, Leader of the Opposition, revealed this prospect in his address to the Annual Conference of the JLP: "It is now known that unless considerable improvement (in the anti-narcotics programme) takes place, Jamaica, like Colombia, could be de-certified by the US government." Seaga's speech notes (mimeo). Also cf. "US aid hanging on drug-war – Seaga", *Daily Gleaner*, 2 December 1996.

53. Cf. Stephen Vasciannie, "Political and policy aspects of the Jamaica/United States Shiprider negotiations", *Caribbean Quarterly* 43, no 3 (September 1997): 34–53. Also cf. Susan M. Smith, " 'We will not grovel': drugs and Jamaican sovereignty" (MSc Research Paper, Department of Government, University of the West Indies, Mona, December 1997), 45–47.

54. For a discussion of this turn-away from unilateral US intervention towards more "collective means" of protecting constitutional democratic governments under forcible assault, cf. Dominguez, *From Pirates to Drug Lords*, 93; Domingo E. Acevedo and Claudio Grossman, "The Organization of American States and the protection of democracy", in *Beyond Sovereignty: Collectively Defending Democracy in the Americas*, edited by Tom Farer (Baltimore and London: Johns Hopkins University Press, 1996), 137–49.

55. Caribbean/United States Summit, *Partnership for Prosperity and Security in the Caribbean*, Bridgetown, Barbados, 10 May 1997 (United States Information Agency, 1997).

56. Ibid., 23–24.

57. Ibid., 25

58. "Inter-American Convention Against Illicit Manufacturing and Trafficking in Firearms, Ammunitions, Explosives, Organization of American States", mimeo.

59. Ibid., 4.

60. Ibid., 5.

61. Planning Institute of Jamaica, *Economic and Social Survey 1997*; *National Master Drug Abuse Prevention and Control Plan 1997–2002*, National Council on Drug Abuse, Ministry of Health, Jamaica, 1996.

62. Moser and Holland, *Urban Poverty*.

63. Cf. Ministry of Agriculture (in collaboration with Rural Agricultural Development Authority), *Alternative Systems for an Illegal Crop* (Kingston: Government of Jamaica, 1994).

64. The first seizure of property under the Asset Forfeiture Legislation took place in 1997.

65. Dreher et al., "Drug consumption and distribution", 99–100.
66. Moser and Holland, *Urban Poverty*, 14–15.
67. Cf. for comprehensive discussion of a public health approach, James F. Mosher and Karen L. Yanagisako, "Public health, not social welfare: a pubic health approach to illegal drug policy", *Journal of Public Health Policy* 12, no. 3 (Autumn 1991): 278–323.
68. This debate has generated an immense body of writing. Cf. e.g., "Political pharmacology: thinking about drugs", *Daedalus Journal of the American Academy of Arts and Sciences* 12, no. 3 (Summer 1992); Rod L. Evans and Irvin M. Berent, *Drug Legalization: For and Against* (Illinois: Open Court, 1992); Eva Bertram, et al., *Drug War Politics: The Price of Denial* (Berkeley: University of California Press, 1996).
69. Ehan N. Nadelmann, "Common sense drug policy", *Foreign Affairs* 77, no. 1 (January/February 1998): 123.
70. Ibid., 124.
71. Ibid., 25.
72. Ibid., 122.
73. "Connecticut tries 'gentler' approach to curb drug use", *Christian Science Monitor*, 21 November 1997, 1.
74. Cf. Two full-page advertisements, *New York Times*, 8 June 1998, A14, A15.
75. Ibid.

Chapter 5

1. The following are representative collections from what has become one of the "growth industries" of political science: John A. Hall, ed., *Civil Society: Theory, History, Comparison* (Cambridge: Polity Press, 1995); Jeff Haynes, *Democracy and Civil Society in the Third World: Politics and New Political Movements.* (Cambridge: Polity Press, 1997); *The Brookings Review* 15, no. 4 (Fall 1997) (Issue on "Civil society – what is it? Why is everybody talking about it"); John Keane, *Civil Society and the State* (London: Verso, 1998); John Harbeson et al., eds., *Civil Society and the State in Africa* (Boulder: Lynne Rienner, 1994).
2. Cf. e.g. Don Robotham, *Vision and Voluntarism – Reviving Voluntarism in Jamaica* (Kingston: Grace, Kennedy, 1998); Brian Meeks, "Careening on the edge of abyss: driving, hegemony and the rule of law in Jamaica", Paper presented for the conference African Diaspora Studies on the Eve of the Twenty-First Century, University of California, Berkeley, 30 April–2 May 1998.
3. For provocative and insightful perspectives on some aspects of this issue, cf. Robert Fine, and Shirin Rai, eds., *Civil Society: Democratic Perspectives* (London: Frank Cass, 1997).
4. For different assumptions and approaches to the policy options in

the United States, cf. the contributions to *The Brookings Review* issue, cited in n. 1 above.

5. Cited in Lawrence Whitehead, "Bowling in the Bronx: the uncivil interstices between civil and political society", in *Civil Society: Democratic Perspectives*, edited by Robert Fine and Shirin Rai, 100.

6. For an interesting article on this question cf. Asef Bayat, "Un-civil society: the politics of the 'informal people' ", *Third World Quarterly* 18, no. 1 (1997): 53–72.

7. Fine, *Civil Society: Democratic Perspectives*, 2.

8. Whitehead, "Bowling in the Bronx", 106.

9. There has been considerable debate surrounding this proposition and its implications following the publication of Robert Putnam's "Bowling alone: America's declining social capital", *Journal of Democracy* (January 1995).

10. Salvador Giner, "Civil society and its future", in *Civil Society: Theory, History, Comparison*, edited by John A. Hall, 321.

11. Ibid.

12. Putnam, "Bowling alone".

13. Joseph S. Nye Jr., Philip D. Zelikow, and David C. King, eds., *Why People Don't Trust Government* (Cambridge: Harvard University Press, 1997), 233–36.

14. Haynes, *Democracy and Civil Society*, 10.

15. Trevor Munroe, *The Politics of Constitutional Decolonization: Jamaica 1944–1962* (Kingston: ISER-Unwin, 1978);

Carl Stone *Democracy and Clientelism in Jamaica* (New York: Praeger, 1986).

16. Trevor Munroe, "The Jamaican industrial relations culture: perspectives on change", in *Jamaica Preparing for the Twenty-first Century*, edited by Patsy Lewis (Kingston: Planning Institute of Jamaica, 1996).

17. For a perspective on this phenomenon from the left, cf. Kim Moddy, *Workers in a Lean World: Unions in the International Economy* (London and New York: Verso, 1997), 183–85.

18. Patricia Anderson and Michael Witter. "Crisis, adjustment and social change: a case study of Jamaica" in *Consequences of Structural Adjustment: A Review of the Jamaican Experience*, edited by Elsie Le Franc (Kingston: Canoe Press, 1994) 1–55.

19. Cf. Carl Stone, "Survey of Jamaican workers' opinions" (manuscript, Department of Government, UWI, Mona, 1987).

20. Damien King "The labour market in Jamaica before and after structural adjustment", mimeo, 15–16.

21. In the mid 1990s, two such cases related to the tourism sector of the economy. In one case, at the island's largest convention hotel, the Jamaica Grande, the company refused, until ordered by the court, to hold a representational rights poll, in accordance with the law, to settle the workers' claim to be represented by a union. In the second case the owners of one of the island's up-market "all inclusive" hotels dismissed all 240-odd of its workers for a strike-demonstration in

support of their request for union representation. In the latter case, the courts upheld the workers' case for reinstatement on grounds of unjustifiable dismissal.

22. Cf. Carl Stone, *The Political Opinions of the Jamaican People 1976–1981* (Kingston: Blackett Publishers, 1982), 38; Stephen Rodriques, *The Jamaican Political Culture: A Theoretical and Empirical Exploration* (MPhil thesis, Department of Government, University of the West Indies, Mona, 1996), 77–78.

23. For a very revealing discussion of the exceptional degree of inequality in Jamaica and its connection to increasing levels of violent crime, cf. Bernard Headley, *The Jamaican Crime Scene: A Perspective* (Washington, DC: Howard University Press), 41–42.

24. Much of the foregoing and the following analysis derives from the author's own experience of over 25 years as a leader in Jamaica's trade union movement.

25. Kenneth L. Carter, *Why Workers Won't Work – The Worker in a Developing Economy: A Case Study of Jamaica* (London and Basingstoke: Macmillan, 1997); Also cf. presentations to the 16th Annual Convention of the Jamaica Employers Federation, 1–3 May 1998, by Douglas Orane, chairman and chief executive officer, Grace, Kennedy and Co. Ltd, Ray Gendron, vice-president and general manager, Alu-

mina Partners of Jamaica, Anthony Bell, managing director, J. Wray and Nephew Ltd. To one extent or another, these presentations from CEOs of leading Jamaican and t ransnational corporations reflected new, more enlightened thinking and experience relating to managerial consultation and communication with labour.

26. Labour Market Reform Committee (LMRC), *Interim Report* (Kingston: LMRC, 1996).

27. Memorandum of Understanding among the Government of Jamaica, Alcan Jamaica Company, Jamalco, Alumina Partners of Jamaica and Kaiser Bauxite Company, the National Workers Union, the University and Allied Workers Union and the Union of Technical Administrative and Supervisory Personnel (mimeo, May 1998).

28. The author has some first-hand experience of a number of enterprises where union-management relations are being reoriented in a more collaborative direction. For example, Grace Meat Processors, a division of Grace, Kennedy and Co. Ltd and J. Wray and Nephew Ltd, a division of the Lascelles DeMercado Group of Companies.

29. Ken Post, *Arise Ye Starvelings* (The Hague: Martinus Nijhoff, 1978).

30. Arthur M. Waters, *Race, Class, and Political Symbols: Rastafari and Reggae in Jamaican Politics* (New Brunswick and Oxford: Transaction Books, 1985).

31. Rodriques, "Jamaican political culture" , 77.

32. *Statistical Yearbook of Jamaica 1996* (Kingston: Statistical Institute of Jamaica, 1996), 80.

33. The author requested and his research assistant was granted access to the records of the Seventh Day Adventists, the Anglican, Baptist, Pentecostal, Roman Catholic and United Churches.

34. Cf. *Daily Gleaner*.

35. For the origin and development of Citizens Action for Free and Fair Elections (CAFFE) cf. *The 1997 General Elections in Jamaica: The Establishment of CAFFE and its Role in the Electoral Process* (Kingston: CAFFE, 1998), chapter 1 and appendix 1. The author was a vice-chairman and one of the founding directors of CAFFE.

36. Robotham, *Vision and Voluntarism*, 47.

37. Ibid., 12.

38. Meeks, "Careening on the edge", 6.

39. Ken Chaplin, *Daily Gleaner*, 24 March 1998.

40. Robotham, *Vision and Voluntarism*, 44.

41. Ibid., 15.

42. Data provided in personal communication to the author (April 1998) from the Jamaican Constabulary Force, Community Relations Division, Information on Police Youth Clubs and Neighbourhood Watch Programmes.

43. Data provided in personal communication to the author from Jamaica 4-H Clubs, April 1998.

44. Data from youth club lists (various years) and youth clubs by parish. Social Development Commission, Research and Documentation Department 1997 (unpublished mimeos).

45. Rodriques, "Jamaican political culture", 64.

46. In 1997, Jamaica became the first Anglophone Caribbean territory to qualify for the World Cup and the smallest of the 32 nations to reach the final rounds of this international tournament in France.

47. The national squad derived the majority of its members from urban, inner-city communities while the leadership and financial support for the Jamaica Football Federation came primarily from the government, elements in the private sector and match attendance from all classes and 'colours' of Jamaicans.

48. The success of the team had a great deal to do with the recruitment of overseas Jamaicans and the overcoming of an 'islandist' tendency amongst sections of the people, which opposed too many foreign based Jamaicans on the Jamaican team.

49. The Brazilian coach, Rene Simoes, was a linchpin in the dramatic improvement of the quality of the national football team. His compensation package of approximately US$700,000 per annum, high by Jamaican standards, stimulated a national controversy in which a substantial minority, and perhaps a majority of the people, sympathized with the

view that Simoes' performance justified the package.

50. Caroline Moser and Jeremy Holland, *Urban Poverty and Violence in Jamaica* (Washington, DC: World Bank, 1997), 34.

51. Rodriques, "Jamaican political culture", 85–86.

52. See also Ministry of Local Government, Youth and Community Development, "Status report on local government reform", mimeo (June 1998).

53. Ministry of Local Government, Youth and Community Development, *Ministry Paper No. 8, Reform of Local Government* (17 February 1993): 13.

Chapter 6

1. For one interesting discussion of the general questions of corruption, see *IDS Bulletin* 24, no. 6 (1996) (special issue on Corruption).

2. Cf. Ronald Inglehart, "Postmaterialist values and the erosion of institutional authority", in *Why People Don't Trust Government*, edited by Joseph S. Nye, Jr., et al. (Cambridge: Harvard University Press, 1997), 217–36.

3. "New realities, new thinking: Report to the task force on campaign finance reform", in *PS: Political Science and Politics* (September 1997): 487–89.

4. *The Times*, 17 November 1997, 22. Also cf. Veron Bogdanor, *Power*

and the People: A Guide to Constitutional Reform (London: Victor Gollancz, 1997), 149–71.

5. Cf. *Economist*, 5 November 1994, 30.

6. David Butler and Austin Ranney, *Referendums Around the World: The Growing Use of Direct Democracy* (Washington, DC: The American Enterprise Institute), 1–10.

7. Bogdanor, *Power and the People*, 145.

8. Vivien A. Schmidt, "The New World Order, Incorporated: the rise of business and the decline of the nation state", *Daedalus* 124 (Spring 1995): 77, cited in James N. Rosenau, *Along the Domestic-Foreign Frontier: Exploring Governance in a Turbulent World* (Cambridge: Cambridge University Press), 410.

9. Adam Przeworski, et al., "What makes democracies endure?" in *Consolidating the Third Wave Democracies: Themes and Perspectives*, edited by Larry Diamond et al. (Baltimore and London: Johns Hopkins University Press, 1997), 410.

10. Juan L. Linz, "Some thoughts on the victory and future of democracy", in *Democracy's Victory and Crises* edited by Axel Hadenius (Cambridge: Cambridge University Press, 1997), 406.

11. Ministry of Local Government, Youth and Community Development, *Ministry Paper No. 44*, 24 November 1995, 4.

12. *Report of the National Committee on Political Tribalism 1997*, 23 July 1997, 26 and passim.

13. Ministry of Local Government, Youth and Community Development, *Ministry Paper No. 8: Reform of Local Government*, 17 February 1993, 13; Ministry of Local Government, Youth and Community Development, *Status Report on Local Government Reform*, June 1998, 4.

14. Joseph C. Rost, *Leadership for the Twenty-first Century* (Westport: Praeger, 1997), 112. Rost's book provides a very useful and comprehensive review of the growing and now massive literature on leadership studies. Cf. also Bryan D. Jones, ed., *Leadership and Politics: New Perspectives in Political Science* (Lawrence: University Press of Kansas, 1989); Bernard M. Bass, *Bass and Stogdill's Handbook of Leadership: Theory, Research and Managerial Applications* (New York: The Free Press, 1990).

Bibliography

Periodicals

The Brookings Review
Christian Science Monitor
Daily Gleaner (Jamaica)
The Economist
Herald (Jamaica)
New York Times
Sunday Gleaner (Jamaica)
Sunday Herald
The Times
Trinidad Guardian
Wall Street Journal

Books and Articles

Abramson, P.R., and R. Inglehart. 1998. "Comparing European publics". *American Political Science Review* 92, no. 1 (March).

Acevedo, D. E., and C. Grossman. 1996. "The Organization of American States and the protection of democracy". In *Beyond Sovereignty: Collectively Defending Democracy in the Americas,* edited by T. Farer. Baltimore and London: Johns Hopkins University Press.

Ake, C. 1973. "Dangerous liaisons: the interface of globalization and democracy". In *Democracy's Victory and Crisis*, edited by A. Hadenius. Cambridge: Cambridge University Press.

Attali, J. 1997. "The clash of Western civilization: the limits of the market and democracy". *Foreign Policy* 107 (Summer).

Bass, B.M. 1990. *Bass and Stogdill's Handbook of Leadership: Theory, Research and Managerial Applications.* New York: Free Press.

Bayat, A. 1997. "Un-civil society: the politics of the 'informal people' ". *Third World Quarterly* 18, no. 1.

Beetham, D. 1994. "Key principles and indices for a democratic audit". In *Defining and Measuring Democracy*, edited by D. Beetham. London: Sage.

Bertram, E., et al. 1996. *Drug War Politics: The Price of Denial*. Berkeley: University of California Press.

Bhalla, S. 1997. "Freedom and economic growth: a virtuous cycle?" In *Democracy's Victory and Crisis*, edited by A. Hadenius. Cambridge: Cambridge University Press.

Blais, A., et al. 1996. "Electoral systems". In *Comparing Democracies: Elections and Voting in Global Perspective*, edited by L. LeDuc et al. Thousand Oaks, Calif.: Sage.

Board of Enquiry. 1997. "Report into disturbances at the Tower Street Adult Correctional Centre and the St Catherine Adult Correctional Centre between 20th–23rd August". Mimeo.

Bogdanor, V. 1997. *Power and the People: A Guide to Electoral Constitutional Reform*. London: Victor Gollancz.

Bogues, A. 1994. *The Limit of Political Sovereignty: A Review of the Jamaican Experience*. Kingston: Friedrick Ebert Stiftung.

Bollen, K.A. 1993. "Political democracy: conceptual and measurement traps". In *On Measuring Democracy: Its Consequences and Constraints*, edited by A. Inkeles. New Brunswick and London: Transaction. *The Brookings Review* 15, no. 4 (Fall 1997).

Budge, I. 1993. "Direct democracy: setting appropriate terms of debate". In *Prospects for Democracy*, edited by D. Held. Palo Alto: Stanford University Press.

Butler, D., and A. Ranney, eds. 1994. *Referendums Around the World: The Growing Use of Direct Democracy*. Washington, DC: American Enterprise Institute.

Carothers, T. 1997. "The observers observed". *Journal of Democracy* 8, no. 55 (July).

Carter Center. 1998. *The Observation of the 1997 Jamaican Elections*. Atlanta: The Carter Center.

Carter, K.L. 1997. *Why Workers Won't Work – The Worker in a Developing Economy: A Case Study of Jamaica*. London and Basingstoke: Macmillan.

Catt, H. 1996. "The other democratic experiment: New Zealand's experience with citizens initiated referendum". *Political Science* 48, no. 1 (July).

Commissioner of Police, Jamaica. 1998. *"Constabulary Force crime review period 1 January 1997 to 31 December 1997 vs 1 January 1996 to 31 December 1996"*. Mimeo, 11 February.

Committee on Political Tribalism. 1997. *Report of the National Committee on Political Tribalism 1997* (23 July). Kingston: Government of Jamaica.

Conference on Security and Cooperation in Europe. 1990. *Document of the Copenhagen Meeting of the Conference on the Human Dimension.* Copenhagen: CSCE.

Conference of Heads of Governments. 1996. "Summary of conclusions of the Fifth Special Meeting held in Barbados, 16 December".

Coppedge, M., and W.H. Reinicke. 1993. "Measuring polyarchy". In *On Measuring Democracy: Its Consequences and Concomitants*, edited by A. Inkeles. New Brunswick and London: Transaction Books.

Cunningham, F. 1987. *Democratic Theory and Socialism.* Cambridge and New York: Cambridge University Press.

Dalton, R. J. 1996. *"Political cleavages, issues, and electoral change".* In *Comparing Democracies: Elections and Voting in Global Perspective*, edited by L. LeDuc et al. Thousand Oaks, Calif.: Sage.

Desch, M.C., J.I. Dominguez, and A. Serbin, eds. 1998. *From Pirates to Drug Lords: The Post-Cold War Caribbean Security Environment.* Albany: State University of New York Press.

Diamond, L. 1993. *Political Culture and Democracy in Developing Countries.* Boulder: Lynne Reinner.

Diamond, L. 1996. "Democracy in Latin America: degrees, illusions and directions for consolidation". In *Beyond Sovereignty: Collectively Defending Democracy in the Americas*, edited by T. Farer. Baltimore and London: Johns Hopkins University Press.

Diamond, L. 1997a. "Promoting democracy in the 1990s: actors, instruments and issues". In *Democracy's Victory and Crisis*, edited by A. Hadenius. Cambridge: Cambridge University Press.

Diamond, L. 1997b. "Is the third wave over?" *Journal of Democracy 7*, no. 3 (July).

Diamond, L., et al. 1997. *Consolidating the Third Wave Democracies: Themes and Perspectives,* Baltimore and London: Johns Hopkins University Press.

Dominguez, J.I. 1998. "The powers, the pirates, and international norms and institutions in the American Mediterranean". In *From Pirates to Drug Lords: The Post-Cold War Caribbean Security Environment*, edited by M.C. Desch, J.I. Dominguez and A. Serbin. Albany: State University of New York Press.

Dominguez, J.I., and A.I. Lowenthal, eds. 1996. *Constructing Democratic Governance.* Baltimore and London: Johns Hopkins University Press.

Dreher, M., S. Shapiro, and A. Stoddard. 1997. "Drug consumption and distribution in Jamaica: a national ethnographic study". Executive summary (mimeo).

Edie, C.J. "Jamaica: clientelism, dependency and democratic stability". In *Democracy in the Caribbean: Myths and Realities*, edited by C.J. Edie. Westport: Praeger.

Electoral Advisory Committee. 1996a. *Report to Parliament on Electoral Reform*, 13 August. Kingston: GPO.

Electoral Advisory Committee. 1996b. *Electoral Advisory Committee Interim Report Part II: Recommendations for Legal Reform*, 24 April. Cited in CAFFE Report. Kingston: CAFFE.

Elklit, J., and P. Svensson. 1997. "What makes elections free and fair?" *Journal of Democracy* 8, no. 3 (July).

Emmanuel, P.A.M. 1993. *Governance and Democracy in the Commonwealth Caribbean: An Introduction*. Barbados: ISER.

Evans, R.L., and I.M. Berent. 1992. *Drug Legalization: For and Against*. Peru, Ill.: Open Court.

Farer, T., ed. *Beyond Sovereignty: Collectively Defending Democracy in the Americas*. Baltimore and London: Johns Hopkins University Press.

Farrell, D.M. 1996. "Campaign strategies and tactics". In *Comparing Democracies: Elections and Voting in Global Perspective*, edited by L. LeDuc et al. Thousand Oaks, Calif.: Sage.

Farrell, D.M. 1997. *Comparing Electoral Systems*. London: Prentice Hall/Harvester Wheatsheaf.

Fine, R., and S. Rai, eds. 1997. *Civil Society: Democratic Perspectives*. London and Portland: Frank Cass.

Franklin, M.N. 1996. "Electoral participation". In *Comparing Democracies: Elections and Voting in Global Perspective*, edited by L. LeDuc et al. Thousand Oaks, Calif.: Sage.

Fukuyama. F. 1992. *The End of History and the Last Man*. New York: Free Press.

Gastil, R.D. 1993. "The Comparative Survey of Freedom: experiences and suggestions". In *On Measuring Democracy: Its Consequences and Concomitants*, edited by A. Inkeles. New Brunswick and London: Transaction Books.

"General Elections 1993: Report of the Ombudsman for Political Matters". Mimeo.

Giner, S. 1997. "Civil society and its future". In *Civil Society: Theory, History, Comparison*, edited by J.A. Hall. Cambridge: Cambridge University Press.

Government of Jamaica. 1987. *Report of the Duffus Commission of Enquiry into the 1986 Local Government Elections*. Kingston: Government Printing Office.

Grant-Wilson, D. 1997. "Globalization, structural adjustment and democracy in Jamaica". In *Democracy and Human Rights in the Caribbean*, edited by I.L. Griffeth and B.N. Sedoc-Dahlberg. Boulder: Westview Press.

Griffith. I.L. 1997. *Drugs and Security in the Caribbean: Sovereignty under Siege*. University Park: Pennsylvania State University Press.

Griffiths, I.L., ed, Forthcoming. *The Political Economy of Drugs in the Caribbean*. London: Macmillan.

Griffith, I.L., and B.N. Sedoc, eds. 1997. *Democracy and Human Rights in the Caribbean*. Boulder: Westview Press.

Hadenius, A., ed. 1997. *Democracy's Victory and Crisis*. Cambridge: Cambridge University Press.

Hall, J.A. 1997. *Civil Society: Theory, History, Comparison*. Cambridge: Cambridge University Press.

Harbeson, J., et al., eds. 1994. *Civil Society and the State in Africa*. Boulder: Lynne Rienner.

Harrigan, J. 1991. "Jamaica". In *Aid and Power: The World Bank and Policy-based Lending Vol. 2: Case Studies*, edited by P. Mosley, J. Harrigan and J. Toye. London and New York: Routledge.

Harriott, A. 1996. "The changing social organization of crime and criminals in Jamaica". *Caribbean Quarterly* 42, nos. 2 and 3 (June–September).

Harrison, F.V. 1989. "Drug trafficking in world capitalism: a perspective on Jamaican posses in the US". *Social Justice* 16 (Winter). Cited in *The Jamaican Crime Scene: A Perspective*, by B. Headley. Washington, DC: Howard University Press.

Hausman, R. 1997. "Will volatility kill democracy?" *Foreign Policy* 108 (Fall).

Haynes, J. 1997. *Democracy and Civil Society in the Third World*. Cambridge: Polity Press.

Headley, B. 1989. *The Jamaican Crime Scene: A Perspective*. Washington, DC: Howard University Press.

Held, D. 1995. *Democracy and the Global Order: From the Modern State to Cosmopolitan Governance*. Palo Alto: Stanford University Press.

Henry-Wilson, M. 1989. "The status of the Jamaican woman, 1962 to the present". In *Jamaica in Independence: Essays on the Early Years*, edited by R. Nettleford. Kingston and London: Heinemann Caribbean and James Currey.

Huntington, S.P. 1991. *The Third Wave: Democratization in the Late Twentieth Century*. Norman and London: University of Oklahoma Press.

Huntington, S.P. 1997. "Democracy for the long haul". In *Consolidating the Third Wave Democracies: Themes and Perspectives*, edited by L. Diamond et al. Baltimore and London: Johns Hopkins University Press.

IDS Bulletin 24, no. 6. 1996.

Inglehart, R. 1997. "Postmaterialist values and the erosion of institutional authority". In *Why People Don't Trust Government,* edited by J.S. Nye, Jr., P.D. Zelikow and D.C. King. Cambridge: Harvard University Press.

Inkeles, A., ed. 1993.*On Measuring Democracy: Its Consequences and Constraints.* New Brunswick and London: Transaction Books.

Jaggers, K., and T.R. Gurr. 1996. "Polity III: regime type and political authority". Inter-university Consortium for Political and Social Research, Ann Arbor. Cited in *World Development Report 1997: The State in a Changing World.* New York: Oxford University Press.

Joint Select Committee. 1995. *Final Report of the Joint Select Committee of the Houses of Parliament on Constitutional and Electoral Reform.* Kingston: Government Printing Office.

Jones, B.D., ed. 1999. *Leadership and Politics: New Perspectives in Political Science.* Lawrence: University Press of Kansas.

Jones, C.O. 1977. "The American presidency: a separationist perspective". In *Presidential Institutions and Democratic Politics: Comparing Regional and National Contexts,* edited by K. von Mettenheim. Baltimore and London: Johns Hopkins Univeristy Press.

Jones, M.P. 1997. "A guide to the electoral systems of the Americas: an update". *Electoral Studies* 16, no. 1 (March).

Jones, M. 1996. "Assuring the public's understanding of constitutional reform: evidence from Argentina". *Political Behaviour* 18, no. 1.

Kaplan, R.D. 1997. "Was democracy just a moment?". *Atlantic Monthly* (December).

Karatnycky, A. et al 1997. *Freedom in the World – The Annual Survey of Political Rights and Civil Liberties, 1996-1997.* New Brunswick and London: Transaction Books.

Katz, R.S. 1996. "Party organizations and finance". In *Comparing Democracies: Elections and Voting in Global Perspective,* edited by L. LeDuc et al. Thousand Oaks, Calif.: Sage.

Keane, J. 1998. *Civil Society and the State.* London: Verso.

Kobach, K. W. 1994. "Switzerland". In *Referendums Around the World: The Growing Use of Direct Democracy,* edited by D. Butler and A. Renney. Washington, DC: American Enterprise Institute.

Labour Market Reform Committee, 1997. *Interim Report.* Kingston: LMRC.

LeDuc, L., R.G. Niemi, and P. Norris, eds. 1996. *Comparing Democracies: Elections and Voting in Global Perspective.* Thousand Oaks, Calif.: Sage.

Lewis, P., ed. 1996. *Jamaica Preparing for the Twenty-first Century.* Kingston: Planning Institute of Jamaica.

Lijphart, A. 1977. *Democracy in Plural Societies.* New Haven: Yale University Press.

Lijphart, A. 1993. "Constitutional choices for new democracies". In *The Global Resurgence of Democracy*, edited by L. Diamond and M.F. Plattner. Baltimore: Johns Hopkins University Press.

Lijphart, A. 1996. "The puzzle of Indian democracy: a consociational interpretation". *American Political Science Review* 90, no. 2 (June).

Lijphart, A. 1997. "Unequal participation: democracy's unresolved dilemma". *American Political Science Review* 91, no. 1 (March).

Lijphart, A., ed. 1992. *Parliamentary Versus Presidential Government.* Oxford: Oxford University Press.

Linz, J.L. 1997. "Some thoughts on the victory and future of democracy". In *Democracy's Victory and Crisis*, edited by A. Hadenius. Cambridge: Cambridge University Press.

Linz, J.L., and A. Valenzuela, eds. 1994. *The Failure of Presidential Democracy: The Case of Latin America.* Baltimore: Johns Hopkins University Press.

Linz, J.L., and A. Stepan. 1997. "Toward consolidated democracies". In *Consolidating the Third Wave Democracies: Themes and Perspectives*, edited by L. Diamond et al. Baltimore and London: Johns Hopkins University Press.

Lowenthal, A. 1997. "Battling the undertow in Latin America". In *Consolidating the Third Wave Democracies: Themes and Perspectives*, edited by L. Diamond et al. Baltimore and London: Johns Hopkins University Press.

Magleby, D.B. 1994. "Direct legislation in the American states". In *Referendums Around the World: The Growing Use of Direct Democracy*, edited by D. Butler and A. Renney. Washington: American Enterprise Institute

Maingot, A.P. 1994. *The United States and the Caribbean.* London: Macmillan.

Mainwaring, S., and M.S. Shugart. 1997. *Presidentialism and Democracy in Latin America.* Cambridge: Cambridge University Press.

Mair, P. 1996. "Party systems and structures of competition". In *Comparing Democracies: Elections and Voting in Global Perspective*, edited by L. LeDuc et al. Thousand Oaks, Calif.: Sage.

Mander, J. and E. Goldsmith. 1996. *The Case Against the Global Economy.* San Francisco: Sierra Books.

March, J.G., and J.P. Olsen. 1984. "The new institutionalism: organizational factors in political life". *American Political Science Review* 78.

McAllister, I. 1996. "Leaders". In *Comparing Democracies: Elections and Voting in Global Perspective,* edited by L. LeDuc et al. Thousand Oaks, Calif.: Sage.

Meeks, B. 1998. "Careening on the edge of abyss: driving, hegemony and the rule of law in Jamaica". Paper presented at the African Diaspora Studies on the Eve of the Twenty-First Century Conference, University of California, Berkeley, 30 April–2 May.

"Memorandum of Understanding among the Government of Jamaica, Alcan Jamaica Company, Jamalco, Alumina Partners of Jamaica and Kaiser Bauxite Company, the National Workers' Union, the University and Allied Workers' Union and the Union of Technical Administrative and Supervisory Personnel". Mimeo, May 1998.

Ministry of Agriculture (in collaboration with Rural Agricultural Development Authority). 1994. *Alternative Systems for an Illegal Crop.* Kingston: Government of Jamaica and RADA.

Ministry of Local Government, Jamaica. 1993. *Ministry Paper No. 8: Reform of Local Government.* Kingston: Government of Jamaica.

Ministry of Local Government, Youth and Community Development, Jamaica. 1998. *Status Report on Local Government Reform.* Kingston: Government of Jamaica.

Ministry of National Security, Trinidad and Tobago. 1993. "Final report for the government of Trinidad and Tobago on investigations . . . in respect of allegations . . . about corruption in the Trinidad and Tobago police service". In *Drugs and Security,* by I.L. Griffith. University Park: Pennsylvania State University Press.

Moddy, K. 1997. *Workers in a Lean World: Unions in the International Economy.* London and New York: Verso.

Moseley, P., J. Harrigan, and J. Toye, eds. 1991. *Aid and Power: The World Bank and Policy-based Lending, Vol. 2, Case Studies.* London and New York: Routledge.

Moser, C., and J. Holland. 1997. *Urban Poverty and Violence in Jamaica,* World Bank Latin American and Caribbean Studies. Washington, DC: World Bank.

Mosher, J.F., and K.L. Yanagisako. 1991. "Public health, not social welfare: a pubic health approach to illegal drug policy". *Journal of Public Health Policy* 12, no. 3 (Autumn).

Munroe, T. 1978. *The Politics of Constitutional Decolonization: Jamaica 1944–1962.* Kingston: ISER and Unwin.

Munroe, T. 1993. Review essay of F. Fukuyama's *The End of History and the Last Man. Social and Economic Studies* 41, no. 4 (December).

Munroe, T. 1994. Review essay of S.P. Huntington's *The Third Wave: Democratization in the Late Twentieth Century. Social and Economic Studies* 43, no. 3 (March).

Munroe, T. 1996a. "Caribbean democracy: decay or renewal?" In *Constructing Democratic Governance*, edited by J.I. Dominguez and A.I. Lowenthal. Baltimore and London: Johns Hopkins University Press.

Munroe, T. 1996b. "The Jamaican industrial relations culture: perspectives on change". In *Jamaica Preparing for the Twenty-first Century*, edited by P. Lewis. Kingston: Planning Institute of Jamaica.

Munroe, T. Forthcoming. "Cooperation and conflict dynamics in the US–Caribbean drug connection". In *The Political Economy of Drugs in the Caribbean*, edited by I.L. Griffiths. London: Macmillan.

Nadelmann, E.N. 1998. "Common sense drug policy". *Foreign Affairs* 77, no. 1 (January/February).

Nader, R., and L. Wallach. 1996. "GATT, NAFTA and the subversion of the democratic process". In *The Case Against the Global Economy*, edited by J. Mander and E. Goldsmith. San Francisco: Sierra Books.

National Defense University, Institute for National Strategic Studies. 1997. *1997 Strategic Assessment: Flashpoints and Force Structure*. Washington, DC: National Defense University.

National Council on Drug Abuse, Jamaica. 1996. *National Master Drug Abuse Prevention and Control Plan 1997–2002*, Kingston: Ministry of Health.

National Democratic Movement. 1997a. *1997 Manifesto of the NDM*. Kingston: Gleaner Co.

National Democratic Movement. 1997b. *A Winnable Alternative*. Kingston: NDM.

Nettleford, R., ed. 1989. *Jamaica in Independence: Essays on the Early Years*. Kingston and London: Heinemann Caribbean and James Currey.

Nevitte, N., and S.A. Canton. 1997. "The role of domestic observers". *Journal of Democracy* 8, no. 3 (July).

Norpoth, H. 1996. "The economy". In *Comparing Democracies: Elections and Voting in Global Perspective*, edited by L. LeDuc et al. Thousand Oaks, CA: Sage.

Norris, P. 1996. "Legislative recruitment". In *Comparing Democracies: Elections and Voting in Global Perspective*, edited by L. LeDuc et al. Thousand Oaks, Calif.: Sage.

Nye, J.S., Jr., P.D. Zelikow, and D.C. King. 1997. *Why People Don't Trust Government*. Cambridge: Harvard University Press.

Organization of American States. *c.*1997. "Inter-American convention against illicit manufacturing and trafficking in firearms, ammunitions, explosives". Mimeo.

Pauly, L.W. 1997. *Who Elected the Bankers? Surveillance and Control in the World Economy.* Ithaca and London: Cornell University Press.

Payne, D.W. 1998a. *Storm Watch: Democracy in the Western Hemisphere into the Next Century.* Policy Papers on the Americas 9, Study 3. Washington, DC: CSIS Americas Program.

Payne, D.W. 1998b. *The 1997 Jamaican Elections: Post-Election Report.* Western Hemisphere Election Study Series 16, Study 1. Washington, DC: CSIS Americas Program.

Planning Institute of Jamaica. 1998. *Economic and Social Survey: Jamaica, 1997.* Kingston: PIOJ.

Plattner, M.F. 1998. "Liberalism and democracy". *Foreign Affairs* 77, no. 2 (March/April).

Post, K. 1979. *Arise Ye Starvelings.* The Hague: Martinus Nijhoff.

Post-Modernity Project Executive Summary. 1996. *The State of Disunion: 1996 Survey of American Political Culture.* Charlottesville: Post-Modernity Project.

Przeworski, A., and F. Limongi. 1997. "Democracy and development". In *Democracy's Victory and Crisis,* edited by A. Hadenius. Cambridge: Cambridge University Press.

Przeworski, A., and F. Limongi. 1997. "What makes democracies endure?". In *Consolidating the Third Wave Democracies: Themes and Perspectives,* edited by L. Diamond et al. Baltimore and London: Johns Hopkins University Press.

Putnam, R. 1995. "Bowling alone: America's declining social capital". *Journal of Democracy* 6, no. 1 (January).

Remmer, K.L. 1995. "New theoretical perspectives on democratization". *Comparative Politics* 28, no. 1 (October).

Rhodes, R.A.W. 1995. "The institutional approach". In *Theory and Methods in Political Science,* edited by D. Marsh and G. Stoken. London: Macmillan.

Robotham, D. 1998. *Vision and Voluntarism – Reviving Voluntarism in Jamaica.* Kingston: Grace, Kennedy Ltd.

Rodriques, S.A. 1996. "The Jamaican political culture: a theoretical and empirical exploration". MPhil Thesis, Department of Government, University of the West Indies, Mona.

Rosenau, J. 1997. *Along the Domestic-Foreign Frontier: Exploring Governance in a Turbulent World.* Cambridge: Cambridge University Press.

Rost, J.C. 1997. *Leadership for the Twenty-first Century.* Westport, CT: Praeger.

Rourke, J.T., R. Hiskes, and C.E. Zirakzakeh. 1992. *Direct Democracy and International Politics: Deciding International Issues Through Referendums.* Boulder and London: Lynne Reinner.

Rowen, H.S. 1995. "The tide underneath the 'Third Wave' ". *Journal of Democracy* (January).

Sangster, A., and L. Barnett, eds. 1998. *The 1997 General Elections in Jamaica: The Establishment of CAFFE and its Role in the Electoral Process*. Kingston: CAFFE

Schmidt, V.A. 1995. "The New World Order, Incorporated: the rise of business and the decline of the nation state". *Daedalus* 124 (Spring). Cited in *Along the Domestic-Foreign Frontier: Exploring Governance in a Turbulent World*, by J.N. Rosenau. Cambridge: Cambridge University Press.

Schmitter, P.C. 1997. "Exploring the problematic triumph of liberal democracy and concluding with a modest proposal for improving its international impact". In *Democracy's Victory and Crisis*, edited by A. Hadenius. Cambridge: Cambridge University Press.

Seaga, E. 1998. Foreword. *A Statement on the Irregularities of Jamaica's General Elections*, 18 December. Kingston: Jamaica Labour Party.

Shugart, M.S., and J.M. Carey. 1992. *Presidents and Assemblies: Constitutional Design and Electoral Dynamics*. Cambridge: Cambridge University Press.

Smith, S.M. 1997. " 'We will not grovel': drugs and Jamaican sovereignty". MSc Research Paper, Department of Government, University of the West Indies, Mona.

Statistical Institute of Jamaica. 1996. *Statistical Yearbook of Jamaica 1996*. Kingston: STATIN.

Statistical Institute of Jamaica. 1997. *Jamaica: Survey of Living Conditions* 1996. Kingston: STATIN and Planning Institute of Jamaica.

Sterling, C. 1994. *Thieves' World*. New York: Simon and Schuster.

Stone, C. 1974. *Electoral Behaviour and Public Opinion in Jamaica*. Mona, Jamaica: ISER.

Stone, C. 1980. *Democracy and Clientelism in Jamaica*. New Brunswick and London: Transaction Books.

Stone, C. 1982. *The Political Opinions of the Jamaican People 1976–1981*. Kingston: Blackett.

Stone, C. 1986. *Class, State and Democracy in Jamaica*. New York: Praeger.

Stone, C. 1987. "Survey of Jamaican workers' opinions". Unpublished manuscript, Department of Government, University of the West Indies, Mona.

Stone, C. 1989a. *Politics Versus Economics: The 1989 Elections in Jamaica*. Kingston: Heinemann.

Stone, C. 1989b. "Power, policy and politics in independent Jamaica". In *Jamaica in Independence: Essays on the Early Years*, edited by

R. Nettleford. Kingston and London: Heinemann Caribbean and James Currey.

Stone Committee. 1990. *Report of the Committee to Examine Ways of Strengthening the Roles and Performance of Parliamentarians, Ministry Paper No. 11*. Kingston: Office of the Prime Minister.

Strange, S. 1996. *The Retreat of the State: The Diffusion of Power in the World Economy*. Cambridge: Cambridge University Press.

Strange, S. 1997. "The erosion of the state". *Current History* (November).

Task Force on Campaign Finance reform. 1977. "New realities, new thinking: Report". *PS: Political Science and Politics* (September).

Troy, G. 1997. "Money and politics: the oldest connection". *Wilson Quarterly* (Summer).

United Nations Development Program. 1995. *Human Development Report 1995*. New York and Oxford: Oxford University Press.

United Nations Development Program. c. 1997a. "Levels of satisfaction with democracy". In *Governance and Democratic Development in Latin America and the Caribbean*. Washington, DC: UNDP.

United Nations Development Program. c. 1997b. "Latin American barometer 1996". In *Governance and Democratic Development in Latin America and the Caribbean*. Washington, DC: UNDP.

United Nations International Drug Control Programme. 1997. *World Drug Report*. Oxford: Oxford University Press

United States Department of State. 1996. *Country Reports on Human Rights Practices for 1995*. Washington, DC: Department of State.

United States Department of State. 1998. *Country Reports on Human Rights Practices for 1997*. Washington, DC: Department of State.

United States Information Agency. 1997. *Partnership for Prosperity and Security in the Caribbean*. Caribbean/United States Summit, 10 May. Bridgetown, Barbados: USIS.

Vanhanen, T. 1997. *Prospects of Democracy: A Study of 172 Countries*. London and New York: Routledge.

Vasciannie, S. 1997. "Political and policy aspects of the Jamaica/United States Shiprider negotiations". *Caribbean Quarterly* 43, no 3 (September).

von Mettenheim, K., ed. 1997. *Presidential Institutions and Democratic Politics: Comparing Regional and National Contexts*. Baltimore and London: Johns Hopkins University Press.

Waters, A.M. 1985. *Race, Class, and Political Symbols: Rastafari and Reggae in Jamaican Politics*. New Brunswick and Oxford: Transaction Books.

West Indian Commission. 1992. *Time for Action: Report of the West Indian Commission*. Black Rock, Barbados: International Development Options.

Whitehead, L. 1997. "Bowling in the Bronx: the uncivil interstices between civil and political society". In *Civil Society: Democratic Perspectives*, edited by R. Fine and S. Rai. London and Portland: Frank Cass.

Williams, P., and C. Florez. 1994. "Transnational criminal organizations and drug trafficking". *Bulletin on Narcotics* (United Nations International Drug Control Programme) 46, no. 2.

Wright, E.O., ed. 1995. *Associations and Democracy*. London and New York: Verso.

Zakaria, F. 1997. "The rise of illiberal democracy?". *Foreign Affairs* 76, no. 6 (November/December).

Zimmermann, J. 1997. *The Recall: Tribunal of the People*. Westport: Praeger.

Index

www.ingramcontent.com/pod-product-compliance
Lightning Source LLC
Chambersburg PA
CBHW062028270326
41929CB00014B/2360